introduction to the principles of language

introduction to the principles of language

PAUL A. GAENG
University of Virginia

HARPER & ROW, PUBLISHERS
New York, Evanston, San Francisco, London

INTRODUCTION TO THE PRINCIPLES OF LANGUAGE
Copyright © 1971 by Paul A. Gaeng

Printed in the United States of America. All rights reserved. No part of this book may be used or reproduced in any manner whatsoever without written permission except in the case of brief quotations embodied in critical articles and reviews. For information address Harper & Row, Publishers, Inc., 49 East 33rd Street, New York, N.Y. 10016.

STANDARD BOOK NUMBER: 06-042218-1

LIBRARY OF CONGRESS CATALOG CARD NUMBER: 78-137810

contents

Preface   vii

1. The origin and prehistory of language   1
2. What is language?   12
3. The structure of language: the study of sounds   24
4. The structure of language: the study of language forms   53
5. The structure of language: revolution in grammar   78
6. Vocabulary: word formation   108
7. Vocabulary: borrowing from foreign sources   125
8. Meaning and etymology   134
9. Writing and its relation to speech   153
10. Regional and social speech variations   166
11. Languages in comparison   184
12. Indo-european and non-indo-european languages   207

A selected bibliography   227

Index   235

preface

The rapid growth of linguistics as an academic subject in recent decades has led to a growing interest in this relatively young science on the part of students and laymen alike. Yet the newcomer has often been bewildered, frustrated, and even alienated by what appear to be esoteric theories, methods, and procedures clothed in the equally esoteric jargon of the professional linguist. This book, which grew out of lectures on language to undergraduate students, is a modest attempt to outline for the beginner the major principles of the science of language in as straightforward and concise terms as possible, without either misrepresenting any school of thought or otherwise doing violence to the discipline through oversimplification. It does not, however, argue any particular theoretical position or methodology but merely aims at presenting the accomplishments and results that have been achieved in the field of linguistics over the past 150 years or so.

I have tried to organize my book in such a way that it could serve as an introductory text in a one-semester undergraduate course in general linguistics. It could also be used, I feel, to cover a unit on linguistics in freshmen English and even in advanced high school English courses, as well as courses in applied linguistics for students preparing for language-teaching careers. Finally, my text is also directed to those English and foreign language teachers who are using linguistically oriented textbooks and, in the absence of formal training in linguistics, need a brief introduction to this field.

To acknowledge my indebtedness to the many scholars upon whose works I have drawn in preparing this book would be impossible, the more so since I would run the risk of unwittingly leaving out some whose contributions to linguistics have been no less important. The notes at the end of each chapter and the bibliography at the end of the book will, I trust, give some indication of my debt to past and contemporary linguistic scholars. As it is, I have not dealt with such recent developments as psycholinguistics, sociolinguistics, computational linguistics, and others, which would have been outside the limitations I set for myself.

I should, nevertheless, like to recognize the following colleagues who have been particularly generous with their advice and constructive criticism: Professor Emeritus Mario A. Pei of Columbia University, for whose encouragement I am particularly grateful; Professor Mathilda Knecht, Chairman of the Department of Linguistics at Montclair State College; Professor B. Ernest Shore of the Department of Germanic and Slavic languages at Montclair State College; and Professor Gilbert Roy of the Department of Romance languages and General Linguistics at the University of Virginia. Their kind assistance has substantially improved many aspects of my treatment. I take this opportunity to thank them for their interest.

Last, but certainly not least, I want to express my indebtedness to my students, both past and present, who have all contributed in one way or another to clarifying my thinking on a number of problems as a result of many interesting and stimulating discussions on matters linguistic. It is to them that I gratefully dedicate this book.

P.G.

introduction to the principles of language

I
the origin and prehistory of language

Language is the most significant and colossal work that human spirit has evolved. Being one of the most characteristic forms of human behavior, it is so familiar a feature of our daily life that we rarely pause to think about it. We take it for granted as we do walking, for instance; but while the latter is an inherent organic, biological function of man, speech is an acquired cultural function. As the late Edward Sapir, one of the most distinguished and revered American anthropologists once said, the normal human being is predestined, in a sense, to walk, not because his elders will teach him this art, but because his organism is prepared from birth to take on all those expenditures of nervous energy and those muscular adaptations that result in walking.[1] We might say then that this particular activity is innate with a physically healthy individual, while language is inherited from the particular society into which an individual is born—from the company he keeps, so to speak. This basic difference in the acquisition of both activities, that is, walking and language, becomes quite evident when we remove a newborn baby from the environment into which he was born and transplant him into an alien one. Chances are he will develop the art of walking in his new social environment very much the way he would have in the old, whereas he will acquire language patterns that differ considerably from those of his native environment.

It is a truism to say that language is not necessary to life but that it is essential to *human* life. There is hardly any human activity which is not dependent on it, and we make use of it in virtually everything we do. There are even those who hold that human thought is not possible without language.[2]

In its broadest sense language is a way of communicating meaning from one human mind to another by vocal sounds, gestures, signals, written symbols, or the like. Of all language activities, however, speech is certainly the most common and widespread. "Speech," said the late British historian Harold Goad, "is the highest of the faculties of man and the one that distinguishes him from animals."[3] What actually separates man from animals is not so much the ability to produce sounds but rather man's mental capacity to link these sounds with meanings which are accepted by other human beings, so that there is a mutual understanding, a real transfer of thought from one mind to another. As a result of patient training, a parakeet may succeed in producing a sentence like "birds can't talk" with proper pitch and intonation. However, he will never be able to say "birds can't write" or "dogs can't talk" (unless we specifically teach him to produce these sentences) because animals are incapable of carrying on language activity, or the kind of word substitution that would allow complex sequences of "organized noises" that add up to definite meanings. The humanlike chatter of a parakeet is *imitation* of language, rather than *use*, because it is spontaneous and it is not, above all, motivated by organized thought.

Whether animals will ever achieve the art of speech is an interesting question. Man, after all, is an animal who is capable of speech, but had he not been endowed with the sort of brain and intelligence which make speech possible, it is doubtful whether he could have achieved it. Man is supposed to have become able to originate language when, unlike the higher primates, he learned to walk upright and altered the contours of his brain in such a way that the development of language centers was made possible.

But just how was it possible for man, or at least some manlike creature, to acquire speech as a means of thought communication? The late Isaac Goldberg, a scholar of many interests and talents, writing about this problem, said: "In linguistic study, as in biological, there appears to be a 'missing link.' Just as we do not know a direct animal ancestor of man, so we cannot establish with unquestionable continuity a mental ancestor, one who definitely bridged the chasm between mere vocalism—howls, hunger calls, love calls—and a flexible system of communication capable of development. Animal vocalism appears today to be just where it was in the ages before history."[4] Sheep have been bleating since time immemorial and cats have been meowing, but only the language of *homo sapiens* has developed into an intricate system of communication by means of vocal symbols.

The origins of language reach deeply into the prehistory of the human race to an epoch in which conceivably only gestures, uncertain vocal cries, and crude markings served to transmit the outlines of human experience. At any rate we have no actual knowledge of language earlier than about 4000 B.C. (the time of the oldest written records that have come down to us from the Sumerians, a people who lived in Mesopotamia), which, in terms of the prehistory of man, is but yesterday. It is clear, furthermore, that language had already had a long course of evolution behind it and that human beings had been speaking for many times that number of years before they got around to recording their speech on either stone or clay, so that we are left without any sort of clue as to how prehistoric man acquired speech as a means of communication. As a matter of fact it is not even possible to establish that the earliest men could speak or that nonvocal communication may have antedated speech in the development of human society, as would be suggested by the prevalence of visual and gestural communication throughout the animal kingdom and by the highly developed system of gestures used by some primitive peoples. That speech was preceded by nonvocal communication is the view of the English scientist Sir Richard Paget. Somewhat influenced by Darwin, he assigns a predominant role to bodily movements in the early history of language and argues that human speech originated in verbal imitations of such movements and gestures, very much the way a person cutting something with a pair of scissors might move his jaw simultaneously with the blades of the scissors or a child learning to write might twist his tongue as his fingers move. An example of this kind of verbal imitation would be the sound sequence *mnyum mnyum* or *mnya mnya*, accompanied by the blowing of air through the vocal cavities, which signifies the gesture sign of eating. Language—that is, speech—is seen as having been produced by a sort of pantomime, the tongue, lip, and jaw unconsciously mimicking the gestures of the hand until the day man realized that he needed his hands for such fundamental tasks as hunting, planting, and toolmaking and that by making mouth gestures vocal he could not only free his hands but also communicate by means of a "new system of conventional gesture of the organs of articulation from which nearly all human speech took its origin."[5] Like all other theories that have been advanced to account for the mystery of how (and when) man first learned to speak, this theory—often referred to as the TA-TA, or mouth-gesture, theory—has found both adherents and critics. Whatever its shortcomings may be (and how are we to pass judgment on the scientific validity of any such theory that must remain, at best, intelligent guesswork?), its most plausible feature would seem to be the fact that it sees language as derived from words signifying human actions.

Other attempts to pierce the mist of linguistic prehistory have not been wanting. Theories advanced in this connection have been named, as a rule, according to the type of words which they claim made up the primitive vocabulary of primeval man.

According to one hypothesis the first words ever uttered by man were imitative of natural sounds, as when a child calls a cow a *moo* or a locomotive a *choo-choo*. This theory, to which the rather unacademic name BOW-WOW was given, holds that the origin of all words is to be sought in *echoism*, or sound imitation (also known as *onomatopoeia*, which is Greek for "name-making"). That is, the first words (like *crash, clang, buzz, bang*, and so forth, which dictionaries describe as echoic) are believed to have approximately reproduced the sound of what they were intended to suggest. For example, we would have to assume in accordance with this view that primitive man copied the barking of dogs and thereby obtained a natural word with the meaning "dog" (hence the name bow-bow theory).

Closely related to the foregoing is the theory that makes interjection the original speech unit. Nicknamed the POOH-POOH theory, it claims that language is derived from instinctive emotional cries called forth by intense sensations and feelings, for example, utterances like *ouch* for mild pain and *oh* for surprise.

Still another theory, called the DING-DONG theory, holds that there is a mystical harmony between sound and sense in language.

This mysterious correspondence was explained by its proponent, the German scholar Max Muller, in one of his Oxonian lectures a century or so ago, as "a law which runs through nearly the whole of nature, that everything which is struck rings. Each substance has its particular ring."[6] This view of language origin fits in with that of some Greek theorists, among them Plato, who thought that language must have arisen by necessity from laws of nature and that there existed a mystical correspondence between the names of things and the objects they stood for.

Another theory, known as the YO-HE-YO theory, seeks the source of speech in the rhythmic chants of a group of men engaged in a common physical task, such as lifting a rock or dragging a heavy log. Accordingly, the beginnings of language would lie in the joint performance of strenuous physical work during which, as a result of intensive effort, strong and repeated breath expulsion would make the vocal cords vibrate, resulting in the kinds of grunts, groans, and other involuntary vocal noises that we make while doing work of this sort. Such noises would then develop into words associated with communal labor, something like *heave* or *haul*.

Quite recently a British lawyer and sociologist, D. S. Diamond, in a book entitled *The History and Origin of Language*,[7] elaborated a theory which is quite reminiscent of the preceding one in that it attempts to find the beginnings of human speech in commands involuntarily uttered in the course of violent or strenuous efforts of the arm that, at first, were calls for assistance accompanied by gestures mimicking the desired action, such as cutting, breaking, crushing, or killing. In fact, Dr. Diamond argues, imperatives like *cut*, *break*, *crush*, *strike* are most likely to have been the first authentic words, and certainly indicate the commonest forms of maximum arm effort. His theory is supported by much philological evidence drawn from a great variety of languages.

Two more theories deserve to be mentioned in this brief survey. One was proposed by the renowned Danish linguist Otto Jespersen, who in his now classic *Language, Its Nature, Development and Origin* sought the genesis of language not in the prosaic but in the poetic side of life, its source not in "gloomy seriousness" but "merry play and youthful hilarity." "There was once a time," he says, "where all speech was sung, or rather when these two actions were not yet differentiated."⁸ The earliest language was expressive rather than communicative, poetic and emotional rather than matter-of-fact and practical; and among the emotions which were most powerful in eliciting outbursts of music and song, love must be placed in the first rank. "Language," this scholar concludes, "was born in the courting days of mankind; the first utterances of speech I fancy to myself like something between the nightly love lyrics of puss upon the tiles and the melodious love songs of the nightingale."⁹ As to the nature of this primitive language which was sung rather than spoken, Jespersen envisions it as consisting of long words and being full of difficult sounds. He arrives at this view, working his way backward into linguistic prehistory, by observing general trends and directions of development. He is particularly impressed by processes of breakdown and simplification whenever he compares the evidence of a later stage of a language with an earlier one, and he concludes that the earlier speech is by far the less broken down and the more complex.

More recently the late G. Révész, professor of psychology at the University of Amsterdam, in his book *The Origin and Prehistory of Language*,¹⁰ advanced his CONTACT theory, which argues that language arose out of man's instinctive need for contact with his companions. He suggests a series of stages through which human speech developed, starting with the contact sound, which is similar to, say, the barking of a dog, and serves no communicative purpose but merely expresses man's desire to identify himself with other members of his species. The next step is the *cry*, the first attempt at communication, which signals a state of emotion, such as fright, anger, or hurt (much like the mating and warning calls heard in the animal world) and is directed, not to a specific individual, but rather to his environment in general. Next comes the *call*, a deliberate message addressed to a particular individual (also found in domestic animals, for example, begging), and finally, the *word*, a specialized development of the call, which has symbolic function and hence is proper to man only. Professor Révész believes that the earliest human speech consisted of commands, but like others before him, he fails to explain how these rudimentary speech forms developed into an articulated and fully functioning language.

In the absence of any scientific foundation (and remember that the only reliable sources in matters of historical investigation are written records), it is no wonder that scholars have reached the conclusions that it is not possible to reconstruct the vestiges of original language and that we may never go beyond the realm of mere speculation. Each of the theories discussed here has been severely criticized and rebutted since, insofar as they are acceptable at all, at best they would explain only small parts of language. To give but one example, the bow-wow theory, among the first and most familiar hypotheses advanced to account for the genesis of human speech, would explain all speech as a gradual evolution from sounds of an imitative nature; yet the overwhelming evidence seems to indicate that echoic (onomatopoeic) words represent only a small segment of the vocabulary of any language, and in some languages of aboriginal peoples of North America they seem to be absent altogether. It is no doubt to obviate speculative and seemingly unprofitable, though sometimes highly ingenious, discussions on a subject beyond our ken that the Linguistic Society of Paris decreed in its bylaws as far back as 1866 that it would not accept papers on the subject of the origin of human speech.

It has been suggested more than once that we could conceivably learn something about man's first attempts at speech by observing children learning their native tongue. As a matter of fact, several experiments are said to have been tried with newborn children to see whether, if isolated from hearing a word of any language whatever, they might evolve a language of their own. The Greek historian Herodotos reports that the Egyptian king Psammatichos secluded two infants in a mountain hut until such a time as they would begin to speak, his assumption being that in the absence of any speech pattern to imitate, they would instinctively evolve their own language, which—so the pharaoh reasoned—would at the same time also provide a clue as to the primitive language of man. With the passing of time, the children were heard to utter something like *bekos*, which was identified as the Phrygian word for "bread." We must presume that King Psammatichos, as well as his court, were convinced that Phrygian (a language once spoken in Asia Minor) was the first language of mankind and that, therefore, it would be instinctively acquired by children. James IV of Scotland is said to have similarly interned two children who, once the experiment was concluded, he determined "spak very guid Ebrew." (This view, incidentally, fits in with the assumption widely held during the Middle Ages that Hebrew was the first language of mankind.)

These experiments are not only totally inconclusive, they are based on the belief that language is *innate* with an individual rather than *inherited* from his elders.[11] From the moment children are born, they are thrown into a world of speaking, and they quite naturally acquire both active and passive mastery of the speech used in their social environment. The child of English-speaking parents who was taken from them at birth and raised by Eskimos would grow up speaking only Eskimo, unless specially instructed in the tongue of his father and mother, in which case he might become bilingual. Children learning their native language can only teach us how an organized language (the language of a given speech community) is acquired; they cannot give us a clue as to the origin of language. In other words, a child repeats what he hears from adults; he returns what is given him.

Nor can we learn anything from observing the speech of primitive societies that are still functioning. Anthropological research has conclusively shown that even the most primitive tribal societies of our time possess highly structured and complex languages with rich vocabularies. Any difference that may exist between the languages of primitive communities and our highly sophisticated cultures lies in the number of ideas and concepts that require expression rather than in the way in which they are expressed. Any hope, therefore, of discovering the specific origin of language from the languages of primitive groups must also be abandoned.

To the question of where language started, the answer must be just as uncertain as it is to the question regarding the precise location of the Garden of Eden. No language spoken today, no language of which we have any sort of record, can suggest what prehistoric language was like. If you ever wondered what language Adam and Eve spoke, you may be interested to know that at a congress held at Stockholm, Sweden, in the late seventeenth century, a Swedish scholar seriously maintained that in the Garden of Eden God spoke Swedish, Adam Danish, and the serpent French. (There is no mention of Eve!) On the other hand, the biblical account of the story of the Tower of Babel (Gen. 11:1–19) seems to suggest a common origin of all languages, although it makes no mention of any specific tongue. Indeed, for many centuries it was widely believed that the human race arose in a single spot of the earth and developed at first a single language which later broke up into different languages as human beings wandered off in different directions. It was believed, furthermore, that this first language of man was Hebrew and that from it all languages were derived. Many languages today, in fact, show a common beginning, with evidence of differences arising in the course of the wanderings of people who at one time lived in one spot and used the same language, but whether all languages can be traced back to a single one and all people to a single locality is very doubtful. Nor is there any evidence to suggest that most languages derive from Hebrew or that the original speech form of man even remotely resembled this language (the Old Testament, which is couched in Hebrew, makes no mention to this effect). This view of the *monogenetic* origin of language (from *mono* + *genesis*, "oneness of origin") has largely been abandoned by modern scholars in favor of the *polygenetic* origin (from *poly* + *genesis*, "plurality of origin"), that is, the theory that several original languages evolved independently in different parts of the globe. Since we are dealing with many, many thousands of years of the prehistory of man and his speech, this latter view is just as unprovable as the former. All we really know for sure is that the human race emerged into the dawn of history equipped with forms of language as fully developed as the ones spoken today.

To sum up our historical sketch, we may say then that there are many guesses about how, when, and where language developed. No one can speak with certainty about the original development of human speech. It may well be, as we have seen, that people first began to communicate by imitating sounds heard in nature, but it may just as well be that attempts at sounds were preceded by the use of signs, gestures, and pictorial representations. The most probable generalization about the origin of language that might be made is that language developed in accordance with man's need to communicate with his fellowman, and that it grew as more and more human beings contributed to its development. In any event, man had to have certain biological capabilities and a psychic constitution before he could use language. As Susanne K. Langer has observed, "It [language] could only have arisen in a race in which the lower forms of symbolistic thinking—dream, ritual, superstitious fancy—were already highly developed, i.e., where the process of symbolization, though primitive, was very active."[12]

notes

1. Edward Sapir, *Language*. New York: Harcourt Brace Jovanovich, 1921, p. 3.
2. Thus Professor Max Black, who states that "Language... appears as the very stuff of which 'ideas' are made. To separate thought from its symbolic manifestation would be as futile as to try separating a mind from its embodiment in a human organism." (*The Labyrinth of Language*. New York: The New American Library, 1969, p. 17.)
3. *Language in History*. Harmondsworth, Middlesex: Penguin Books, 1958, p. 11.
4. *The Wonder of Words*. New York: Appleton-Century-Crofts, 1938, p. 16.
5. Sir Richard Paget, *Human Speech*. New York: Harcourt Brace Jovanovich, 1930, pp. 133–134.
6. Quoted in Otto Jespersen, *Language, Its Nature, Development and Origin*. London: G. Allen & Unwin, 1922, p. 415.
7. New York: Philosophical Society, 1959.
8. Jespersen, *op. cit.*, p. 420.
9. *Ibid.*, p. 434.
10. Translated from the German by J. Butler. New York: Philosophical Library, 1956.
11. By saying that language is not innate we do not mean that the individual does not have the innate *capacity* of acquiring language. What must be learned from one's elders is a *specific linguistic competence*, for example, English, French, or Russian. The experiments described above were all based on the premise that it is this competence which is innate with the individual. For a recent study suggesting a certain biological predisposition for the development of speech and language, consult Eric H. Lenneberg, "The Capacity for Language Acquisition," in Jerry A. Fodor and Jerold J. Katz, eds., *The Structure of Language: Readings in the Philosophy of Language*. Englewood Cliffs, N.J.: Prentice-Hall, 1964, pp. 579–603.
12. *Philosophy in a New Key*. Cambridge, Mass.: Harvard University Press, 1951, p. 127.

2
what is language?

Human language is primarily a spoken means of communication. The very term language, which is ultimately derived from the Latin word *lingua* meaning "tongue," underscores the importance of this particular speech organ, so that in the last analysis language comes to mean a "tonguing" or "wagging of the tongue." The use of the word *tongue* as a synonym for language is but further proof of the essential part it plays in speech production.[1]

An observation might be in order before we attempt to find out what language is and how it works. We all too often assume that firsthand acquaintance with a form of human behavior (and what could be a more typical one than language?) is sufficient for an understanding of its nature; but the nature of language has been, and still is, widely misunderstood. For instance, many people still view language as a particular arrangement of letters on a piece of paper, in a book, or on other printed material about which some learned gentlemen, called grammarians, have set down immutable rules. Thus they confuse writing with language. Others believe that there is an inherent relationship between language and race or nationality or culture; still others maintain that primitive people must of necessity speak "primitive" languages. The fact of the matter is that writing is *not* language, except to the extent that it reproduces, more or less faithfully, the vocal sounds which people produce when they speak to each other. There is *no* inherent relationship between language and race, nationality, or culture. And primitive people of our time do not speak "primitive" languages.

Indeed, it might be worth mentioning at this point that people continue to confuse language with nationality and to associate race and culture with both.

If by the term *race* we mean a grouping of people sprung from the same stock or breed and, therefore, possessing certain characteristics in common (as when we refer to what anthropologists have called the Nordic, Alpine, and Mediterranean races in Europe), we find that none of the major languages (that is, major in terms of distribution and number of speakers) follow ethnic geography closely at all. French is spoken by a people of the same mixed stock that is also represented in areas where languages other than French are spoken. English, German, and Russian are spoken by no less heterogeneous groups.

Another no less widespread notion seems to be that every language represents the expression of a distinct nationality. It is true, of course, that a national unit once established by political forces finds in a language the clearest and most obvious expression of its identity. Some attempts toward linguistic centralization are being made now; Mao Tse Tung's effort to bring about *one* national language uniformly spoken and written throughout the Chinese Peoples' Republic by making Mandarin Chinese (the Peking form of Chinese) the official speech form is one example. The fact remains, however, that in contrast to such centralizing trends we find instances where law and government are still administered in more than one officially recognized language. The classic example is Switzerland, where the business of the central government is conducted in three *official* languages—French, German, and Italian—to which a fourth *national* language, called Rheto-Rumansch, must be added. National unity in this case clearly transcends linguistic unity.

Nor is there any intrinsic association between language and *culture* (that is, the socially inherited ways, customs, and beliefs that shape the lives of a group of human beings), although close ties between the two in terms of literary production or folklore are not denied. By intrinsic or inherent association is meant that closely related languages or even a single language may belong to separate cultural spheres, as is the case with Great Britain and the United States, where a community of language does not make for a community of culture. And while a common language is most certainly the best means to a mutual cultural understanding, it can no longer function as a vehicle of a common culture when the geographical, political, and economic determinants of the culture are no longer the same throughout its area of use.

What, then, is language? In attempting to give a definition of this most complex of human activities, students of language—those professional people who study language for its own sake—proceed from certain assumptions. The most fundamental of these are that humans communicate by means of audible sound signals and that this form of human behavior may be studied and described objectively. Hence, any definition we may want to adopt for our purposes will set forth speech as the salient feature that gives language its character and quality. From time to time, different definitions, emphasizing one or another aspect of language, have been advanced by various scholars; but no matter how their viewpoints or their wording may differ, at the root of all their definitions is the concept that language is speech.

The late Edgar Sturtevant, a distinguished scholar from Yale University, proposed a definition in his *Introduction to Linguistic Science*[2] which is both concise and inclusive. He viewed language as *a system of arbitrary vocal symbols by which members of a social group cooperate and interact*. Accordingly, language is (1) a *system* and (2) it is made up of *arbitrary vocal symbols*. Let us examine the terms of this definition more closely.

To begin with, let us take the phrase *arbitrary vocal symbols*. The key word here is *symbols*, and symbols are things that stand for other things. We speak of mathematical, chemical, and logical symbols, and all of them have one feature in common—namely, that there is nothing in the nature of things that gives these symbols the meanings assigned. Instead, people have given them meaning by some sort of agreement or convention. The relationship between symbols and the things they symbolize is neither self-evident nor as natural a one as might exist, say, between dark clouds in the sky and the imminence of rain or between a running nose and an incipient cold (especially when accompanied by body temperature). These are *signs*, which are indicative of certain events or things, and they stand in some natural or causal relationship to the phenomena they suggest and direct attention to. *Symbols*, on the other hand, which derive their specific function from group consensus, have no validity for those not acquainted with such an agreement and convey no immediate information to the uninitiated. A symbol, of course, could also be defined as a "conventional sign" because it is only conventionally related to events or things.

Symbolism is at the very heart of language, and because symbols are based on convention and acquire an *arbitrary* nature, it follows that certain sounds and sequences of sounds have certain meanings only by agreement of a particular speech community and become unintelligible outside the community where they are used. Indeed, words are symbols for objects or ideas, but there is no direct relationship between the symbol and the message it conveys. The English word *horse* means roughly the same as German *Pferd*, French *cheval*, Spanish *cabballo*, and Hungarian *ló*, and the only reason *horse* carries this meaning is that the speakers of English agree to use this meaning with this particular sequence of sounds rather than with another sequence of sounds, *mook*, for example, just as the German, the Frenchman, the Spaniard, and the Hungarian use other sound sequences to symbolize the same object. There is, then, no intrinsic necessity for any word to mean what it does, because there is nothing in the perceivable physical nature of the symbol that could be taken as corresponding to any feature of the thing (or idea) symbolized. The mere fact that the concept "horse" could be represented by another sequence is proved by differences among languages and by the very existence of different languages. The term *arbitrary*, however, by no means implies that the choice of the word symbol is left entirely to the speaker or that he can modify it at will. Language is a kind of social contract, and both the sounds of speech and their connection with the messages they express are passed on to all members of a speech community by the older members of that community.

There is a special class of words that purport to imitate the sounds they represent. They are called ONOMATOPOEIC words (that is, sound-imitative or echoic words) and are exemplified by such words as *bang*, *boom*, *clang*, *clatter*, *splash*, *swish*, *whisper*, and others for which there would seem to be a special relationship between symbol and meaning. But apart from instances of exceptional identity, like English *meow*, French *miaou*, and German *miau*—all of which imitate the sound made by a cat, identical meanings in different languages are never expressed by the same sound sequence. The English word *whisper*, for instance, is *flüstern* in German, *susurrar* in Spanish, *chuchoter* in French, and *susogni* (with the sound represented by *s* pronounced like the initial sound of *show*) in Hungarian. Even the same natural sound seems to strike the ear of different people differently; to an Englishman the rooster sounds like *cock-a-doodle-do*, while the Frenchman hears the same bird cry *cocorico*, the Italian *chicchirichi* (with a *k*-sound for written *ch*), and the Hungarian *kukoriku*. A dog becomes a *bow-wow* in English but a *Wauwau* in German (with a *v*-sound as in *very* for written *w*), while a French child will generally refer to him as a *toutou*. Clearly, then, even these sound-imitative words are chosen somewhat arbitrarily and are to a large extent conventionalized, despite a certain amount of direct phonetic imitation. In any event a speaker must learn the correct imitations used in his language.

Closely related to onomatopoeia, that is, sound imitation, are those spontaneous expressions that we call INTERJECTIONS. Here again, when we compare two or more languages, we find that these expressions differ from one language to the next. The Englishman utters *ouch* for mild pain, whereas the Frenchman says *aïe*, the German *au*, and the Hungarian *jaj* (pronounced approximately like *yoy*). Interjections, in other words, are not involuntarily or instinctively uttered sounds (like groans, for instance) but must be learned as would any other conventional sound sequence in a language.

Both onomatopoeic words and interjections, though a significant part of any language, form but a proportionately small segment of the total word stock and, in any event, do not altogether escape the arbitrariness of the association between symbol and meaning.[3]

The word *vocal* in Sturtevant's definition underscores the fact that human language activity is primarily speech, that is, it is made up of sounds produced by the interaction of various organs associated with the respiratory tract.

When we say that language is a *system*, we mean that even though the relationship between sound symbol and meaning is arbitrary, there is a good deal of consistency in the way sounds (the smallest building blocks of language) and sound combinations (the larger units that carry grammatical and lexical meaning) are put together in a given language. Hence, when human beings talk, their talk is not a mere succession of sounds put together in a haphazard fashion like the prattling of babies or the chattering of monkeys. Quite the contrary. We notice that in any particular language the same sounds and sound combinations keep recurring and that there emerges a pattern of partial resemblances in the sequences that people utter; therefore, we say that language has system in the way sounds are put together and in the way they are patterned into larger units. Certain sounds, for instance, may not appear in the beginning of a word; others may not appear at the end. Thus, while the native English speaker will have no trouble pronouncing words like *desks*, *lisps*, *hosts*, *ends*, *strengths*, and *paths*, or a combination like *is dry*, he would have a great deal of difficulty with words that begin with *sks-*, *sps-*, *sts-*, *ndz-*, or *zdr-* (the final *s* in *ends* and the *s* in *is dry* being pronounced as a *z* sound). On the other hand, these consonant clusters, which English tolerates in final position, would definitely be rejected by languages like French, Spanish, and Italian. Italian, however, permits such initial clusters as *zdr-*, *zbr-*, and *zg-* (written *g* representing the initial sound in *judge*), for example, *sdraiarsi* 'to stretch out,' *sbrigarsi* 'to hurry,' and *sgelare* 'to thaw' (the *s* automatically becoming a *z*-sound in Italian before a voiced consonant), which an English speaker would find to be quite a mouthful. The same sound or cluster of sounds that seems so easy and natural to pronounce in one position may require quite a tongue-twisting effort in another.

Let us take another example. Initial consonant groups like *str-*, *spr-*, *skr-*, and *spl-* are perfectly permissible clusters in English in words like *stripe*, *spray*, *script*, and *splendid* but are not tolerated, for instance, in Spanish, whose sound system happens to require that an *e*-sound be put before all initial groups made up of *s* plus consonant. English *stirrup*, then, becomes Spanish *estribo*, *spouse* becomes *esposo*, *script* becomes *escrito*, and *splendid* becomes *espléndido*. Conversely, the English speaker may find some difficulty pronouncing the Spanish word *ñato* 'flat-nosed' (which begins with a sound whose approximate equivalent would be the one represented by the combination *ny* in the word *canyon*), or the German interjection *ach* and the proper name *Bach* (both of which end with the guttural sound heard in Scottish *Loch*), simply because these sounds do not fit into the familiar English sound pattern.

These few examples should suffice to show that any sound or sound cluster must meet certain criteria of compatibility which differ from language to language, so that what seems difficult to handle for speakers of one language will not only be easy but quite natural for speakers of another language.

Sounds are combined into entities that carry meaning, that is, entities that classify our experiences of the outside world, and we find that these are arranged in recurrent designs. And just as in the case of a triangle, which can be drawn if only one side and two angles are given, there is a great deal we can predict about a design even if only part of it is known. Professor Archibald Hill illustrates this point in his *Introduction to Linguistic Structures*[4] on the basis of an incomplete sentence such as *John ____s Mary an ____*. A native English speaker would have no trouble filling these two blanks, the first one with a verb and the second one with a noun. Furthermore, he would also be able to determine that not all verbs fit into the first slot, since it requires a verb form which takes an *s* in the third person singular and can also take *two* objects. As to the second slot, not all nouns would fit into it, since whatever form we select must be one that begins with a vowel and takes an article. A native English speaker is most likely to come up with something like *John gives Mary an apple* or *John brings Mary an orange* and is not likely to produce a sentence like *John *boughts Mary *an dress.*[5]

The English speaker, then, is able to predict, on the basis of certain grammatical devices such as the final *s* and the article *an* in our example, what the correct utterance would be, just as the French, Spanish, German, and Hungarian speakers would be able to predict from an incomplete sentence a good deal about what a complete sentence should sound like in their languages. We must keep in mind, of course, that each speaker would use different grammatical devices to signal a present tense verb form or a noun object. In French and Spanish, for instance, the latter would be signaled by word order, as in English, whereas in German it would sometimes be shown by word order and sometimes by a special ending of the preceding article, for example, *der Mann* 'the man' (subject) versus *den Mann* 'the man' (direct object). In Hungarian, on the other hand, the noun itself would take an ending, for example, the subject form *ember* 'man' becomes *embert* when used as a direct object. Examples of this sort would fill several pages, and it could be shown, for instance, how nouns are variously classified by gender, by form, by designating animate or inanimate objects, and how verbs are classified from the standpoint of tense (present, past, future) or aspect (incompleted versus completed action), and so forth. But all of them would boil down to one basic principle, namely, that every language has its *own* system, that is, every language shows order, consistency, and patterning in its sounds and in the way these sounds are combined into larger units.[6] Anything that has system can be described in terms of its elements, and so we are able to make detailed analytic statements about language by describing as briefly and concisely as possible the aural–oral signaling system used by human beings in their daily affairs.

It is the merit of modern linguistics, the objective study of language as a system, to have recognized the extent to which every language has a system of its own and to have developed techniques for describing the structure of individual linguistic systems.

The last part of Sturtevant's definition, namely, *by which members of a social group cooperate and interact*, designates the chief function of language in society, since without transfer of thought from one human mind to another there can be little or no cooperation and interaction. This is illustrated by the well-known Bible story of the Tower of Babel in which the building of the tower, which was to have reached the sky to prove man's might, suddenly comes to a stop when God, as punishment for man's foolish pride, causes the language of each member of the community to change so that things begin to go haywire through lack of communication. Life in society, therefore, presupposes that members of a given group of people, called a speech community, be able to communicate through a common, agreed-upon symbol system.

Linguistics is very much a part of the social sciences since it is concerned with a universal part of human behavior and with one of the most essential human faculties. And just as social science is referred to as a "science," we are justified in calling linguistics a science too, since it fulfills the criteria that any form of study must meet to call itself one. The specialist concerned with the subject matter of linguistics—who is called the linguistic scientist, or LINGUIST (to be distinguished from the sense of the word as it is often used to refer to someone who has a practical knowledge of several languages or a facility to acquire them)—sets himself the task of reporting about the facts of language (for a science must direct its attention to a coherent body of fact) as they emerge from his observations, with the ultimate aim of furnishing a body of information that may be useful to whoever is concerned with language in any way. In doing so, he is intent on discovering the contrasts in the system of the language that enable the speaker to make his hearer perceive and react to different meanings and on identifying things as they are, and not as he would wish them to be. To this extent, then, and because the linguist deals with observable truths that are publicly verifiable, linguistics can be justified as a science. The field of the linguist is language, *any* language, in all its forms and manifestations without regard for the number of speakers who use it or for the level of civilization that its speakers may have achieved. His study encompasses both living languages, that is, languages used today as a means of communication, and so-called "dead" languages, namely, languages like classical Latin and ancient Greek or former stages of languages now in use, like Old French and Old English (spoken about 1000 years ago), which are known only from written records, such as manuscripts, inscriptions, and printed texts. Furthermore, the linguist considers languages with long literary traditions as well as hitherto unrecorded ones (for example, many African and American Indian languages) equally valuable and worthy objects of study.

The linguistic scientist may approach his analysis from either of the following points of view: (1) the SYNCHRONIC study (from the Greek *syn* 'with' and *chronos* 'time'), also called *descriptive* study, refers to the study of the state of language at a given point of time, either past or present, while (2) the DIACHRONIC study (from the Greek *dia* 'across' and *chronos* 'time'), or *historical* study, deals with the developments in languages in the course of time, the various stages that languages go through, and the causes and results of language changes.

There is also a third aspect, called CONTRASTIVE ANALYSIS, under which language can be studied, such as when we *compare* two or more language structures either diachronically, with a view to determining historical relationships among languages and their common ancestry, or synchronically, in which case our study is based on the comparison between different languages as they appear at a given time (say English and Swedish) without any historical considerations involved. Such a descriptive comparison serves to show how languages differ in their sound patterns, grammatical structure, and vocabulary. This type of analysis has received a great deal of attention of late in connection with language teaching and learning, where the learner's language is compared with the so-called target language in order to point out those areas where the contrast between the two languages is greatest.

Modern descriptive linguistics has often been referred to as "structural" linguistics and is considered by many scholars to be the fundamental aspect of the science of language, since before engaging in historical or comparative studies, the linguist must first ascertain the interrelationship and patterns which make up the structure of language. The descriptive, synchronic approach has been particularly prevalent since the days of the Swiss linguist Ferdinand de Saussure in the 1920s, the key figure in modern linguistic scholarship, and, in America, since the days of Franz Boas, Edward Sapir, and Leonard Bloomfield in the early 1930s, the "founding fathers" of the American school of linguistic studies.

The linguist's task, as was said earlier, is to report the facts of language as they emerge from his observations. In describing a language spoken at a particular point in time, the linguistic scientist progresses through three levels of structure. These are

1. the system of speech sounds as used by native speakers of the language under consideration, called PHONOLOGY (from Greek *phonē* 'sound' and *logos* 'study');
2. the meaningful forms into which speech sounds are combined, that is, the study of words and word parts, called MORPHOLOGY (from Greek *morphē* 'form'); and
3. the study of the arrangement of words to form sentences, called SYNTAX (ultimately derived from Greek *syntassein* 'to put in order').

Sometimes levels 2 and 3 are subsumed under the heading of *morphosyntactic* level because of the rather tenuous dividing line between the study of language forms and their combination into larger structures, but for pedagogical purposes it would seem convenient to keep the two levels separate.

Structurally oriented linguists, the so-called *structuralists*, have generally assumed that the description and analysis of language must begin with the description of the raw material of language, that is, the sounds and their patterning into larger units, and that description of meaning should be put off until the analysis of the rigidly observable normal language behavior of people is completed. The heavy emphasis on the sound system is largely due to the methods developed by Bloomfield and those other linguistic scientists who were interested in studying relatively unknown languages, particularly those of the American Indians, for which they had to devise a system of notation for transcribing sounds and sound sequences.

As a result of a "revolution" in grammatical theory (see Chapter 5), many linguists have come to recognize meaning as crucial to an understanding of language. Viewing language as an essentially abstract set of psychological principles of which people's verbal behavior (the system of speech sounds) is but an indirect manifestation, they contend that a description of the abstract linguistic system should logically precede observable speech activity. These scholars would rather approach their analysis from the top downward, so to speak, that is, by starting with syntactic structures and working their way down through the level of forms (morphology) to the ultimate level of speech sounds (phonology).

In this presentation we are going to follow the traditional structuralist approach. The next three chapters will be concerned with the description of the three levels of linguistic structures.

notes

1. In many languages *tongue* and *language* are the same word: for example, French *langue*, Italian *lingua*, Spanish *lengua*, German *Zunge*, Greek *glossa*, Russian *yazyk*, and Hungarian *nyelv*, to mention a few.
2. New Haven: Yale University Press, 1947, p. 5.
3. Sound imitation in particular plays a significant role in the creation of new words. Think, for instance, of a sound-imitative word like *coo*, which originally denoted the soft murmuring sound of a pigeon or dove and was then extended to mean the "cooing of lovers."
4. New York: Harcourt Brace Jovanovich, 1958, p. 5.
5. It is a convention among linguists to mark an unacceptable form or construction with an asterisk.
6. Chapters 3 and 4 are essentially devoted to demonstrating this proposition.

3
the structure of language: the study of sounds

In keeping with the definition of language as a structured system of arbitrary vocal symbols, which underscores the fact that human language activity is primarily speech, it seems logical to begin the descriptive analysis of language on the level of speech sounds. In order to understand a language as a *system* of sounds, however, we must first have some knowledge of the individual sounds and of the way they are produced by the human vocal apparatus.

THE SPEECH PROCESS

"The essence of speech," says R. H. Robins, "is that one human being, by movements beginning at his diaphragm and involving various parts of his chest, throat, mouth, and nasal passages, creates disturbances in the air around him, which within a limited distance from him have a perceptible effect on the eardrums and through them on the brains of other people, and that the hearers can, if they belong to the same language community, respond to these disturbances, or noises, and find them meaningful."[1] Accordingly, the act of communication, which requires the presence of at least two people, operates on three levels: the *psychological*, the *physiological*, and the *physical*. Using the diagram proposed by the late Ferdinand de Saussure, one of the most distinguished structural linguists of this century, the complete speech process, which is a complicated one, could be represented as follows.

To illustrate this speaking circuit between two people, let us suppose that the speaker A wishes to convey a message—say, the notion of "book"—to the hearer B, who uses the same language. To do this, A's brain, which has received the concept (c) of "book" from one of its billions of cells, must first translate this

The Speaking Circuit

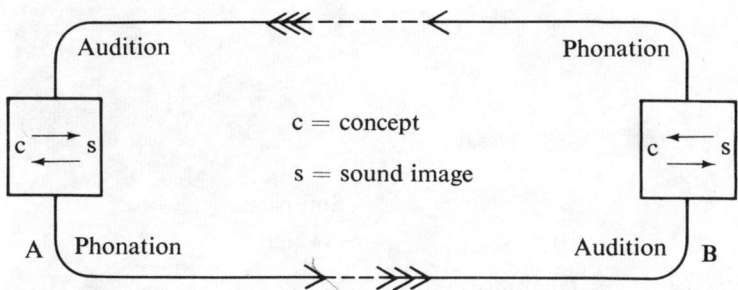

Adapted from Ferdinand de Saussure, *Cours de linguistique générale*, 3rd. ed. Paris: Payot, 1935.

concept into the appropriate sound image (s), made up of the set of sounds that are used to symbolize this concept, the kind of nonvocal sound symbol we use when we talk to ourselves without moving the lips or the tongue or when we do some kind of mental recitation. This purely *psychological* process is immediately followed by a *physiological* response to a nerve impulse from the brain which causes the organs of speech to produce the sound sequence that A wishes to convey to B. This is where the act of PHONATION—that is, the production of speech sounds by the vocal organs—sets in.[2] The *lungs*, which provide the source of energy for speech, drive the breathstream, by means of constriction of the chest muscles, upward through the *windpipe* and the *vocal cords* housed in the *larynx* (popularly referred to as the Adam's apple) into the *mouth* or *nasal passage*, where the flow of air is shaped into the desired sounds by the interplay of the *articulators* (tongue, teeth, lips, palate). The air vibrations thus produced are propelled from the mouth or nose as sound waves through the air—the *physical* process—and reach the hearer's ear. At this point, the point of AUDITION, the order is reversed: By a physiological process the vibrations caused by the sound sequence (the sounds in "book" in this case) are transmitted to B's brain, which, in turn, translates the audible sound symbols into the appropriate sound image. Finally the message is decoded in terms of the psychological association of this sound image (s) with the corresponding concept (c). Since speaker and hearer speak the

The Organs of Speech

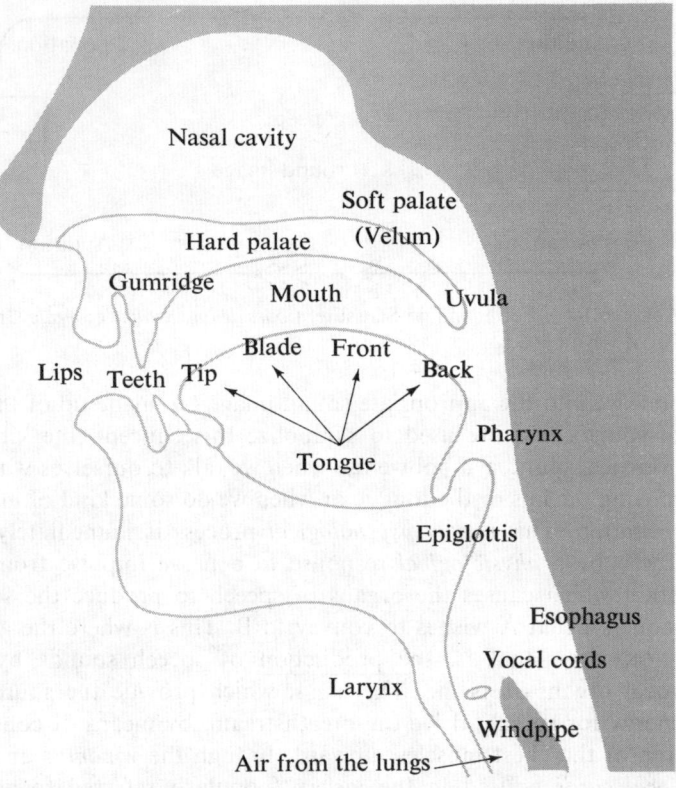

same language, A's concept will more or less coincide with that of B.

Mario Pei has summarized the speech process in six operations, as follows:

Operation 1: Speaker gets concept of "book" from brain cell, transfers it to speech center, where concept is exchanged for sound symbol.
Operation 2: Speech center sends order to utter "book" to speech organs.
Operation 3: The word is uttered by the speech organs.
Operation 4: It is transmitted by airwaves to the listener's ear.
Operation 5: The listener's ear refers it to the speech center of the listener's brain.

Operation 6: The word is referred to the decoding center, where the word symbol gives rise to the concept "book" in the listener's brain.[3]

A more detailed study of the anatomy and physiology of speech and hearing would not be in keeping with the purpose of this book.[4] Having briefly sketched the speaking process, let us now take a closer look at the speech sounds themselves, with the view of describing and classifying them and, finally, examining how they are used—that is, how they *function* in a given language.

THE DESCRIPTION OF SPEECH SOUNDS

Speech sounds can be described in various ways. You have, no doubt, heard people refer to a "flat" or "broad" *a*-sound (presumably the sounds in *cash* and *father*) or a "hard *g*," as in *go*. And what is a "harsh" or a "bright" sound? It is quite obvious that whatever may strike your ear as "harsh" may strike mine in a completely different fashion. Hence, a sound description of this kind, based on the impression of the hearer's ear—his *auditory* impression—would hardly be useful for objective analysis, just as a botanist's description of flowers and plants in terms of their colors or smell would have no scientific value. Furthermore, the study of the sounds of speech from an auditory point of view does not provide the kinds of terms, with precisely defined meanings, that are required for identifying the characteristics of speech sounds. We must turn, therefore, either to the physical structure of the sounds themselves and analyze the properties of the sound waves as they are revealed to us by precision instruments or to the study of the movements and positions of the vocal organs and the way in which the sounds of language are produced. Since the measurement of sound waves presupposes extensive training in mathematics and physics, particularly the branch that is called *acoustics*, linguists have chosen to describe speech sounds in *articulatory* terms, basing their terminology on the physiological production of sounds, or their articulation. To the linguist, then, the study of PHONETICS—the study of the sounds of language—means, for all intents and purposes, the study of *articulatory phonetics*.

The human speech mechanism has been compared to a clarinet

or a flute, since "in both, sounds are produced by stopping, obstructing, or otherwise interfering with the free flow of a column of air through an enclosed passage."⁵ The current of air coming from the lungs may be stopped or obstructed at various points along its passage, and the shape of the chambers through which it passes may be variously modified. Sounds produced with a relatively free passage—that is, sounds in which the breathstream passes through resonance chambers formed in the oral cavity by various movements of the tongue and the lips—are called VOWELS; sounds involving audible obstruction or even momentarily complete stoppage of the airstream, are called CONSONANTS. Some linguists prefer to speak of *vocoids* and *contoids* instead of vowel and consonant sounds, reserving the terms *vowel* and *consonant* as labels for the significant sound units, or PHONEMES, of specific languages (see page 42).⁶ The latter terms are consecrated by usage, however, and continue to be used by linguists and phoneticians alike to refer to the actual sounds of language; we shall follow this usage.

In addition to the division of speech sounds into vowels and consonants, we must also distinguish between VOICED and VOICELESS sounds, according to whether the airstream forced through the larynx is restricted by the vocal cords or not. During respiration these cords, which are really two bands of muscle stretching across the larynx, are drawn apart for the air to pass through without obstruction. Voiceless speech sounds are those produced with the vocal cords in this position. On the other hand, these elastic vocal bands may also be set into vibration by the passing air current and thereby produce audible sound waves; this we call *voicing*, and the sounds produced in this way are said to be voiced. While vowels in English are regularly voiced, consonants may be either voiced or voiceless. Thus the sound written with *p* in *pit* is voiceless, but the sound written with *b* in *bit* is voiced.

The space between the vocal cords is technically known as the *glottis*. Its primary biological function (see note 2) is to open and close the entrance to the pulmonary tract. When completely closed, the glottis keeps the air locked in the lungs and allows the necessary muscular strength to build up above the hips for the purpose of lifting or pushing heavy objects (like pushing your car out of the snow). Upon sudden release of this closure, a *glottal stop* results. This is an important speech sound in many languages and can occasionally be heard in English also, as in the mildly reproachful "oh-oh."

Another major division of speech sounds can be made in terms of whether the airstream is directed into the mouth or nose. Accordingly, we speak of ORAL and NASAL sounds. Whether a given sound will be pronounced with or without nasal resonance is determined by the flexible soft palate also called the *velum* (the Latin word for "sail"), which may rise to shut off the nasal cavity. Conversely, when the velum is lowered, the nasal passage is kept free and the air may escape, either partially or totally, through the nose. This, incidentally, is the normal breathing position.

In addition to the mouth, or oral cavity, and the nasal cavity, the *pharynx* (the cavity in the back of the mouth which connects the larynx and the mouth and nasal passages) plays an important part as a resonance chamber. It is possible, indeed, to produce speech sounds by contracting the pharyngeal muscles, and some languages—for instance, Arabic—make full use of this organ of speech. The mouth, nasal cavity, and pharynx are often brought under the general heading of *supraglottal* ("above the glottis") *cavities*.

Finally, speech sounds may be divided into NONCONTINUANTS and CONTINUANTS. The former involve a complete stoppage of the breathstream and an interval of silence during their production. Sounds thus formed are called *stops*. Some examples are the initial sounds in *pin*, *bin*, *time*, *dime*, *cane*, and *gain*. Phoneticians also refer to these sounds as *plosives*, since the breath, which has temporarily been compressed, escapes upon release with a mild explosion. A special type of stop, called an *affricate*, results from the gradual release of a stop sound accompanied by a slight friction noise, as in the initial and final sounds of *church* and *judge*. Stops can be either voiced or voiceless.

Continuants are produced without complete blocking of the airstream. According to the degree of obstruction of the airstream, starting with those sounds that show the greatest amount, we may distinguish several types.

1. *Fricatives* These are produced with enough constriction of the speech organs at some point in the mouth passage to cause

a noticeable friction noise as the air squeezes through. The initial sounds of *fine, vine, thigh, thy, seal, zeal* and *ship*, as well as the medial sound written with an *s* in *pleasure*, are fricative sounds. These sounds are also known as *spirants* (from the Latin *spirare* 'to breath' or 'to blow,' while the word *fricative* ultimately derives from the Latin *fricare* 'to rub'). The affricates mentioned earlier may be considered as a combination of a stop and a fricative sound. It is customary to make a distinction between *slit* and *groove fricatives*. In the foregoing examples slit fricatives are heard in the first four words, while the fricative sounds in the last four are of the groove type. The difference between the two lies in the shape of the narrow opening, which in the case of *fine, vine, thigh,* and *thy* is slitlike, in contrast to the much narrower opening for *seal, zeal, ship,* and *pleasure*. In addition, in the latter group the tongue is bunched up so as to form a groove, a kind of channel through which the airstream can escape. Because of the accompanying hissing noise, the sounds of [s] and [z] are also known as *sibilant-fricative sounds* or simply *sibilants*. (For the use of square brackets to represent sounds rather than letters, see page 34.)

A special type of fricative is represented by the initial sound in *house*. Here the friction is caused by the air passing through the glottis; hence this sound is called a *glottal fricative*. Fricatives are also either voiced or voiceless.

2. *Nasals* The initial sounds heard in *mad* and *no* and the final sound in *ring* differ in articulation from those in *bad, dough,* and *rig* only insofar as during their emission the nasal passage is kept open for the air to issue through the nose. This is why you are most likely to substitute [b] for [m], [d] for [n], and [g] for [ŋ] (the symbol for written *ng*) when you have a bad head cold and are unable to let your breath escape through the nose. While there are no nasalized vowels as such in English, as there are in some languages (French, for example), they are sometimes heard from speakers who do not, or cannot, properly close off the nasal cavity for oral sounds and thus give their speech a "nasal twang." Nasals are normally voiced sounds, except that in words like *smoke* and *snow* they may be partially "devoiced" because of the preceding voiceless consonant.

3. *Laterals* The sound [l] in *live, well,* and *milk* is classified as a lateral sound (from the Latin *latus* 'side'). Lateral sounds are

made by blocking the mouth passage with the tongue along a median line, leaving an opening along one or both sides for the breathstream to pass through. There are two major varieties of the English [l], sometimes called "clear" and "dark," depending on whether the stoppage occurs in the front of the mouth or in the back of it (with the back of the tongue slightly raised). As a rule the former occurs initially and the latter either in final position or when followed by a consonant: The word *lilt* is a good illustration. Laterals in English are generally voiced except in contact with a preceding voiceless consonant sound, as in *plan* or *clean*, when they become partially devoiced. An initial voiceless [l] is heard in some Welsh proper names spelled *Ll-*, for example, *Lloyd*, which sounds to an English speaker as though the word began with a voiceless fricative sound.

4. *Glides* These could also be termed "transitional sounds," since they are characterized by a moving, rather than a stationary, tongue position as they pass to and from the place where a speech sound is articulated. The sounds represented by written *y*, *w*, and *r* as in *yes*, *well*, and *red* are generally regarded as glides, though not all phoneticians include the initial sound of *red* in this category. Leaving the [r] sound aside for a moment, let us consider the nature of the initial sounds in *yes* and *well* (or the final sounds in *say* and *how*, for that matter), which are usually represented by the symbols [j] and [w]. The vowellike quality of these glides is borne out by the fact that there is no stoppage or noticeable friction involved in their production; yet they cannot be classified as vowels because they never form a syllable center (as vowels do, by definition). And because they are always found associated with a vowel, though functioning as consonants on account of their nonsyllabic nature, these glides are also known as *semivowels* or *semiconsonants*. They could just as well be called nonsyllabic vowels because their role in language is to partake in the formation of vowel sequences called *diphthongs* and *triphthongs* (see page 41). Linguists and phoneticians are generally agreed that the sound of [r] is "probably the most variable of all consonants in our language."[7] Its many variations, we are told, are due to the history of its development. It seems that at an earlier stage of the English language, this was a *trilled* sound, that is, a sound formed by making the tip of the tongue vibrate against the upper gums

under the pressure of the escaping breath, producing a series of taps. It is still common in some varieties of present-day English, notably Scottish and Irish speech, as well as in many other European and non-European languages. Sometimes the vibration is reduced to a single tap, in which case we speak of a *flap*, as in the southern British pronunciation of *very, merry, American,* and the like.

The American English [r] is generally considered to be a glide, comparable to [j] and [w]. It involves no oral closure either and has therefore a vowellike quality. It differs from the preceding glides, however, in that it does not enter into the formation of diphthongs and triphthongs, but it lends definite " r-coloring " to the preceding and following vowels. Because it is formed by curling the tip of the tongue back toward the roof of the mouth, the American [r] is technically known as a *retroflex glide* (from the Latin *retro* ' backwards ' + *flectere* ' to bend ').

5. *Vowels* In the production of these sounds, the continuous airstream is unobstructed, save for modifications of the oral cavity by various movements of the tongue and the lips, causing however, no audible friction. These will be treated separately later on.

Nasals, vibrants (the trilled [r]), laterals, glides, and vowels are sometimes subsumed under the general heading of RESONANTS.

It will be seen from the foregoing discussion that the dividing line between vowels and consonants is, at best, tenuous and blurred. There is actually a continuum between vowel- and consonantlike sounds; we start with the position of maximum sonority—say, the sound written with an *a* in *father*—and progress through ever-increasing constriction and friction in the oral passage until we reach the point of complete closure and blocking of the breathstream. This continuum is illustrated on page 33.

THE REPRESENTATION OF SPEECH SOUNDS

If we are to talk about them, speech sounds must somehow be represented in writing. As members of a literate community we are accustomed to thinking of speech in terms of the written language, the more so since the letters of the alphabet make an attempt at representing specific types of speech sounds. Thus, we associate the letter *b* with the sound of [b] and the letter *m* with the sound of [m]. Though this may work out in a handful of cases,

The Continuum of Articulation Between Vowellike and Consonantlike Sounds

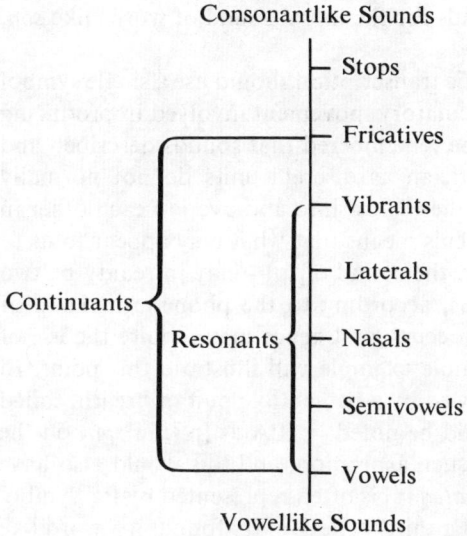

the representation of a sound by a letter of the alphabet is, more often than not, quite misleading. Take, for instance, the letter *a* and compare it with the sounds it stands for in such words as *name, man, father, fall, many,* and *alone*. Are these sounds identical or even similar? And how about the second sound in *pot*? It is written with the letter *o*, and yet it is pronounced by many speakers of American English with the same vowel sound as in *father*. The limitations of traditional orthography, not only of English but of many other languages, are obvious, hence the necessity of devising an objective system of recording the sounds of speech. The International Phonetic Association, recognizing as early as 1886 the need for such a system of notation, has developed over the years a set of symbols that provides a frame of reference in which the sounds of all the languages of the world can be classified. The International Phonetic Alphabet (IPA) is a *phonetic spelling system* in which the same sound is always represented by the same symbol, regardless of how the sound is spelled, very much the way the mathematician uses but one symbol for each numerical concept.

Because IPA uses essentially the letters of our Roman alphabet as phonetic symbols it is customary to enclose the symbols in square brackets: [ ]. For instance, [s] is a phonetic symbol with a specific value which stands for the initial sound of words like *son*, *scene*, and *cent*.

Ideally, then, a phonetic transcription should use a single symbol for each discernible articulatory movement involved in producing a given sound. It must be remembered that sounds described and classified by the phonetician as discrete units do not normally occur in isolation but rather "flow into and overlap each other in a modulated stream."[8] This means that what may appear to us to be the same sound—say, the sound of [p]—may in reality be two or more different sounds, according to the phonetic makeup of the word in which each occurs, and hence may require the use of different symbols. A simple example will illustrate this point. In *pit* the [p] sound is followed by a perceptible puff of breath, called *aspiration*, and this would be noted in IPA as [p']; in *spit*, on the other hand, there is no such aspiration, and this would also have to be noted. The *unaspirated* [p] is often represented by the symbol [p⁼]. We could even add a third variety of [p] found in a word like *lipstick*, where this sound is said to be *unreleased*, that is, where the lips close after the vowel is pronounced. This could be symbolized as [p']. It is the phonetician's task to record all these particular features of which a speaker may not even be conscious. (In fact, it is doubtful whether the average English speaker is aware of the three different [p] sounds in the above examples.)

Linguists (and phoneticians too) have found that the sounds of a given language can be classified without describing every observable and identifiable detail, concentrating only on those features that are significant because they keep utterances apart. Whether the initial sound in *pin* is aspirated or not is, for the speaker of English, rather irrelevant in terms of the meaning of the word (as a matter of fact, some foreign speakers are likely to pronounce the word without the accompanying puff of breath), as long as the [p] is not replaced by, say, the sound [b], in which case we would get the word *bin*. Recognizing that not all phonetic features in a language are *distinctive*, or *relevant*—that is, features which may change the meaning of a word—linguistic scholars have devised for each language they wish to analyze a system of transcription that will represent distinctive sounds only, leaving aside all nondistinctive (or nonrelevant) features—that is, those which do not alter the meaning of a word. This system is known as a *phonemic transcription*, since it represents only the phonemes, the distinctive sound units of a language. Using, on the whole, the letters of the Roman alphabet, this system has the advantage of reducing the potentially unlimited number of symbols used to represent the infinite number of actual speech sounds (it has never been estimated just how many sounds the human speech organs are theoretically capable of producing) to a rather *limited* number of distinct symbols because the sounds of a language are organized into a *finite* number of distinctive units. While the *phonetic* symbols of IPA or existing adaptations thereof may be used to represent the phonetic material of any language, *phonemic* symbols, which it is customary to enclose within slanted bars / /, must be defined in terms of the particular language under study.

THE CLASSIFICATION OF ENGLISH CONSONANTS AND VOWELS

In the following classification of the consonant and vowel sounds of English, keep in mind that reference will be made to sound *ranges* rather than actual sounds; hence we will find it more convenient to speak of consonant and vowel *phonemes*.

Speech sounds are named according to those parts of the speech mechanism that are used in making them. The nomenclature involved is not really difficult, even though expressions like "voiceless bilabial stop" (which happens to be the description of the phoneme /p/) may appear rather formidable at first. There are a series of questions that must be answered in connection with the articulatory description of speech sounds. For the *consonants* we may phrase them as follows:

1. What happens at the glottis? Is there any vocal vibration in the larynx during the production of a given sound, or is the glottis wide open to let the breathstream through without obstacle?
2. What is the *place of articulation* above the glottis? At what point, in other words, are the articulators (lips, teeth, tongue, gums, palate) brought together to form a given consonant sound?

3. What is the *manner of articulation*, that is, the degree of obstruction along the oral and nasal channels?

For the division of speech sounds into *voiced* and *voiceless*, see page 28.

The *points of articulation* are best studied in conjunction with the diagram on page 26, showing the organs of speech. Since all consonants are characterized by either a closure or a narrowing at some point in the mouth, there are always *two* articulators that come into contact at the point of articulation. The most mobile organ of speech is, of course, the *tongue*, which is responsible for more varieties of articulation than any other speech organ. The principal places of contact of the various parts of the tongue (tip, blade, front, and back) with other speech organs are the teeth, the upper gumridge, the hard palate, the soft palate, or velum, and the uvula (though the latter is not used by speakers of English except for gargling). The only time the tongue does not intervene is when the two lips or the lower lip and upper teeth are involved in the articulation of a speech sound, as in [p], [b], [f], and [v]. The *lower lip*, which moves freely against and away from the upper lip and upper teeth, is another highly movable organ. Because of their relative position, and to distinguish them from the rest of the speech organs, the tongue and lower lip are sometimes referred to as the *lower articulators*, whereas the others are the *upper articulators*. Here, then, is a rather convenient table that may serve to define the various articulations according to the articulators involved.

Lower Articulators	Upper Articulators	Name of Articulation
lower lip	upper lip	bilabial
lower lip	upper teeth	labiodental
tip of the tongue	upper teeth	dental
tip of the tongue	upper gumridge	alveolar
front of the tongue	hard (bony) palate	prepalatal
back of the tongue	soft palate (velum)	velar
the two vocal cords		glottal

Adapted from Gleasons's table of English Articulations, from *An Introduction to Descriptive Linguistics*, Revised Edition, by H. A. Gleason, Jr. Copyright © 1955, 1961 by Holt, Rinehart and Winston, Inc. Used by permission of Holt, Rinehart and Winston, Inc.

The *manner of articulation* tells us *how* a given sound is articulated. As we have already seen in our discussion of noncontinuants and continuants (page 29), there are many ways of modifying the release of the airstream. (You may want to refer again to the diagram on page 33, which illustrates the continuum of articulation between consonantlike and vowellike sounds.)

The diagram on page 38 charts the consonant phonemes of English. An illustrative word is given for each phoneme, and the letter (or combination of letters) representing it is underlined. Manners of articulation are shown vertically, while points of articulation are listed horizontally. When you describe consonants according to the three criteria that are important for keeping phonemes apart, begin by stating whether the articulation is voiced or voiceless, then identify the place of articulation, and finally the manner. Thus the initial sound of the English word *pool* is defined as a " voiceless bilabial stop " and that of *goal* as a " voiced velar stop." Remember that laterals, nasals, and semivowels (glides) are usually voiced. Also notice that the latter are classified as consonants because they occur in much the same position as traditional consonants.

Unlike consonants, *vowel sounds* are normally voiced, though voiceless vowels do occur in some non-European languages. (We are, of course, not concerned with whispered speech, in which vowels would naturally be voiceless.) Hence, the question as to what happens at the glottis in the pronunciation of a vowel is irrelevant. Since the articulation of vowels does not involve contact between two articulators (such as the tongue and the upper gumridge), their classification and description must follow different criteria. There are two basic questions we must ask: (1) What is the position of the tongue in the mouth? and (2) What is the shape of the lips? Take, for instance, the words *beat*, *but*, and *boot*. You will notice that in pronouncing these words, your tongue moves along a horizontal axis from the front part of the mouth to the back. Accordingly, we speak of *front* (*beat*), *central* (*but*), and *back* (*boot*) vowels. Now pronounce the words *beat*, *bit*, *book*, and *boot*. Observe that in all instances your tongue is quite close to the palate (both hard and soft); that is, it is raised *high* in the mouth. Conversely, for words like *bat* and *pot* the tongue lies *low*, that is, away from the palate. In between these two extremes on the vertical axis, there is a *mid* position of the tongue, as in the words *bait*, *bet*, *boat*, and *bought*. These two

The Consonant Phonemes of English

	Point of articulation / Manner of articulation	Bilabial	Labiodental	Dental	Alveolar	Prepalatal	Velar	Glottal
Stops	voiceless	/p/ (pin)			/t/ (tin)		/k/ (coal)	
	voiced	/b/ (bin)			/d/ (din)		/g/ (goal)	
Affricates	voiceless				tš	/č/ (church)		
	voiced					/j/ (judge)		
Fricatives — slit	voiceless		/f/ (fine)	/θ/ (think)			✗	/h/ (house)
	voiced	β	/v/ (vine)	/ð/ (this)			ɣ	
Fricatives — groove	voiceless				/s/ (seal)	/š/ (shoe)		
	voiced				/z/ (zeal)	/ž/ (azure)		
Laterals					/l/ (life)			
Nasals		/m/ (man)			/n/ (now)	ñ ɱ	/ŋ/ (sing)	
Semivowels		/w/ (water)			/r/ (red)	/j/ (yes)		

voiced { (Laterals, Nasals, Semivowels)

factors, *tongue height* (high, mid, low) and *tongue position* (front, central, back), intersect with a third one, namely, the shape of the lips in the production of vowel sounds. These can be rounded or spread (unrounded). Except for the back vowels in *bought*, *boat*, *book*, and *boot*, which are automatically accompanied by lip-rounding, all vowels in English are unrounded. It is, of course, possible to pronounce front vowels with rounded lips and back vowels with lip-spreading; rounded front vowels are quite common in languages like French, German, Swedish, Hungarian, and Turkish, to name but a few. Using these criteria, the vowel in *beat* will be called an "unrounded high front" vowel, while that in *boot* will be a "rounded high back" vowel; the first vowel in *about* is an "unrounded mid central" vowel, and that in *pot* is an "unrounded low back" vowel. As you study the diagram below, see if you can identify all the vowel phonemes in English according to (1) lip shape, (2) tongue height, and (3) tongue position.

THE CARDINAL VOWEL SYSTEM

Phoneticians and linguists have used various frameworks for classifying vowels. One such frame, in which vowels are defined with reference to a set of arbitrarily chosen vowels and without reference to any particular language, has been suggested by the British phonetician Daniel Jones. Recognizing the difficulty of accurate vowel description, since "the shade of vowel used depends on the locality from which the speaker comes," he proposes "a scale of 'Cardinal Vowels,' that is, a set of fixed vowel sounds having known acoustic qualities and known tongue and lip positions."[9] Jones' system consists of eight of these "theoretical" vowel sounds, four front vowels and four back vowels, represented by the phonetic symbols [i], [e], [ɛ], [a], [ɑ], [ɔ], [o], and [u]. The following diagram shows the cardinal vowels and their approximate relationship to English vowels. Again, an illustrative word is given for each vowel phoneme, and the letter or letter combination which represents it is underlined.

It should not be assumed that the cardinal vowels in any way coincide with the English vowel phonemes, although some of them, like those in *bet*, *bought*, and the American English *pot*, are fairly good approximations. In the words *beat*, *bait*, *boat*, and *boot*, where vowels are the nearest to the cardinal vowels

The Cardinal Vowels and their Relation to English Vowel Phonemes*

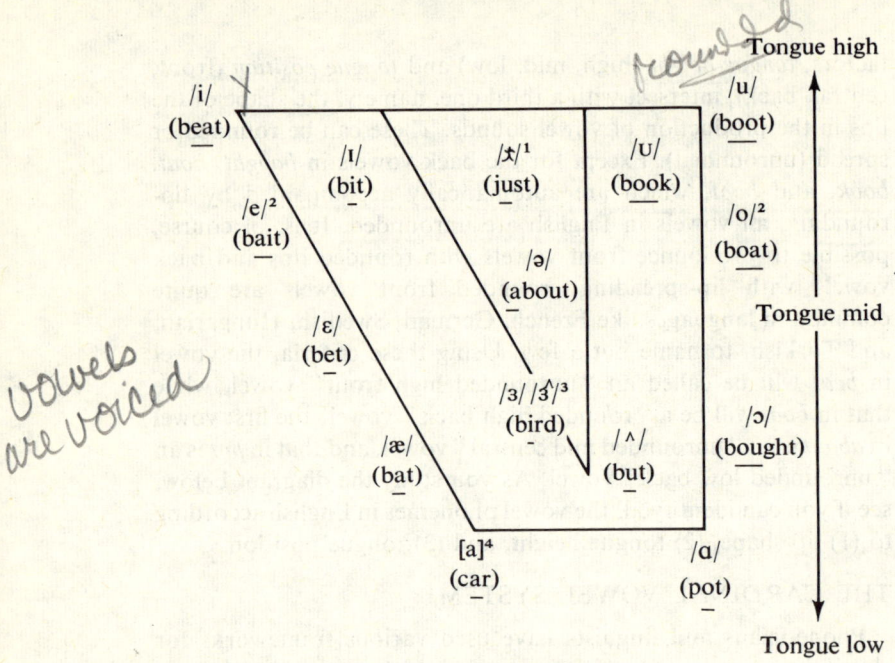

* This chart follows Charles K. Thomas' analysis in *An Introduction to the Phonetics of American English,* 2nd ed. New York: The Ronald Press, 1958, pp. 55–130.
[1] As in "just a minute" in some speakers' pronunciation. More common in unstressed syllable.
[2] Note that in *bait* and *boat* the /e/ and /o/ phonemes are realized as diphthongs; that is, the sounds of [e] and [o] are always followed by the glides [j] and [w] respectively.
[3] The symbol ɜ stands for the "r-less" vowel sound, whereas the symbol ɜ˞ represents the "r-colored" sound, which is the more common in American English. These vowel sounds occur only in stressed position.
[4] As pronounced by an Eastern New Englander. The symbol is enclosed in square brackets because this is not a separate phoneme of English. In English phonemic transcription, the letter symbol "a" is, therefore, often used to represent the phonemes in *pot* and *father* rather than the IPA symbol ɑ.

rounding of only back vowels in English

[i], [e], [o], and [u], you may notice that while pronouncing the vowel sounds, your tongue moves from one vowel position to another. In the first two instances the tongue glides forward and upward toward the roof of the mouth (the palate), while in the latter two cases there is a backward and upward gliding of this speech organ. This is because in English these four vowel sounds are articulated with some tension of the tongue muscles (hence the name *tense vowels*). It is a characteristic feature of the English sound system, as distinguished from many other languages where tense vowels are "pure" vowels—that is, single sounds pronounced with no change in the position of the speech organs—that all such vowel sounds assume a diphthongal quality. This difference in tension is quite noticeable as you move from *beat* to *bit*, from *bait* to *bet*, or from *boot* to *book*. (Put your finger on the muscles underneath your chin and you will feel it.) Because of the relative absence of tension in *bit*, *bet*, and *book*, the vowel sounds in these words are called *lax*.

The pronunciation of vowels differs greatly from speaker to speaker. The Scotsman is likely to pronounce the words *bait* and *boat* without the glide that is heard in the speech of most speakers of English, and the same vowel that appears as a single sound in the speech of the Easterner may come out as a diphthong, that is, a single vowel followed by a glide, in the Southerner's mouth. Accordingly, one linguist's transcription may differ from that of another. Indeed, some will note, even in phonemic transcription, the diphthongal nature of the vowel sounds in *beat*, *bait*, *boat*, and *boot* and transcribe the words /bijt/, /bejt/, /bowt/, and /buwt/, using the glide symbols /j/ and /w/; others, on the other hand, may dispense with the glide symbols altogether and transcribe the same words /bit/, /bet/, /bot/, and /but/. How speech sounds are represented and what symbols we use is unimportant in the last analysis, as long as we clearly define the symbols in terms of the sounds they are supposed to stand for.

DIPHTHONGS AND TRIPHTHONGS

Single vowel sounds are also known as *simple vowel nuclei* (a vowel being the *nucleus*, or *peak*, of a syllable), while a single vowel followed by a glide is called a *complex vowel nucleus*. More familiar terms are *monophthong* (from the Greek *mono* 'one' + *phthongos* 'sound') to designate the former and *diphthong* (from the Greek *dis* 'twice' + *phthongos*) to denote the latter. Traditionally a diphthong is defined as a sequence of two vowel sounds belonging to the same syllable. Since the function of a vowel is to be a syllable carrier in speech, it follows that one of the vowel sounds making up a diphthong must be *nonsyllabic*; hence, we might bring the following precision to our definition and say that a diphthong is a combination of a syllabic and a nonsyllabic vowel. In *house* the [a] sound is syllabic, whereas in *yes* it is the [ɛ]. According to the position of the nonsyllabic, or semivocalic, element with respect to the syllabic vowel, we speak of *rising* (for example, *yes*) and *falling* (for example, *house*) diphthongs. When a syllabic vowel is both preceded and followed by a nonsyllabic vowel, we speak of a *triphthong* (from the Greek *tri*, relating to "three"), for example, the word *way*.

SYLLABIC CONSONANTS

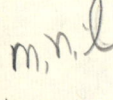

In the preceding paragraph we spoke of syllabic vowels and diphthongs. There are, however, instances in both English and many other languages where consonant sounds may become syllabic, in which case they take on a vowellike function in that they alone suffice to constitute a syllable. In expressions like *stop'em* (for *stop them*) or *kill'em* (for *kill them*) or in words like *button*, *sudden*, *cattle*, and *beetle*, the [m], [n], and [l] regularly become syllabic nuclei, as does the [r] glide in *butter*, *matter*, and *better*.

THE PHONEME

In the foregoing pages we have attempted to describe and identify, as briefly and succinctly as possible, the characteristics of the "raw material," that is, the speech sounds out of which language is made. As was stated earlier (see page 35), the number of sounds that the human speech organs are capable of producing is theoretically infinite. No language actually makes use of all the possibilities, but even so, the great variety of sounds used by members of a given speech community is quite bewildering. Linguists have discovered, however, that not all phonetic elements serve to keep meanings apart. Thus in the examples *pit*, *spit*, and *lipstick* already mentioned, phonetically speaking, there are three distinct though closely related [p] sounds, which we call "aspirated," "unaspirated," and "unreleased," respectively. However, the substitution of, say, [p-] (unaspirated) for [pʻ] (aspirated) in *pit* would be irrelevant in terms of the meaning of the word. When the [p] in *pit* is replaced by a [b] sound, though, the result is the word *bit*, with a change in meaning.

What, then, makes the speaker of English accept the two varieties of the initial [p] sound in *pit* as the same sound and reject the identity of [p] and [b] in *pit* and *bit*? It so happens that in normal English speech the presence versus absence of aspiration is not a *distinctive* difference, one that would be capable of distinguishing one meaning from another, while voicing versus voicelessness is distinctive and hence perceptible to the average native speaker as a different sound. Furthermore, the aspirated and unaspirated (as well as the unreleased) varieties of [p] do not usually occur in similar positions, since their phonetic features are automatically determined by their position in the word, while [p] and [b] are likely to occur in the same position. And when they do, they change the meaning of a word (for example, from *pit* to *bit* or from *rip* to *rib*) because, as linguists say, they are *in contrast*. We can state, therefore, that /p/ and /b/ are *phonemes* of the English language, while [pʻ], [p⁼], and [pʼ] are *variants* (technically known as ALLOPHONES). Because these variants are in mutually exclusive positions—that is, they normally do not get in each other's way—we call them *positional variants* and say they are in *complementary distribution*. (*Distribution* is the sum total of all the positions in which a sound may occur.)

The concept of the phoneme is not really difficult to understand. Paul Roberts once characterized it as follows:

A phoneme is not exactly a single sound. It is more a collection of similar sounds which, in spite of their slight differences, sound the same to a native speaker of the language. If the native speaker hears them as the same, they are the same for him, and they make up one phoneme.[10]

It follows from this definition that a phoneme cannot actually be pronounced, since it is not a single, objective sound of speech but rather a group of related sounds that are referred to the consciousness of the speaker of a specific language as the same sound. The phoneme is an abstraction, so to speak, which exists only by virtue of its members—the variants, or allophones. Thus the English phoneme /p/ comes into being through [pʻ], [p⁼], and [pʼ], as the case may be. (Note that there may be great variation in the number of recognizable variants that make up a phoneme. The English /p/ shows greater variation than does English /f/.)

In order further to clarify the concept of the phoneme and to show, at the same time, that a particular sound or class of sounds does not function in the same way when we pass from one language to another, we offer the following examples:

1. Let us come back to the examples of *pit*, *spit*, and *lipstick*. You will have been convinced by now, we hope, that there are three different [p] sounds involved here which, for the sake of argument, we shall call p_1, p_2, and p_3, that is, aspirated, unaspirated, and unreleased, respectively. Since aspiration is *not* a relevant feature in English, the word *pit* will not change meaning, whether we pronounce it with p_1 or p_2. Because these are both members of the English phoneme /p/, it will be sufficient to define the latter as a "voiceless bilabial stop," as opposed to a "voiced bilabial stop," the English phoneme /b/. Not so in Mandarin Chinese. Aspiration in this particular language happens to be a *relevant* feature, since both the aspirated and the unaspirated [p] normally occur in the same position, so that there is a *contrast* between /pʻa/ and /pa/, with a corresponding change in meaning. Contrary to English, then, p_1 and p_2 are not merely variants whose phonetic features are determined by their position in the word (or the phonetic context) but two separate phonemes. The learner of Mandarin Chinese would have to be especially careful to observe this *phonemic* contrast which in his language is only a matter of positional variants.

2. When we say *keep*, *calm*, and *cool*, we may not be at once aware that these are three distinct [k] articulations, since they are interpreted by speakers of English as the "same" sound, that is, as belonging to the /k/ phoneme. Actually, each [k] sound is selected in accordance with the following vowel sound; although

the phoneme /k/ is usually classified as a "voiceless velar stop," the [k] in *keep* is much farther forward along the hard palate than it is for *calm* or *cool*. Again, these three varieties would never contrast with each other in normal English speech; for instance, the [k] in *keep* would not usually occur before the back vowel [u]. In Arabic, on the other hand, both the palatal [k] and the velar [k] can be followed by the same vowel sound, for example, /kalb/ 'dog' (with palatal [k]) versus /qalb/ 'heart' (with velar [k]). Because they are thus in opposition to each other, we would have to state that these two varieties of [k] in English are two separate phonemes in Arabic, generally represented as /k/ and /q/.

3. Nasalized vowels do not normally occur in English, although they can often be heard in the speech of some people who "talk through their noses," as the saying goes. In any event, nasalized vowels, if and when they occur, are not distinctive in English. In French, on the other hand, the phonetic feature called *nasalization* (the pronunciation of vowel sounds with the breathstream passing partly through the nose and the mouth) alone distinguishes /bo/ 'beautiful' from /bõ/ 'good.'

4. A Spanish speaker is likely to say *leave* for *live* and *live* when he really means *leave*. (A Spanish student of mine actually wrote "I am now *leaving* in New York" on an examination paper.) This is because the speaker of Spanish has only one /i/ phoneme in his language, which seems to encompass the ranges of both the /i/ and the /ɪ/ phonemes of English. Whether a word like *vivo* 'I live' is pronounced with a long or short [i] sound, the meaning remains the same. And unless the Spanish speaker is aware that these two vowel sounds, which function as variants in his language, are two separate phonemes in English, he is most likely to mispronounce all words in which the difference in meaning is determined by the sole contrast between English /i/ and /ɪ/, for example, "Yesterday he *bit* me" (for *beat*), "I want a *pitch*" (for *peach*), "*Seat* down!" (for *sit*).

Examples of this sort could be extended almost indefinitely; but all of them would merely serve to confirm the fact that languages differ considerably in both the number and the types of contrasts in the sound pattern. It is the merit of the structuralists to have worked out a method of analysis to sort out, so to speak, the distinctive features of the sounds of a language in context and from the point of view of their function. Thanks to this *phonemic analysis*, it is possible to organize the infinite variety of speech sounds into a limited number of units, ranging from about fifteen to fifty, depending on the language. The method linguists have used to determine whether a difference in sound is correlated with a difference in meaning is often called the *commutation*, or *substitution*, test. It seeks to establish the so-called *binary oppositions* that exist between, say, /p/ and /b/ in *pit* versus *bit*, or /t/ and /d/ in *pat* versus *pad*, or /i/ and /ɪ/ in *seat* versus *sit*, and so forth, in otherwise identical pairs of words.

STRESS, PITCH, AND JUNCTURE

Consonant and vowel phonemes occur as successive units, or *segments*, in the stream of speech. Because of this sequential arrangement in the spoken chain, they are referred to as SEGMENTAL PHONEMES. There is, however, much more to speech than a mere assemblage of sounds in a kind of linear order, such as the linear arrangement of the letters of the alphabet. The fundamental qualities of the human voice are comparable to those of any musical instrument (or should we say any *other* musical instrument?) in that it has variability of pitch and varying intensity of volume. We know that not all syllables are pronounced exactly alike, either in respect to *stress*—that is, the force with which the voice bears upon one syllable rather than another—or to *pitch*—that is, the musical tone, or the frequency of vibration imparted to them. Stress and pitch have been found to be important features of the English signaling system in that they perform a *distinctive* function in the language. They are, in other words, phonemes of English; and because they occur above the vowel and consonant segments, at least in written representation, and usually affect more than one segmental phoneme, they are called SUPRASEGMENTAL PHONEMES.

Stress involves the loudness or softness with which sounds are uttered, that is, the degree of prominence given to a particular syllable. It is a signal that is capable of lexical differentiation, as, for instance, in *pérmit* versus *permít*, *súbject* versus *subjéct*, and *ímport* versus *impórt*, where it distinguishes between noun and verb. In some languages it can also distinguish between verb forms, as in Spanish *cánto* 'I sing' versus *cantó* 'he sang' or Italian *párlo* 'I speak' versus *parló* 'he spoke.' In other languages, for example Czech and Hungarian, the position of stress is a fixed one (always on the first syllable), and it is not a relevant linguistic feature.

It has been traditional to distinguish four stress phonemes in English, to which the following names and symbols have been assigned:

1. *Primary stress* / ´ /, the most prominent
2. *Secondary stress* / ^/, next to the loudest
3. *Tertiary stress* / ` /, or *medium* stress
4. *Weak stress* / ˘ /[11]

It is clear that not all stress contrasts appear in every utterance. Thus, in *Sît dówn*! there are only two stresses, whereas in a sentence like *Whêre's the máilbòx*? we have a good illustration of the four stress levels.

Stress alone distinguishes such ambiguities in writing as *He's a sweet salesman*, in which we wonder whether *sweet* is to be considered a modifying adjective or a noun modifying another noun. In other words, is the salesman sweet or does he sell sweets? The stress pattern will, of course, give us the answer:

Hê's ă swêet sálesmăn. (The salesman is sweet.)
Hĕ's ă swéet sâlesmăn. (He sells candy.)[12]

The improper use of stress may lead to some rather amusing nonsense. As Roberts puts it: "You might not be surprised to get a "wríting desk" for Christmas. But you would probably be very much surprised if you got a "wrîting désk."[13]

Pitch could be defined as the acoustic result of the frequency of vibration of the vocal cords. The greater the number of vibrations, the higher the pitch, and conversely, the slower the vibrations, the lower the pitch. In some languages voice pitch functions at word level, while in others only at utterance level. To put it in more technical terms, pitch in some languages is phonemically distinct *on individual syllables*, whereas in others it is functionally significant only as *terminal contour*, or *clause terminal*. That is, it is distinct only at the end of an utterance, as when the change of pitch distinguishes between *John is my friend* as a simple statement (with falling tone), a question (with rising tone), or a suspended statement (with sustained pitch level).

Examples of languages in which a difference in pitch on an otherwise identical sound sequence may distinguish one meaning from another are the languages of China, Southeast Asia (Thai, Burmese, Vietnamese), parts of Africa (languages of the Sudan, the Bantu, and the Hottentot groups), and some Indian languages of North America. Since pitch differences used to signal phonemic differences are called *tones*, these languages are often referred to as TONE, or tonal, languages. "Each syllable in a tone language," says Professor Kenneth L. Pike, "has a pitch as fully basic to the word in which it occurs as *p*, *t*, and *f* are inherent in English *pie*, *time*, and *wife*."[14] Tones on a given syllable may be either *level* (in which case they contrast with each other in terms of relative height) or *gliding* (involving a rise, a fall, or a combination of both during the pronunciation of the syllable). A frequently quoted example from Mandarin Chinese is the word *ma*, which means "mother" with high level, "hemp" with high rising, "horse" with a combination of falling and rising, and "scold" with low falling tones.

In English, as in many other languages, pitch contrasts are significant only to the extent that they serve to characterize speech segments uttered between pauses, technically known as *phonological phrases*. Although there is great variation among speakers in the use of these contrasts, it has been customary to distinguish four relative pitch levels as phonemes of English. These are usually numbered /1/, /2/, /3/, and /4/, using the lowest number for the lowest pitch, followed by *mid* (or normal), *high*, and *extra high*, respectively. In transcription these numbers are written above the words that receive the pitch. Occasionally, especially for pedagogical purposes, lines are used underneath or above the words, as in the following example:

2 3 1
I'm going home now.

I'm going | home | now.

Notice that the line directly underneath a word (or words) corresponds to level 2, considered to be the normal pitch at which you begin to speak; the line directly above a word (*home* in our example) corresponds to level 3; while the lines representing levels 1 and 4 are drawn one space below and above the words they refer to, respectively. Pitches combine into melody patterns that end in one of the three terminals already mentioned. Each utterance, then, consists of one or more pitch phonemes and one terminal. These are usually symbolized by arrows: ↑ for rising, ↓ for falling, and → for level terminals. (Slanted arrows for rising ↗ and falling ↘ contours are also in use.) In the sentence *John is my friend*, we could illustrate the various possibilities as follows:

2   3   1
John is my friend ↓ (simple statement)
2   3   4
John is my friend ↑ (surprised question)[15]
2   3
John is my friend → (suspension, indicating that more is to come)

Some scholars, following the Trager and Smith analysis (see note 11), prefer to call these terminal contours *terminal junctures* (a juncture being a significant break or division in the speech stream) and use the following symbols: / || / (double-bar juncture) for rising, / # / (double-cross juncture) for falling, and / | / (single-bar juncture) for level terminals. The last, which indicates a pause in an utterance, is frequently used to set off nonrestrictive clauses and appositives and would roughly correspond to a comma in writing.

There is obviously a close relationship between the stress and pitch patterns of an utterance in that the stressed syllable is likely to receive a different pitch from the immediately preceding or following syllables. But while *syllabic stress* is generally fixed by convention and may, as we have seen, alter the meaning of a word, the intonational pattern of an utterance—the *phrasal stress*, as we might call it—merely reflects the emotional content of the information that the speaker wishes to convey.

Stress, pitch, and terminal junctures, subsumed under the

general heading of INTONATION, represent contrasts in the English language; hence they are phonemic. To complete the inventory of the phonemes of English, however, there is one more contrast that remains to be discussed briefly. It is the contrast that is found in the transition between syllables and words in such items as *I scream* versus *ice cream*, *a nice man* versus *an ice man*, *a name* versus *an aim*, and many others. The pause between, say, *ice* and *cream*, and *I* and *scream*, the only feature that differentiates the meaning between these otherwise identical sound sequences, is known as an *internal open, or plus, juncture*. It is symbolized in transcription by a plus sign /+/; thus /ajs+krim/ versus /aj+skrim/. And just as terminal junctures do, a plus juncture also breaks the flow of speech, except that it does so on the syllable and word levels rather than the phrase level.

Some linguists also speak of a *close juncture* to refer to an uninterrupted sequence of phonemes, as in *nitrate*, which would be distinguished from *night rate* by the presence of a close rather than an open juncture.

A more detailed account of the sound structure of English would not be in keeping with the scope of this text. On the other hand, since language is primarily an oral means of communication, we felt it was important to acquaint you with the principles of phonetics, the objective analysis of speech sounds as universal realities, and phonemics, the study of the phonemes, or the significant sound units of a language.

Sound units, which are basically meaningless, combine into larger units that become carriers of meaning. To examine these combinations we must now proceed to the next level of linguistic structure, the level of language forms.

notes

1. *General Linguistics: An Introductory Survey.* London: Longmans, Green, 1964, pp. 83–84.
2. Note that the vocal organs have more basic biological functions, such as breathing (lungs, larynx) and eating and drinking (lips, teeth, tongue).
3. Adapted by permission from *Language for Everybody.* New York: Devin-Adair, 1961, p. 71.
4. There are a number of excellent manuals that deal with the anatomy and physiology of speech. For a suggested list, consult the Bibliography.
5. Bernard Bloch and George L. Trager, *Outline of Linguistic Analysis* (Special Publication of the Linguistic Society of America). Baltimore: Linguistic Society of America, 1942, p. 12.
6. See Charles F. Hockett, *A Course in Modern Linguistics.* New York: Macmillan, 1958, pp. 67 ff.
7. Arthur J. Bronstein, *The Pronunciation of American English.* New York: Appleton-Century-Crofts, 1960, p. 117.
8. W. Nelson Francis, *The Structure of American English.* New York: Ronald Press, 1958, p. 59.
9. *An Outline of English Phonetics*, 9th ed. Cambridge: W. Heffer and Sons, 1964, p. 28.
10. *Patterns of English.* New York: Harcourt Brace Jovanovich, 1956, p. 223.
11. This view has been prevalent among American linguists ever since it was first proposed by George L. Trager and Henry Lee Smith, Jr., in *An Outline of English Structure* (Studies in Linguistics: Occasional Papers 3). 7th printing. Washington: American Council of Learned Societies, 1957, pp. 35–39.
12. Examples taken from Roberts, *op. cit.*, p. 229.
13. Roberts, *loc. cit.*
14. *Tone Languages.* Ann Arbor: The University of Michigan Press, 1948, p. 5.
15. We say "surprised" question, since all questions do not follow the same pattern. Those introduced by the so-called *wh*-words,

such as *who*, *where*, *what*, and *why*, closely follow that of the simple statement, with the voice dropping to a lower pitch level. Conversely, the *yes–no* question is often pronounced rather like a suspended utterance, ending in a level tone. For a good summary of these pitch patterns, see Paul Roberts, *Understanding English*, New York: Harper & Row, 1958. pp. 237 ff.

4
the structure of language: the study of language forms

The phonological system of a language is concerned with the selection and organization of sounds into basic units called phonemes. These units are not meaningful elements in and of themselves, except to the extent that they serve to differentiate the meaning of words, as in *pit* versus *bit*. The phonemes, the building blocks of language, as it were, are combined into larger units, usually thought of as words, that have recognizable meaning. The concept of the word is not easy to define, and, in any case, a definition of what a word is may be attempted only in terms of the particular language under study. We could say that in English, for example, a word is a basic and meaningful sentence component that speakers recognize as the smallest speech unit because it admits of a momentary pause before and after it and, furthermore, is marked off in writing by a space on either side. Thus, *woman* is a word and so is *womanly*; yet, it is possible to isolate the *-ly* element and tack it on to the word *brother* with the identical meaning with which it is used when added to *woman*, namely, "in the manner of a . . ."

Consider the following sentence:

Yesterday John ran away with the baker's younger daughter.

You will agree that all these words can occur in other contexts with the same or, at least, similar meanings. They are reusable, so to speak, as in *Yesterday I went shopping*, *In terms of man's history, the invention of writing is but of yesterday*; *John is my friend*, *I like John* (but not *I am going to the john* or *I bought a demijohn of wine*, where the requirement of similarity of meaning is not met); *The prisoner ran away with a hostage*, *He was scared and ran away*; *John is older than I am*, *The older of his two daughters*, and so forth.

The question is whether these words can be broken up into smaller units that still have some sort of separate meaning and whether they, too, can be reused with approximately the same meaning.

Let us look at these words individually:

1. *Yesterday* is obviously made up of *yester* and *day*. The first element, which corresponds to the German *gestern* 'yesterday,' also occurs in a combination like *yesteryear*, but only *day* has an independent existence, as in, *It is a good day for swimming*, *The last day of the month*, and so forth.

2. In the compound verb *ran away* (which speakers may well consider as one word, since they are unlikely to pause between *ran* and *away*), both *ran* and *away* can be used independently in other contexts, for example, *He ran two miles* and *The bird flew away*. But what about the word *away*? The *a*-element recurs in the forms *aground*, *ashore*, *around*, and *aloft*, so that *away*, in turn, may be said to consist of two components, *a-* and *way*.

3. The definite article *the* and the preposition *with* may, indeed, be considered "words" if we use the criterion of a potential pause before and after either form as a definition of a word. Yet none of these elements could stand as a complete meaningful utterance within a context like the verb "read" in answer to the question *What are you going to do now?—Read*, or the utterance "John's" in the context *Whose hat is this?—John's*.

4. Now look at the word *baker's*. If we take off the final *-s*, we are left with the form *baker*. This involves no change in the basic meaning of the word. The effect of the *s* (pronounced [z] in this instance) is merely to specify *baker* with respect to possession, as in the case of *Mary's new hat*, *my wife's relatives*, *children's corner*, *what in heaven's name*, and so forth. (The apostrophe before the *s* in writing simply serves to differentiate this particular *s*, which shows possession, from the *s* which indicates "more than one.") The *s* in *baker's*, then, does have a meaning, namely, "belonging to" (let us call it the possessive *s*), though it acquires this meaning only when tacked on to a noun.

We can further divide *baker* into *bake* and *-er*. This latter element occurs also in *builder, singer, dancer, caterer* and many other words where it carries the meaning of agent, that is, "one who performs the action expressed by the verb." We may, therefore, conclude that the form *baker's* is a combination of three elements, namely, *bake + er + s*, which are all meaningful. Of the three however, only *bake* can stand by itself as a word.

5. The native speaker of English will at once realize that *younger* is made up of *young* and *-er*, since the former can occur in utterances like *He is a young man, This tree is quite young*, and so forth, while the latter is found in forms like *prettier, finer, wider, longer*—and now even in *coffee-er!* This *-er* element is not to be confused with the *-er* discussed under (4), since it has an entirely different function. It is also meaningful, though only in conjunction with another speech unit, and can also be reused in other contexts, where it indicates "more."

6. Finally, let's take the word *daughter*. Can it be broken up into *daught-* and *-er* and used in other contexts with similar meanings for each element? The *daught-* element does not occur anywhere except in *daughter* and the *-er* is certainly not identical in meaning with the *-er*'s in *baker* and *younger*.

It might, of course, be argued that the *-er* element in *daughter* also occurs in the words *father, mother, brother,* and *sister* and that since these are terms of family relationship, this particular *-er* form may indicate some common feature of meaning. But just as *daught-* does not occur in other contexts with the meaning it has in *daughter*, the forms *fath-, moth-, broth-,* and *sist-* are not reusable elements with the meaning each has in *father, mother, brother,* and *sister*.[1]

Our sentence, *Yesterday John ran away with the baker's younger daughter*, according to our analysis, is made up of the following fourteen *smallest meaningful reusable* units of speech:

yester + day + John + ran + a + way + with + the + bake + er + s + young + er + daughter

THE CONCEPT OF THE MORPHEME

The units of speech we have just discussed are technically known as MORPHEMES. Scientifically speaking, the morpheme is a much more precise and definite linguistic unit than the word. Some morphemes may, indeed, be words, that is, meaningful forms that can stand by themselves, such as *day, John, ran, bake, daughter* and thousands of others like them. Others have no independent existence and assume meaning only insofar as they are attached to other morphemes, like *yester-, a-* (in *away*), *the, -er* and, *-s*. Accordingly, linguists speak of FREE and BOUND MORPHEMES. A free morpheme may also be called a *free form*, though the two terms are by no means synonymous, since a free form may also be a combination of a free and one or more bound morphemes, as in *huckleberry* (*huckle + berry*), *boyish* (*boy + ish*), *manly* (*man + ly*), and *unpredictable* (*un + predict + able*), or of two or more bound morphemes, as in *conceive* (*con + ceive*), *perceptive* (*per + cept + ive*), and *incomprehensible* (*in + com + prehens + ible*). A free form which cannot be further divided into lesser *free* forms is a *minimum free form*, which Bloomfield equates with the *word*.[2] Hence, *boy* is a word because it cannot be broken down into lesser free forms, but so is *boyish*, since it consists of only one free form combined with a bound form (a synonym for bound morpheme). Words of this latter type, containing one or more bound forms, are called *complex words*, in contrast to *compound words*, which are made up entirely of minimum free forms, such as *gentleman, blackbird*, and *altogether*.[3]

Any linguistic form, then, which cannot be broken down into smaller meaningful units is a morpheme. Some of these minimum units may consist of merely one sound (for example, the final *-s* in *baker's*); others may be of syllable length (for example, *-er* in *baker*); and others may be made up of several syllables, as in the name *Connecticut* or the word *crocodile*. It is important to remember that a given sound sequence that functions as a morpheme in certain words is not necessarily a morpheme wherever it shows up. The *-cut* element in *Connecticut* is not identical with the like-sounding morpheme in *glasscutter*, nor is the *-ile* in *crocodile* the same as that in *virile, senile,* and *puerile*, where *-ile* is a bound morpheme and means "having the quality of . . .," or in the word *vile*, which is a free morpheme.

A morpheme, either free or bound, that carries the basic meaning of a word is called a BASE or, in more traditional terminology, a ROOT, to which one or more bound forms may be "affixed." These are properly referred to as AFFIXES, which are of three kinds according to their *position* with respect to the base:

1. PREFIXES are added before the base (for example, *rewrite*).
2. SUFFIXES are attached to the end of the base (for example, *manly, boys*).
3. INFIXES are inserted in the base (for example, Arabic *katab* 'he wrote' from the root *k-t-b* 'write').

DERIVATIONAL AND INFLECTIONAL AFFIXES

According to their *function*, affixes are of two kinds:

1. DERIVATIONAL AFFIXES, which serve to *derive* related words that contain a common base (for example, *boyish, boyhood, rewrite, underwrite*, derived from the bases *boy* and *write*, respectively)[4]
2. INFLECTIONAL AFFIXES (also called *grammatical affixes*), which serve as signaling devices to show such grammatical relationships and aspects as *number* (*baker* versus *bakers* or *man* versus *men*), *person* (*I love* versus *he loves*), *tense* (*dream* versus *dreamed* or *sing* versus *sang*), *possession* (*baker* versus *baker's*), and *comparison* (*pretty* versus *prettier* versus *prettiest*)

Derivational affixes in English may be either prefixes or suffixes. Prefixes like *de-* (*de+escalate*), *ex-* (*ex+clude*), *inter-* (*inter+vene*), *re-* (*re+write*), *trans-* (*trans+gress*), and others, operate very much like prepositions (*de = down, away; ex = from, out of; inter = between; re = again, back; trans = across, beyond*) and are not entirely devoid of meaning content, that is, dictionary meaning. They serve to delimit the meaning of the base. Conversely, derivational suffixes like *-ly* (*man+ly*), *-ness* (*great+ness*), *-er* (*play+er*), *-age* (*shrink+age*), and so forth, are "empty" as far as actual meaning goes, except to the extent that they serve to determine the word class (part of speech) of a particular linguistic form. Thus, *man* is a noun, but *manly* is an adjective; *great* is an adjective, while *greatness* is a noun; *shrink* is a verb, but *shrinkage* is a noun; and so forth. English makes a great deal of use of derivational affixes to make new words from existing bases. A set of related words with a common base, for instance *man* and its derivatives *manly, mannish, manful, manliness manhood, manikin* ('little man'), and *superman*, is called a DERIVATIONAL PARADIGM.

In English, as in many other languages, inflectional affixes that indicate the grammatical function of words in a sentence are always placed *after* the base or the STEM.[5] They differ from derivational suffixes mainly in following ways:

1. They do not change the word class, for example, *boy, boys, boy's,* and *boys'* are nouns and both *work* and *worked* are verbs.
2. They may be added to *all* bases or stems of a given word class, for instance, *fail*s, *manage*s, and *shrink*s (while *-age* can only combine with *shrink* to form a noun but not with *fail* or *manage*, which require the suffixes *-ure* and *-ment*, respectively).
3. They always appear last in a word, for example, *stiffen*s or *greatness*es.
4. In principle, only one inflectional affix may be used with a given word.[6]

Inflectional prefixes are by no means uncommon. Thus, in *Swahili*, the most important member of the Bantu group of languages spoken in eastern, central, and southern Africa, the noun consists of a base *and* a prefix which shows whether it is singular or plural. For instance, from the base *-toto* are formed *mtoto* 'child' and *watoto* 'children' and from *-tu* we get *mtu* 'man' and *watu* 'men.'[7] Time of the action expressed by the verb is also marked by a "tense prefix" which is *na-* for present, *li-* for past and *ta-* for future. Taking the verb base *soma* 'read,' we have *watoto wanasoma* 'the children are reading' versus *watoto walisoma* 'the children were reading.[8]

In addition to the use of suffixes to show grammatical relationship, English also uses a device known as INTERNAL VOWEL CHANGE, that involves variation in the vowel of related bases. This linguistic process, whereby one morpheme replaces another within the word, is illustrated by such plural forms as *men, women, mice, geese* and by past tense forms like *shrunk, led, swam, found*, and many others. These vowel alterations, which are characteristic of the Germanic languages (those languages historically closely related to English), are often quite unsystematic and unpredictable and pose a difficult learning problem for the student.

INFIXES AND OTHER GRAMMATICAL PROCESSES

Infixes are inserted in the base within either vowel or consonant sequences. They are not found in English, although some linguists (Hockett among them) have interpreted internal vowel changes as kinds of infixes. (Accordingly, the plural form *men* would consist of the base *m-n* into which the inflectional morpheme *e* has been inserted.) Infixes are used as regular grammatical devices in many languages. A classic example is *Arabic*, which is characterized by a large number of bases represented by a sequence of three consonants, so-called "triliteral roots," into which infixes may be inserted on either side of the middle consonant. For instance, from the base *k-t-b* 'write,' we can form the words *katab* 'he wrote,' *kitab* 'book,' *katib* 'writer,' and so on. This does not mean that Arabic operates exclusively with infixes, since both prefixes and suffixes may also be added to the triconsonantal roots, for example, *yiktib* 'he writes,' *tiktib* 'she writes,' *katabt* 'I wrote,' *katabit* 'she wrote,' and so on. Infixes inserted between vowels or between vowel and consonant may be illustrated by the following examples taken from *Ilocano*, a language spoken in the Philippines by about three million people: *panaw* 'go,' the base form, but *pumanaw* 'he goes,' *pimmanaw* 'he went'; or *kita* 'sight,' but *kinita* 'thing seen.'

A special type of grammatical process, called REDUPLICATION, involves repetition of a part or the whole of the base within the same word. Ancient *Greek* offers a good illustration of this process; it regularly occurs in the perfect tense formation of most verbs, for example, *léipo* 'I leave,' but *léloipa* 'I have left' (with an internal vowel change of the base *léip-* to *loip-*); or *grapho* 'I write,' but *gégrapha* 'I have written.' This partial reduplication, that is, the repetition of the initial consonant of the base followed by the vowel /ĕ/, also occurs sporadically in *Latin*, as in *canō* 'I sing,' but *cecinī* 'I sang'; *fallō* 'I deceive,' but *fefellī* 'I deceived,' and so on. It is generally accompanied by a vowel change in the base (*can-* versus *cin-*; *fall-* versus *fell-*). In a language like *Malay*, on the other hand, reduplication of the entire word is a regular device for forming noun plurals, as in *bunga* 'flower,' but *bunga-bunga* 'flowers'; *kapal* 'ship,' but *kapalkapal* 'ships.'

A set of related forms which contain a common base, such as *man* and its derivatives, is a derivational paradigm. In the same fashion we may also list the *inflected* forms of a given base or stem (that is, a base or stem to which inflectional affixes have been added), for example, *boy, boy's, boys, boys'* or *work, works, worked, working*. This is an INFLECTIONAL PARADIGM. Anyone who has ever studied *Latin* is familiar with the orderly listing of inflectional forms of nouns, adjectives, and pronouns, the so-called DECLENSIONAL PARADIGM of the *amīcus, amīcī, amīcō, amīcum* type, or with the CONJUGATIONAL PARADIGM like *amō, amās, amat, amāmus, amātis, amant*, in which the changes in the base form of the verb *am-* 'love' signal the notions of person, number, tense, mood, and voice.

Most bases in English are free forms, but bound forms do occur, as shown by the word *occur* itself, where the element *-cur* may also appear with the prefixes *in-* and *re-*. Another example is *-ceive*, which can only stand on its own in the forms *conceive, deceive, receive,* or *perceive*, or in words like *deceiver, perceived, receiving*, where the base is both preceded and followed by an affix. The relative proportion of free and bound bases differs from language to language; but whether free or bound, it is always the base that expresses the vocabulary meaning of the word, while the affixes merely serve to convey some kind of modification of the basic message.

CONTENT AND FUNCTION WORDS

The concept of free and bound morphemes is linked to the distinction that linguists make between CONTENT WORDS, or *contentives*, and FUNCTION WORDS, or *functors* (also called *structure words*). These have been appropriately called the bricks and mortar of language, the bricks (content words) being those linguistic forms that provide the substance of a sentence (the nouns, verbs, adjectives, and adverbs), while the mortar (function words) holds them together in a meaningful grammatical order. (The function words are inflectional suffixes, articles, prepositions, conjunctions, and auxiliary verbs.) The *grammatical* meaning of a sentence, as opposed to its *dictionary* meaning, is expressed precisely by these functors. They do not, normally, occur independently, though some of them, like auxiliaries and prepositions, do have limited semantic content, in addition to their primary function, which is to connect the content words into a coherent structure. In the sentence *The player hits the ball with a bat*, the grammatical meaning is expressed by the articles *the* and *a*, the final *-s* ending of *hits*, and the preposition *with*, and by the sequence of the words. The grammatical pattern of this sentence would, therefore, look something like this:

The ____ ____s the ____ with a ____ .

Even if we should fill the blanks with meaningless syllables, for instance, *The clater pafs the lat with a koob*, the sentence would still convey the meaning that somebody (or something) does something to somebody (or something) with something (or somebody), even though the meaning of *clater, paf, lat,* and *koob* is not known. But let us replace the function words *the, a,* and *with* by nonsense syllables and omit the final *-s*, as in *Dou clater paf dou lat goum lou koob* (which might be a perfectly acceptable sentence in a language whose structure and phonemes we do not know), and we shall find that it makes no sense at all because it no longer conveys any kind of grammatical relationship. We must conclude, then, that the pattern of an English sentence is expressed by precisely those morphemes that convey grammatical meaning; hence, they cannot be replaced by meaningless syllables lest total loss of any recognizable meaning should result.

PLURAL AND PAST TENSE MORPHEMES IN ENGLISH: THE ALLOMORPH

Consider now the verb form *hits* in the above sentence. The final *-s* represents the third person singular present tense morpheme and is pronounced [s] in speech. If you now replace *hits* by either *holds* or *catches*, you will notice that this same verb ending is pronounced [z] and [əz] ([ɨz] in some people's pronunciation), respectively. In other words, the same morpheme may appear in different phonetic shapes, depending on the preceding sound. This kind of variation is quite predictable and is generally determined by the final vowel or consonant of the base or stem of the verb. In fact, we may even set up a rule to this effect and say that written final -*s* (or -*es*) is pronounced as [z] after voiced nonsibilant consonants and all vowels (for example, *holds, lives, begs, seems, sees, lies*), as [s] after nonsibilant voiceless consonants (for example, *hits, takes, laughs, dumps*) and [əz] after sibilants (for example, *catches, hisses, judges, pushes*). The same rule, incidentally, also holds true for the plural suffix of English nouns, represented in writing by final -*s* or -*es* (except for *dice*, the plural of *die*), for example, *hats* /hæts/, *dogs* /dɔgz/, and *churches* /čɜ^čəz/, as well as the possessive morpheme, as in *John's* /janz/, *Jack's* /jæks/, and *George's* /jɔrjəz/. These variations in the phonetic shape of a given morpheme are known as ALLOMORPHS, paralleling the concept of the allophones, the phoneme variants. And just as allophones are determined by their phonetic environment (for instance, the three different [p] sounds in *pit, spit,* and *lipstick*) and do not, normally, get in each other's way, so the allomorphs are noncontrastive positional variants of a grammatically relevant morpheme class. The allomorphs /s/, /z/, and /əz/, which happen to be identical in three different morpheme classes, —the noun plural, the possessive, and the third person singular present, respectively—and can be symbolized as {-S_1}, {-S_2}, {-S_3}, all have the same meaning within their particular class, regardless of difference in pronunciation or spelling.[9]

Similarly, the past tense morpheme represented in spelling by -*t*, -*d*, and -*ed* (for example, *kept, deceived, walked, started*) has three phonetic manifestations which are predictable on the basis of the preceding sound. Again, the rule which determines the automatic use of one or the other allomorphs of this morpheme class—symbolized as {-D_1}[10]—is quite simple: use /d/ after a voiced consonant except /d/ (as in *called* /kɔld/), /t/ after a voiceless consonant other than /t/ (as in *laughed* /læft/), and /əd/ (or /id/) after the alveolar stops /t/ and /d/ (as in *started* /startəd/).

In addition to the predictable allomorphs, the past tense and past participle morphemes, {-D_1} and {-D_2}, also include variants that are not phonologically conditioned (that is, they are not determined by the phonetic environment). Some of these fall into a pattern, for instance those that change the base vowel /ɪ/ to /æ/ in the past tense, like *sit–sat, sing–sang, ring–rang, drink–drank,* or the class of verbs of the *read, meet,* and *speed* type which change the base vowel to [ɛ] in both the past and the past participle, namely /rɛd/, /mɛt/, and /spɛd/. Other verbs, on the other hand, are quite irregular, for example, *be–was* and *go–went*, because they are isolated cases and involve a complete replacement of forms. A complete statement of the {-D$_1$} morpheme class, for instance, would have to make provisions for all its possible allomorphs. The following formula, incomplete as it is in terms of the many subclasses that the English past tense comprises, may give you an idea of the kind of concise descriptive symbolization that linguists have used to illustrate a morpheme paradigm:

$$\{-D_1\} = /\text{-d}/ \sim /\text{-t}/ \sim /\text{-əd}/ \sim /æ{\leftarrow}(\text{ɪ})/ \sim /ɛ{\leftarrow}(\text{i})/ \sim /\text{t}/ + /ɛ{\leftarrow}(\text{i})/ \ldots$$

The first subclass given in this formula includes the phonologically conditioned alternation (symbolized by $\sim$) of the allomorphs /d/, /t/, and /əd/, as in *deceived, walked*, and *started*; the second one comprises verbs of the *sing–sang, swim–swam* type; the third includes the *meet–met, read–read, speed–sped* subclass; and the fourth that of the *sleep–slept, keep–kept*, and *leap–lept* type. Professor Gleason distinguishes a total of fifty-three subclasses of the English verb.[11]

The plural suffix of the English noun that we symbolized as {-S$_1$} has allomorphs other than /s/, /z/, and /əz/ (as in *hats, dogs*, and *churches*) though these are by far the most common ones, since they not only occur with the great majority of nouns but are also used with new nouns that constantly enrich the English vocabulary. These allomorphs are, in fact, so productive that in many instances they have replaced such foreign plurals as *curricula* (singular, *curriculum*), *criteria* (singular, *criterion*), *dicta* (singular, *dictum*), and *cherubim* (singular, *cherub*), to name those that readily come to mind, and have been "anglicized" to *curriculums, criterions* (even *criterias*), *dictums*, and *cherubs*, respectively. While the allomorphs /s/, /z/, and /əz/ are conditioned by their phonetic environment and, hence, are predictable, other allomorphs of the English plural are not predictable. Consider, for example, the plural forms *oxen, children, sheep, aircraft, men*, and *feet*. Grammatically speaking, all of them parallel the *-s* (or *-es*) plural, which makes them members of the {-S$_1$} class. Let us briefly examine these three subclasses separately:

1. There is nothing in the base forms *ox* and *child* that would lead us to predict the *-en* /ən/ ending in the plural. After all, plural forms like *boxes* and *wilds* (in *the wilds of Africa*) are perfectly acceptable, so why not *oxes and *childs? We must conclude, therefore, that for some reason the bases *ox* and *child* require the plural suffix *-en* and that's that, unless we do some linguistic detective work by going back into the history of the language. Then we will find that both *oxen* and *children* are survivors of an earlier stage of English in which the plural of nouns was often shown by *-en*.

In connection with the form *children*, an additional remark may be in order. You will have noticed that the bases differ in the singular and the plural, namely /čajld/ versus /čild-/ or /čildr-/, depending upon whether we analyze the plural allomorph as /ən/ or /rən/ (either choice being legitimate). This is a good illustration of the fact that some bases in English have free and bound variants. Other cases in point are *brethren*, the archaic plural of *brother*; the plural bases *wive-* /wajv-/, *hous-* /hawz-/, and *path-* /pæð-/, which are allomorphs of the singular bases *wife* /wajf/, *house* /haws/, and *path* /pæθ/, respectively; and past tense bases like *kep* /kɛp-/, *slep-* /slɛp-/, and *deal-* /dɛl-/, which are bound variants of the present tense bases *keep* /kip/, *sleep* /slip/, and *deal* /dil/.[12]

2. The words *sheep* and *aircraft* (and some others like *swine*, *deer*, and *grouse*) may occur in different grammatical environments without any change of shape. When we refer to Bach's well-known cantata-aria "Sheep May Safely Graze," the form *sheep* is obviously used as a plural; yet we can also use the very same form in the singular and say *The sheep is grazing in the meadow*. In the case of *aircraft*, we can say *The aircraft flies* or *The aircraft fly at* 30,000 *feet*. Since *sheep* and *aircraft* function in these contexts similarly to words that take an inflectional ending in the plural (for example, *The ox is*/*The oxen are in the meadow* or *The plane flies*/*The planes fly at* 30,000 *feet*), it is convenient to consider words with identical shapes in singular and plural to consist, in a plural environment, of a base morpheme plus a plural *zero* allomorph, symbolized as /∅/.[13] Thus, the plural of these words can be represented as /šip/ + /∅/ and /ærkræft/ + /∅/, respectively.

3. The plural forms *men* and *feet* (as well as *women, geese, mice,* and others) illustrate the formation of certain English plurals by the change of the base vowel of the singular—the so-called internal vowel change (see page 58). A description of the English plural morpheme {-S_1} will have to include all these changes as well.

Again we may use a formula to account for all the allomorphs of the plural morpheme in English, similar to the one used in connection with {-D_1}. The following description does not purport to be in any way exhaustive and includes only those variants discussed in the preceding paragraphs:

$$\{-S_1\} = /-s/ \sim /-z/ \sim /-əz/ \sim /-ən/ \sim /ɛ \leftarrow (æ)/ \sim /i \leftarrow (ʊ)/ \sim /\emptyset/ \ldots \,^{14}$$

In addition to other vowel changes not listed (for example, *women, geese, mice*), a complete description of {-S_1} would also have to make provision for changes in the plural base, like *childr-, wive-, house-,* as well as for foreign plurals of the *alumni, alumnae, criteria* type.

MORPHOPHONEMIC CHANGES

Allomorphs, as was shown in the foregoing discussion, may be conditioned by surrounding sounds and are, therefore, predictable as to their distribution. On the other hand, there are a good many examples of allomorphs whose occurrence is not predictable in terms of phonological factors. The changes in the phonetic shapes of allomorphs brought about by phonetic environment are technically known as MORPHOPHONEMIC CHANGES or MORPHOPHONEMIC ALTERNATIONS.[15] These changes, which may or may not be reflected in spelling, can also occur as a result of adding derivational suffixes to bases, as in *mónograph, monógrapher,* and *monográphic*. In these cases there is a change in the vowel sound in the second and third word (though not in the spelling) due to a shift in accent. Morphophonemic alternations also serve as a process of derivation, for instance *life* (noun) versus *live* (adjective), *house* (noun) versus *house* (verb), or *safe* (adjective) versus *save* (verb).

The phonemic shape of words may also be affected by adjacent words in the sentence, as when *Did you eat?* becomes substandard

/jit/ or *Does she?* becomes /dʌšši/ in rapid speech. A more familiar example of this kind of change within a word group is the retention or the loss of a final consonant in French, according to whether the following word begins with a vowel or a consonant sound. For instance, the form *est* 'is' is pronounced /ɛ/ before consonants (and also when it occurs in isolation), as in *il est pauvre* /ilɛpovʀ/ 'he is poor,' but /ɛt/ before a word that begins with a vowel, as in *il est aimé* /ilɛtɛme/ 'he is loved.' This kind of morphophonemic feature which occurs not within individual words but rather between words is known as SANDHI, a term first used by Sanskrit grammarians that means 'combination' or 'putting together.' Sandhi variation, which really amounts to the creation of a new form because of contact with two other forms, is also known by the name of SYNTACTIC PHONOLOGY.

The study of these phonemic variations between allomorphs of a given morpheme class is called MORPHOPHONEMICS, which is a branch of MORPHEMICS, the study of the distribution and classification of morphemes in general and the ways they combine into words. This study, in turn, falls within the larger scope of MORPHOLOGY, which could be defined as the study of the construction of words and parts of words, that is, of free *and* bound morphemes. Morphology is distinct from the construction of phrases and sentences which traditionally comes under the heading of syntax and deals with free forms exclusively.

CLASSIFICATION OF LANGUAGES ACCORDING TO STRUCTURE

The preceding pages have shown that languages are unique both in their inventory of sounds and in the manner in which these are used to combine into meaningful sequences. At the same time, it was also shown that some languages resemble one another in their phonemic and morphemic structures and, conversely, show striking differences with respect to other languages. The systematic comparison of languages in terms of significant structural features has occupied linguists ever since the dawn of linguistic science in the early nineteenth century. A classification of languages according to their present *type*, a so-called TYPOLOGICAL CLASSIFICATION, has repeatedly been suggested, taking different criteria as a basis for such a classification. Thus, on the basis of differing articulatory features, a phonetic typology could be established, distinguishing, for instance, between languages that regularly make use of front rounded vowels and those that do not. Another classification involving the sound system might be based not on phonetic features per se, but rather on the way in which sounds are organized into a system and the way in which they function in the language. Such a phonological typology might classify languages according to whether they are tonal or nontonal, that is, whether there exists, in their system, sets of phonemes which are differentiated solely by levels of pitch, as in Chinese and some languages of Southeast Asia and West Africa.

On the grammatical level, different levels of classifications have also been suggested. One such classification would be based on word order and word-class (that is, part of speech) membership in the sentence structure. Such a system would differentiate the Chinese languages, for instance, in which the function of a word is determined by its position in the sentence, from ancient Greek or Latin, where word order is relatively unimportant since relationships within a sentence are marked by inflectional endings and changes in the shape of words. In this kind of classification English would come quite close to Chinese because of its great reliance on word order and because a great many words may belong to more than one word class. On the other hand, in a classification according to *grammatical* rather than *natural* gender of the noun,[16] English would go with languages like Finnish, Hungarian, or Japanese, which, in other respects, are very different from our language. You can see that typological classification largely depends on the kind of criteria that are used.

A typological classification that has been traditional in linguistic studies and that, in essence, goes back to nineteenth century scholarship, divides the languages of the world into *analytic* (or *isolating*), *synthetic* (or *inflectional*), and *agglutinative* types, according to the structure of the word as a grammatical unit and the number of concepts that languages combine into a single word. Let us consider each division individually:

1. A SYNTHETIC, or INFLECTIONAL, language is one which depends heavily on grammatical devices like affixes and internal changes in words to show grammatical relationships and

meanings. To put it another way, a synthetic language groups several units of meaning within a single word, for instance, Latin *ibō* 'I shall go,' in which the base *i*, the future tense morpheme *b(i)*,[17] and the first person singular ending *-ō*, three bound morphemes, are fused into one word. The classical languages like Latin, ancient Greek, and Sanskrit are good examples of synthetic language structures in which bases (whether they be nouns, adjectives, or verbs) cannot be used in isolation but only in conjunction with an ending. The Latin base *amīc-*, for example, which carries the meaning of 'friend,' may only appear in the forms *amīcus* 'friend' (subject), *amīcī* 'friend's,' *amīcum* 'friend' (direct object), *amīcō* 'for or to the friend.'

Many of the modern European languages have preserved an elaborate system of inflections, for instance, Lithuanian, Lettish (two languages spoken along the Baltic seacoast), and the Slavic languages (Russian, Ukranian, Polish, Czech, and Serbo-Croatian). On the other hand, the so-called Neo-Latin, or Romance, languages (French, Spanish, Italian, and so on), the historical descendants of Latin, have largely discarded inflectional endings in the noun system but keep them very much alive in the conjugational paradigm. The Germanic languages (such relatives of English as Dutch, German, Swedish, Danish, and Norwegian) have further simplified their verb system by using auxiliaries, while the Romance languages still use inflectional endings, (the future tense). English, possibly the least inflectional of all Indo-European languages,[18] can hardly qualify as a typical synthetic language structure because of its predominant use of free morphemes, the hallmark of analytic languages. Indeed, on a sliding scale indicating degrees of synthesis, English would have to be placed very low.

Among inflectional languages we must classify the Semitic tongues like Arabic and Hebrew with their characteristic triconsonantal roots which have no independent existence of their own. The root *k-t-b* (as was seen on page 59) can only appear with infixes and affixes, for example *katab* 'he wrote,' *yaktubu* 'he will write,' and *yuktabu* 'it will be written.'

2. What is called an AGGLUTINATIVE language is, in reality, a special kind of inflectional (hence synthetic) structure. Agglutinative languages are differentiated from inflectional ones in that

the bases, which are usually free morphemes, and the affixes are 'glued' to each other but preserve their individuality, thus keeping bases and affixes distinct. Turkish, Finnish, Hungarian, Japanese, and Swahili are considered to be typically agglutinative in structure, with Turkish and Hungarian being most frequently cited as stock illustrations of the process of agglutination. For instance, the Turkish base *ev* 'house' remains unchanged in *evler* 'houses,' *evden* 'from the house,' and *evlerden* 'from houses.' Similarly, the Hungarian base *ház* 'house' is also unchanged in *házban* 'in the house,' *házak* 'houses,' and *házakban* 'in the houses.' Furthermore, contrary to English, more than one inflectional ending may be added to a base form and bases, as a rule, do not undergo morphophonemic alternations of the /haws/ ∼ /hawzəz/ kind.[19]

As a parenthetical note, another interesting feature concerning Turkish and Hungarian may be mentioned. In both languages the vowels of all suffixes (most function words are expressed by suffixes) must "harmonize" with the vowel of the base. If, for example, the base has a front vowel, then the suffix must have a front vowel also—Turkish *ev-ler*; conversely, a back vowel in the base will automatically require a back vowel in the suffix—Turkish *oda-lar* 'rooms.' In the same vein, the Hungarian speaker says *ház-ak* but *kép-ek* 'pictures.'

An example of an agglutinative structure in Japanese is the form *tabesaserareru*, literally 'to be caused to eat,' that is, 'to be fed,' where *tabe-* represents the base with the meaning of 'eat,' *-sase-* the causative element (to cause someone to do something), *-rare-* the passive, and *-ru* the infinitive. Each element here has a fixed meaning (either lexical or grammatical) and can be mechanically added to or separated from a complex word structure. Thus, we may have the forms *taberareru* '(something) is eaten,' or *tabesaseru* 'to cause someone to eat,' that is, 'to feed someone.'

In Swahili, as was stated earlier (see page 58), grammatical changes are shown by prefixes. The form *ninasoma* 'I am reading' may be broken up into its component parts as follows: the base *-soma* 'read,' the continuous present tense affix (the present progressive) *-na-*, and the first person singular affix *ni-*. Substituting, for instance, *u-*, the second person singular affix, for *ni-*, we would have the form *unasoma* 'you are reading,' which in the simple past becomes *ulisoma* 'you have read' and in the future *utisoma* 'you will read,' where *-li-* and *-ta-* represent the past and future tense morphemes, respectively.

3. In an ANALYTIC language the sentence is of prime importance. The classic example of a language that makes no formal distinction between verb, noun, adjective, or any other part of speech is Chinese, together with several languages of Southeast Asia, notably Vietnamese. The word is an unalterable unit whose function in the sentence is not usually marked by some grammatical device (ending, preposition, auxiliary) but by position—hence the term ISOLATING. The following example may illustrate this point, where the Chinese form *wŏ* may mean 'I,' 'me,' 'my,' and 'to me':

Wŏ kan tá   'I see him'
Tá kan wŏ   'He sees me'
Tá kan wŏ peng yŏu   'He sees my friend'
Tá gei wŏ chyan   'He gives me money'

4. With the discovery of some American Indian languages, a fourth type of language structure called POLYSYNTHETIC, or INCORPORATING, was added to the traditional typological classification. This structural type combines into a single unit a number of concepts, notably those of subject, object, and verb, which have no separate existence. These languages, in other words, make the sentence coextensive with the word. Actually, however, this type of structure merely represents a synthetic structure carried to an extreme, by multiplying the number of bound morphemes within a grammatical unit which stands for an entire phrase or sentence. Here are two examples, one from Eskimo and the other from Oneida (an American Indian language of the Iroquois group) to illustrate a polysynthetic structure:

Eskimo *qasuiiġasġbigsagsiññitluinaġnaġ-puq* which, roughly translated means 'someone has completely failed to find a resting place.' This "word" could be analyzed as follows: *-puq* is the third person singular ending referring to the subject of an intransitive verb; *qasu-* 'to be tired,' an intransitive verb; *-iiq* 'not to be'; *-saq* is a suffix with causative value; *-bbik* 'place for . . .'; *-saq* is a suffix showing repetition; *-si* 'to find'; *-ññit* is a negative suffix; *-luinaq* 'completely'; *-naq* is a suffix showing accomplished action. (Note:

the *g* in this example is to be pronounced as a voiced velar fricative as in the Spanish word *pagar*, while *ññ* is a palatal nasal as in Spanish *año*. Notice also that the final *k* (a palatal sound like our [k] in *kin*) and *q* (corresponding to our [k] sound in *calm* and *cool*) become in the utterance the homorganic voiced fricatives written *g* and *ġ*, respectively.)

Oneida *gnaglaslizaks* 'I am looking for a village,' where *g* carries the meaning of 'I'; *-nagla* conveys the idea of 'living'; *-sl* is a suffix that makes *nagla* a noun, so that *naglasl* comes to mean 'village'; *i-* is a verbal prefix which gives *-zak* the verbal idea of 'look for'; *-s* is a morpheme to indicate continuous action. If used by itself, none of these elements would convey any definite meaning; for instance, one could not say *gizak* 'I search,' without specifying what one is searching for.[20]

The terms synthetic, agglutinative, analytic, and polysynthetic are relative and by no means mutually exclusive. English, for example, shows features of an inflecting language with its paradigms *man, man's, men, men's* or *drink, drinks, drank, drunk, drinking*, but the use of *mail* as a noun (*the mail*), a verb (*to mail a letter*), and an adjective (*mailbox*), and its reliance on word order puts it squarely in the class of isolating languages. On the other hand, words like *baker, goodness, ungodly,* and many others in which affixes are mechanically added to an independent base are characteristic of agglutinative languages. Nor does Eskimo show purely polysynthetic features. To a free base like *anut* 'father,' one can add the possessive suffix *-iga*, so that *anutiga* comes to mean 'my father,' while *iglu* 'house' becomes *igluk* in the dual ('two houses') and *iglut* in the plural ('houses').[21] These features are certainly reminiscent of an agglutinative structure like Hungarian (compare *ház* 'house' and *házak* 'houses').

It would appear that except for cases of extreme synthesis or analysis, which, admittedly, are few and far between, languages usually reveal features that partake of two or more structural types. It might be more appropriate, therefore, to set up a continuous scale for the comparison of grammatical systems, with isolating structures given at the extreme analytical pole and incorporating structures at the opposite end. You would find that most languages fall somewhere in between the two extremes. A language having relatively few morphemes per word would then be placed toward the analytic pole of the scale, while a language with a relatively large number of morphemes per word would be placed closer to the synthetic side.

More recently, Professor Joseph H. Greenberg suggested a system of indexes to determine the type of language by dividing the number of morphemes by the number of words in a given text. By this kind of mathematical operation, Greenberg arrives at an "index of synthesis." For example, our earlier sentence *Yesterday John ran away with the baker's younger daughter* has nine words but consists of fourteen morphemes. If we now divide the number of morphemes by the number of words we get an index of 1.55. A Hungarian sentence, on the other hand, might consist of twice as many morphemes as there are words (an index of 2.00), while a Chinese sentence might contain as many morphemes as there are words (an index of 1.00).[22] Of course, individual sentences are far too insufficient evidence to yield reliable results, but they serve to illustrate the procedure to follow for arriving at these indexes of synthesis.

Greenberg suggests that a low index of synthesis, say, 1.00 to 2.22, would define a language as analytic, an index of 2.22 to 3.00 as synthetic, and over 3.00 as polysynthetic. The highest value encountered by him so far is 3.72 for Eskimo.[23] The index for a language would tell us the average number of morphemes in a word. It may well be that classifications made on the basis of this procedure will confirm the traditional typological classification of languages that modern linguists have generally abandoned.

When we have determined which are the free and which are the bound morphemes of a given language, we look at the combinations in which they can occur and find out what FORM CLASSES they fall into, or, to use a more traditional terminology, what parts of speech they belong to. The concept of parts of speech into which traditional English grammar (a grammar largely constructed by British grammarians of the eighteenth century along the lines of Latin grammar) classifies words is based on a system that originated with the ancient Greek grammarians. It is a system which *defines* parts of speech on the basis of the meaning of words, as well as their function and form. Traditionally, for instance, certain forms are called nouns because they name a person, a place, or a thing, rather than because they show certain linguistic characteristics and can be used in specific functions, as nouns would be described in a modern grammar.[24]

In the next chapter we shall have a look at the "revolution" against traditional grammar brought about by the advances of linguistic science in recent decades.

notes

1. Professor Charles F. Hockett points this out, using the word *sister*. Though the sequence of phonemes /sist/ occurs in environments other than those in which it is immediately followed by /ər/, for instance *cyst, system, consist, insist*, there is no similarity in meaning between *sist-* in *sister* and the same sound sequence in these other words. Hence, he concludes, the word *sister* cannot be regarded as a combination of the elements *sist-* and *-er*. (*A Course in Modern Linguistics*. New York: Macmillan, 1958, p. 125.)
2. Leonard Bloomfield, *Language*. New York: Holt, Rinehart and Winston, 1933, p. 178. The concept of free and bound morphemes has largely been abandoned in current linguistic theory, which deals primarily with sentence structures whose components are words, that is, free forms. See Chapter 5.
3. Do not confuse compound words with phrases, which are constructions involving two or more free forms. Thus, the compound word *gentleman* differs from the phrase *gentle man*, *blackbird* from *black bird*, and *altogether* from *all together*.
4. Derivation is used here in a descriptive sense, that is, in terms of present-day English grammar, referring to the process of forming words from bases by the addition of one or more affixes and the relationship of a word to its base.

    In a historical sense, derivation refers to the formation or development of a word from an earlier one, as when we say that the English word *knight* derives from Old English *cniht* 'servant, attendant'.
5. Base (or root) and stem are not necessarily identical. In addition to the base, a stem may also include one or more derivational affixes. The stem of *boys* is *boy* (which is also the base) but that of *greatnesses* is *greatness* and not *great* (the base); while in the form *solidified*, the base is *solid* but the stem is *solidify*.
6. An exception to this principle is the plural possessive form which

includes two morphemes, one to show plurality and one to show possession, as in *children's*, *brethren's*, and *oxen's*, or foreign forms like *alumni's*, *alumnae's*, and so on. Technically speaking, of course, words like *boys'* and *girls'* also add two morphemes, the *-s* plural and the *-s* possessive, which coalesce in speech.

7. Derivation in this language is also shown by means of prefixes; thus, *kitoto* 'childish' and *utoto* 'childhood.'
8. Notice that the verb showing the action of the noun must "agree" with it, that is, the verb has to repeat the noun prefix showing number.
9. It is customary to enclose morphemes within braces, while slants are used for allomorphs. Some linguists prefer to use $\{-Z_1\}$, $\{-Z_2\}$, $\{-Z_3\}$, to indicate the morpheme class, depending on which allomorph is selected as a base form, namely /z/, /s/, or /əz/.
10. The subscript $_1$ is used to distinguish the past tense morpheme from the past participle morpheme (traditionally the third principal part of the verb), which is symbolized as $\{-D_2\}$. In the case of the so-called "weak" (or "regular") verbs the two morpheme classes are identical (for example, *walk*, *walked*, *walked*) but this distinction is important in connection with the so-called "strong" (or "irregular") verbs that undergo internal vowel change and often have different forms in the past and the past participle (for example, *sing*, *sang*, *sung* or *rise*, *rose*, *risen*).
11. In his *Introduction to Descriptive Linguistics* (rev. ed., Holt, Rinehart and Winston: New York, 1955, 1961), you will find a complete description of thirteen subclasses, pp. 102–103.
12. The phonemic shapes of the plural allomorphs /wajv-/, /hawz-/, and /pæð-/ are phonologically conditioned in that the final voiceless consonant of the singular base changes to its voiced counterpart at the same time that the plural suffix becomes the voiced allomorph /z/. (Notice, however, that this change does not occur in the possessive case of the singular, for example, *my wife's name is Mary*.) Since neither of these bases may occur in isolation, they must also be interpreted as bound morphemes.
13. By the same token we may also say that verbs of the *let* and *cut* type take a zero allomorph in the past tense and the past participle.
14. For a complete description of the plural morpheme in English, see Gleason, *op. cit.*, pp. 98–99.
15. Do not confuse *morphophonemic changes* with the *morphophonemic rules* of transformational grammar, which convert sentences

obtained by transformations into phonemic sequences, see Chapter 5.
16. In *natural gender* animate beings and inanimate things are classified as masculine, feminine, and neuter in accordance with their sex or lack of it. In *grammatical gender*, which is characteristic of a great majority of languages, a word is masculine, feminine, or neuter not because of a sex classification, though it may be found in obvious cases (for example, German *Mann* 'man' being masculine, *Frau* 'woman' feminine, and *Wasser* 'water' neuter), but because in some remote past a conventional gender has been attached to a particular word. In French the word for 'sun' (*soleil*) is masculine, but in German (*Sonne*) it is feminine. In Russian it is neuter. The German word for 'child' (*Kind*) is also neuter in gender.
17. The future tense sign of Latin verbs belonging to the first and second conjugational classes is *-bi-* with the loss of *i* before the personal ending *-ō*.
18. Indo-European is an important group of historically related languages that all descend from an unrecorded parent language. Now spoken by about one half of the earth's population, Indo-European languages extend all the way from Iceland to Northern India, covering most of Europe, large parts of Asia, Australia, portions of Africa, and the Western Hemisphere.
19. This does not mean that morphophonemic changes never occur. For instance, the singular form of Hungarian *ökör* 'ox' becomes *ökrök* in the plural, instead of **ökörök*, which means that the plural base becomes a bound form *ökr-*, much like the English plural base *childr-*.
20. The Eskimo example is adapted from A. Meillet and Marcel Cohen, *Les langues du monde*, rev. ed., vol. 2. Paris: H. Champion, 1952, p. 1169. The Oneida example is from Louis H. Gray, *Foundations of Language*. New York: Macmillan, 1939, p. 300.
21. Besides the plural, some languages have a dual, a grammatical number indicating two. Many of the Indo-European languages in their older stages (for example, Sanskrit, ancient Greek, Old Irish, Old Church Slavic) have a dual number (Greek *ánthropos* 'man,' *anthrópo* 'two men,' and *ánthropoi* '[more than two] men'). Among present-day languages we find a dual, beside the plural, in Hebrew, Arabic, some languages of India, Asia, the Pacific, and aboriginal languages of the Americas.
22. Due to increasing use of compounding and affixation in modern

Chinese, a one-to-one correlation between word and morpheme is not universal throughout the language.
23. Joseph H. Greenberg, *Anthropological Linguistics*. New York: Random House, 1968, p. 129.
24. A noun, in English, would be described as a linguistic element which, in *form*, makes a distinction between singular and plural (with a minimum of exceptions) and between base form and possessive, while in terms of *position* it fits into certain frames, like *The* ——— *is/are good, I see the* ———, *He goes to a* ———. See Chapter 5.

5
the structure of language: revolution in grammar

If you look up the word GRAMMAR in *Webster's New Collegiate Dictionary* (the 1969 edition) you will read that it is "the study of the classes of words, their inflections, and their syntactical relations and functions." Grammar, accordingly, is that part of the system of language which deals with the organization of morphemes and combinations of morphemes into larger meaningful utterances. One can nevertheless still hear people say that expressions like *I didn't see nobody*, *It is her*, and *I ain't got none* are "ungrammatical" or that Mr. So-and-So is very literate because he "uses good grammar" (presumably because he uses no double negatives and never splits his infinitives). The implication is that grammar is some kind of "body of laws" that legislate upon "correctness" and "appropriateness" of speech. Obviously, then, *grammar* means different things to different people.

THE MEANING OF GRAMMAR

In a now classic article entitled "Revolution in Grammar,"[1] Professor W. Nelson Francis examines this much-maligned word in terms of both its linguistic and its social implications. Rejecting as inadequate the traditional notion of grammar as a fixed and unalterable set of "rules," he shows how it can become a clear, useful, and scientific concept. Francis feels that much of the "emotional thinking about matters grammatical"[2] arises from failure to keep three different meanings of the word *grammar* apart. Assigning to them the names *Grammar 1*, *Grammar 2*, and *Grammar 3*, he defines the three concepts as follows:

Grammar 1, according to Francis, is "the set of formal patterns in which the words of a language are arranged in order to convey larger meanings."³ Taken in this sense the word *grammar* refers to a specific part of the total structure of language, that is, the complex system which constitutes the subject matter of Grammar 2, which Francis defines as "the branch of linguistic science which is concerned with the description, analysis, and formulization of formal language patterns."⁴ Putting it in different terms, we might say that Grammar 1 is the built-in mechanism that enables the native speaker of a language to produce a theoretically infinite number of utterances, while Grammar 2 is the study that permits us to understand the operation of this mechanism. "Just as gravity was in full operation before Newton's apple fell, so grammar in the first sense [that is, Grammar 1] was in full operation before anyone formulated the first rule that began the history of grammar as a study,"⁵ Francis goes on, clarifying the essential difference between the two concepts.

The third meaning of *grammar* (or Grammar 3), the meaning which is popularly applied to the word, refers to what is "right" or "wrong" in the use of language. Grammar in this sense concerns the kinds of judgments that we are wont to pass on expressions like *He don't like nobody* or *Him and me grabbed us a bite to eat*, which are termed "ungrammatical," although they conform to the pattern of English just as completely as *He doesn't like anybody* or *He and I had a bite to eat*. Since such "ungrammatical" utterances are "wrong" only in terms of social acceptability (because they do not conform to the speech habits of educated people), this meaning of *grammar* could be labeled "linguistic etiquette." Accordingly, the use of *Him and me grabbed us a bite to eat* would be considered "bad linguistic manners" in some circles (but presumably quite acceptable among stevedores in a shipyard), just as putting your feet on the table would be frowned upon at the Dean's party, though you may feel perfectly free to do so in your own home. *Grammar* used in this sense, that is, with reference to correctness and appropriateness of the use of language, is now generally called USAGE.

THE TRADITIONAL POINT OF VIEW

What we call the "traditional point of view" in grammar, or simply "traditional grammar" (sometimes also referred to as "school grammar") is essentially the code of linguistic behavior enshrined in handbooks and manuals of English, upon which some kind of stamp of "authority" has been placed to lend weight to statements about "right" and "wrong" uses of language. This conventional attitude in matters of language has deep-seated roots that go back to the doctrine worked out and codified by the Greek grammarians of the Alexandrine period (second century B.C.), who under the influence of Aristotelian logic, endeavored to give a systematic treatment to this most important aspect of human behavior. Believing that their language "embodied the universal form of human thought,"[6] they confined their grammatical observations to Greek and defined grammatical categories and terminology, such as the parts of speech and the chief inflectional categories, that largely prevail today. Subsequently taken over by Latin grammarians and adapted to the requirements of the Latin language, this system (now clothed in Latin terms) became the basis of traditional grammatical thought throughout medieval and Renaissance Europe. Eventually it was espoused by influential grammarians of eighteenth-century England, notably *Bishop Lowth* (to whom we owe the "rule" that two negatives in English cancel themselves out and are equivalent to an affirmative), *Joseph Priestly, George Campbell,* and *Lindley Murray,* who sought to discover and formulate definitive rules of syntax and usage.[7] Since many of these scholars had a thorough grounding in Latin, which through the years had come to be regarded as the most logical form of human speech, they developed grammars based mainly on the rules of Latin, though they also relied on their own intuition about what *they* considered to be "logical" and "reasonable" rules for English. This kind of grammar, modeled on the grammar of Latin and prescribing what speakers should say and write lest they incur the censure of linguistic "authorities," is called a PRESCRIPTIVE, or NORMATIVE, GRAMMAR.[8]

The influence exerted by Bishop Lowth and his fellow scholars was very strong indeed. His Latin-inspired and dogmatically prescriptive *Short Introduction to English Grammar*, published in London in 1762, became both authoritative and widely accepted. It is said that the adaptation and popularization of his work by the American-born Lindley Murray under the title of *English Grammar, Adapted to the Different Classes of Learners*, first published in New York in 1795, went through hundreds of editions and sold in the millions. The following is an example of this "Latinate" English grammar. Starting from the assumption that English is an inflectional language like Latin and Greek, it was thought that English would have to be inflected in similar fashion. For instance, since Latin has six cases, English necessarily must have just as many; indeed, the declensional pattern of a noun, *man* for example, was stated in these terms:

Nominative case: the man (Latin *homō*)
Genitive case: the man's or of the man (Latin *hominis*)
Dative case: to the man (Latin *hominī*)
Accusative case: the man (Latin *hominem*)
Ablative case: by, from the man (Latin *homine*)
Vocative case: oh man! (Latin *homō*)

The Latin equivalents are given in brackets for the sake of comparison. Notice that the English form *man* does not change its shape throughout the pattern, while the Latin word *homo* takes five different forms, according to its function in the sentence.

This traditional way of looking at English grammar (and that of many other languages) in terms of Latin and applying the devices and distinctions of Latin grammar, whether they fitted a particular situation or not, was not seriously challenged until the late nineteenth and early twentieth centuries.

THE SCIENTIFIC APPROACH

As a result of new insights into language structure gained through the scientific historico-comparative approach to language study (see Chapter 11), which rejected the notion of a standard and "ideal" language norm, it was inevitable that scholars should reach conclusions that made traditional concepts of language largely untenable. This new attitude toward language structure is clearly reflected in the work of one of the pioneers of the scientific approach to English grammar, Henry Sweet (also the founder of the science of phonetics and said to have been the prototype for Professor Henry Higgins in Shaw's *Pygmalion*). Recognizing that a prescriptive rule of grammar has no authority, by itself, to legislate whether a given usage is correct or incorrect, Sweet made the "revolutionary" statement that "rules of grammar have no value except as statements of facts: Whatever is in general use in a language is for that very reason grammatically correct."⁹ Since he considered grammar a science, he felt that its first business is to observe the facts and phenomena with which it has to deal, and to classify and state them methodically. Sweet did not believe that grammar is of much use in correcting vulgarisms, provincialisms, and other "linguistic defects," that is, in improving linguistic manners, for these depend more on social influences at home and at school than on grammatical training. While, for instance, his American colleague, William Dwight Whitney, then Professor at Yale University and also a pioneer in the scientific study of grammar, mildly lamented the use of *It is me* even by "respectable authorities," Sweet accepted the fact that this expression is in general use among educated people and merely noted that it is avoided in literary language.¹⁰

These ideas were ahead of their times. Contemporary grammarians did not seriously heed them, being too steeped in the traditional concept of prescriptivism in grammar. It was not until 1914, when Leonard Bloomfield's *Introduction to the Study of Language* appeared (subsequently expanded into what has become the basic work of American structuralism, under the title of *Language*, and published in 1933), that a new theory of DESCRIPTIVE, or STRUCTURAL, GRAMMAR was proposed which put on a firm basis the *inductive* rather than *deductive* (or normative) approach to language analysis. Bloomfield and his followers set out to describe language as it exists, without being concerned, as were the traditionalists, with questions of "correct" or "incorrect" usage. Their aim was to describe *all* usage, whether or not sanctioned by the "rules" of traditional grammar. In doing so, Bloomfield and his fellow structuralists directed their attention primarily to the external manifestations, the *formal* features, of language—that is, those phenomena which are most accessible to objective analysis and description, and ultimately to verification.

Thus the concepts and definitions favored by traditional grammar, which were based essentially on meaning, were replaced by highly objective and precise definitions based on the description of language units. The structural grammarian, in his attempt to avoid admitting *subjective* criteria into his analysis, left meaning aside until the formal characteristics of these units (let's call them words, for the sake of convenience), as well as their relationships to other units, had been established. A concrete example may help to clarify this point: While a traditional grammar would normally identify a noun as "the name of a person, place, or thing," the structural grammarian is likely to define it instead as a word which patterns, or "behaves," like *boy, boys* (singular–plural contrast), *boy's,* and *boys'* (possessive relationships) and can enter into constructions like *The boy is tall, I see the boy,* and *John is a boy.*

One of the chief exponents of this "new" structural grammar ("new" not primarily because of the discovery of new facts but rather because of the new ways of looking at old data) was Charles Carpenter Fries, whose important study of the structure of English sentences, *The Structure of English,*[11] has been most influential in incorporating the results of American structuralism into textbooks on English grammar. Challenging the validity of the analysis of parts of speech in terms of traditional terminology, Fries devised a structurally based system for identifying them. Using the sentence as his unit of analysis and basing his definitions not on what a given word means but on the way it fits into a sentence pattern, Fries' chief aim was consistency, simplicity, and exactness of description.

This unique analysis of English sentence structure is based on a collection of fifty hours of telephone conversations (yielding about 250,000 words) among speakers of standard American English who did not know that their utterances, covering a wide range of topics, were being recorded. It will be worthwhile to devote some of the following pages to a brief discussion of the key ideas of this important work. In the author's own words, this book is intended for all those "interested in learning something about how the English language accomplishes its communicative function—about the mechanism of its utterances."[12]

THE FRIES FRAMEWORK

To begin with, Fries challenges the conventional approach to the grammatical analysis of a sentence, which makes use of *meaning* as the basic tool of analysis. His position is clearly stated in the following passage:

In the usual approach to the grammatical analysis of sentences, one must know the total meaning of the utterance before beginning any analysis. The process of analysis consists almost wholly of giving technical names to portions of this total meaning. For example, given the sentence *the man gave the boy the money*, the conventional grammatical analysis would consist in attaching the name "subject" to the word *man*, the name "predicate" to the word *gave*, the name "indirect object" to the word *boy*, the name "direct object" to the word *money*, and the name "declarative sentence" to the whole utterance. If pressed for the basis upon which these names are given to these words, one would, in accord with the traditional method, say that the word *man* is called "subject" because it "designates the person about whom an assertion is made"; that the word *gave* is called "predicate" because it is "the word that asserts something about the subject"; that the word *boy* is called "indirect object" because it "indicates the person to or for whom the action is done"; and that the word *money* is called "direct object" because it "indicates the thing that receives the action of the verb." The sentence is called a "declarative sentence" because it "makes a statement." The total procedure begins with the total meaning of the sentence and consists solely in ascribing the technical terms "subject," "predicate," "indirect object," direct object," and "declarative sentence" to certain parts of that meaning.[13]

Fries believes, as a general principle, that in the study of sentence structure (and linguistic study generally), any use of meaning is unscientific whenever the fact that we know the meaning makes us stop short of finding the precise *formal signals* at work to convey that meaning. In other words, it must be "discovered" through the *structure* rather than the *thought content* of the sentence. As an illustration of his point, Fries cites the now classic example of Lewis Carroll's Jabberwocky:

'Twas brillig, and the slithy toves
   Did gyre and gimble in the wabe;
All mimsy were the borogroves,
   And the mome raths outgrabe.

Despite the "ideas" that this poem conjures up in Alice's mind ("It seems to fill my head with ideas," she says), the words mean nothing; and yet the *frames* in which they appear are clearly recognizable:

'Twas ____, and the ____y ____s
   Did ____ and ____ in the ____;

All ――y were the ――s,
And the ―― ――s ――.

It would seem, then, that there is a structural framework which has a meaning independent of the dictionary meanings of the words. To distinguish between these two different kinds of meaning, Fries assigns the name STRUCTURAL MEANING to those signals that show grammatical function (such as performer of an action, number of persons or things involved, time of the action, and so forth) and LEXICAL MEANING to the dictionary definitions of words themselves. In the sentence *The man gave the boy the money*, the dictionary would tell us something about the meaning of *man, boy, money*, and *give*, but beyond these lexical meanings we would get no further information. Yet the sentence expresses a whole range of meanings not expressed by the words themselves. It tells us, for instance, that the man performed the action rather than the boy and that only one of each was involved; it also tells us that the action has already taken place and that the information conveyed is a statement of fact and not a question or a negative. Therefore, the total meaning of this utterance must consist of both the lexical meanings of the individual words and the structural meanings just illustrated. An alteration of either kind of meaning will bring about a change in the *total* meaning, as in *The boy gave the man the money* (change in structural meaning) or *The man gave the girl the money* (change in lexical meaning).

Structural meanings, according to Fries, are fundamental and necessary meanings; and in order to understand a sentence, we must know not only what the words mean but also what their grammatical functions—signaled by specific and definite devices —are. "It is the devices that signal structural meanings which constitute the grammar of a language," he concludes[14] and points out that whenever appropriate structural signals (part-of-speech markers) are absent from a sentence, we may run into structural ambiguity. For instance, the sentence *Ship sails today* could have more than one structural meaning. Among the possible signals that would clear up this ambiguity is the part-of-speech marker *the*, which, put before the first word, would make this sentence the unambiguous statement *The ship sails today*;

conversely, should this same marker be placed before the second word, the result would be *Ship the sails today*, which is equally unambiguous. The utterance, however, would be different in that it would now have become a request. The ambiguity could also be resolved by means of another marker, for instance the ending *-ed*, so that we could have either *Shipped sail today* or *Ship sailed today*. In all these cases the *the* and *-ed* have been used to signal the structural meaning of the words *ship* and *sail*.

An English sentence, Fries tells us, is not a group of words as such—that is, a group of lexical units—but rather a *structural pattern* made up of parts of speech which are properly identified by formal markers (such as final *-s* meaning 'more than one' or the contrast between *fun* and *funny* in *This exercise is fun* versus *This exercise is funny*) and by their position in the pattern, so as to make the structural meaning of the utterance clear. Rejecting the quasi-philosophical definitions of traditional grammar (for example, "a noun is the name of a person, place, or thing"), Fries uses exclusively the criteria of form and grammatical arrangement for defining parts of speech and shows by the application of so-called *test frames* how it is possible to identify various kinds of units in a sentence. Starting out with the frame

    The concert was good

he collects all the words in his recorded material that could substitute for the word *concert* with no change of structural meaning, for instance

    The food was good
        coffee
        family
        taste

To the words in this list, which all occupy an identical position in the structural frame, Fries assigns the designation of Class 1 words. (FORM CLASS is the term he uses for parts of speech.) Making proper allowances for words occurring in his material with the same function but with an *-s* ending, like *meals, reports, lessons*, as well as for those that occasionally show up without a preceding *the*, as in *Coffee is good, Reports were good*, and so forth, he is able to set up the following adjusted frame for Class 1 words:

(The) ____ is/was good
____s are/were

It follows, then, that all words that are mutually substitutable in this pattern belong to the same grammatical class. Thus, in *The fintal was good*, although we do not know the meaning of *fintal*, it is a Class 1 word because it "behaves" the way *food*, *coffee*, *taste*, and so forth, do in this pattern.

By a similar process of substitution, Fries sets up three additional form classes, applying the same frames already tested out for Class 1 words, which in addition to *The concert was good* (Frame A), also include *The clerk remembered the tax* (Frame B), and *The team went there* (Frame C).

Class 2 words fit the following positions.

Frame A   (The) *Class 1* is/was good
                      ____s are/were
                      seems/seemed
                      seem
                      sounds/sounded
                      sound
                      becomes/became
                      become

Frame B   (The) *Class 1* remembered (the) *Class 1*
                      ____s wanted   ____s
                      saw
                      discussed
                      suggested

Frame C   (The) *Class 1* went there
                      ____s came
                      ran
                      moved
                      lived

Class 3 words pattern like the word *good* in Frame A. In addition, for an item to qualify as belonging to Class 3, so Fries tells us, it must be one that can fit both in the position following the Class 2 word and between *the* and the Class 1 word.

	Class 3	Class 1	Class 2	Class 3
(The)	good	_____	is/was	good
		_____s	are/were	
	large			large
	necessary			necessary
	foreign			foreign

Class 4 words fit the following structural positions in the three test frames.

		Class 3	Class 1	Class 2	Class 3	Class 4
Frame A	(The)	_____	_____	is/was	_____	there
						here
						always
Frame B	(The)	*Class 1*	remembered	(the)	*Class 1*	clearly
		_____s				sufficiently
						especially
						soon
Frame C	(The)	*Class 1*	went			there/upstairs
						back/away
						out/rapidly

Our utterances, Fries concludes, are mainly made up of arrangements of these four form classes, or parts of speech. They constitute the bulk of the words we use.

In addition to the form class words identified above, English sentences contain a number of other words which, though comparatively few in number, are very frequently used (the 154 items of this kind found by Fries make up about one third of the material he recorded). These he calls FUNCTION WORDS because they serve to signal structural meanings, and in the absence of general identifying characteristics, they must be recognized and learned as separate items. By the same process of substitution within test frames made up of utterances taken from his material, Fries sets up fifteen separate groups that he identifies merely by the letter codes A through O. These groups include what traditionally have been called articles and determiners (*the, a, every, some*), auxiliaries (*may, can, must, should*), qualifiers (*very, more, rather*), connectives (*and, or, but*), prepositions (*for, by, in, from*), subordinators (*because, after, when*), and so forth. For the sake of illustration, here are some examples to show how function-word class affiliation is determined.

Group A consists of all items that can occur in the position of *the* in the following frame.

    A   1   2   3
The concert was good

The main items are *a/an, every, no, my, our, your, some, any, John's, this,* and so forth.

Group B includes words for the position in which *may* occurs in the following sentence frame.

    A   1   B   2   3
The concert may be good

Some possibilities are *might, can, could, will,* and *would.*

    A   1   B   2
The ____ had moved
            was
            got
The ____ was moving
            got
            kept
The ____ had to move
            did

Fries notes that Group B words all go with Class 2 words and that when they appear in this position, they serve as structural markers of Class 2 words.

Having established by this process of substitution within test frames various speech classes whose members behave identically, or at least similarly, Fries turns to the question of how users of English recognize each of these "functioning units" in the stream of speech. What other identifying features are there, in addition to positional relationships in the frame, that enable the users of the language to recognize what class a word belongs to? Since Fries finds no general identifying characteristics by which to recognize the fifteen groups of function words (which must be learned as separate items), his investigation concerns only the four part-of-speech classes.

We have already alluded to formal markers, such as the *-s* ending which correlates with the meaning of "more than one" and the contrast between *fun* and *funny* in *This exercise is fun* versus *This exercise is funny* (p. 86). Indeed, Fries points to contrastive identifying forms of individual words that provide additional clues to form class classification. He finds regular patterns of contrast between, say, Class 1 words like *arrival, departure, discovery, acceptance, accomplishment, helper,* and *applicant* and Class 2 words like *arrive, depart, discover, accept, accomplish, help,* and *apply*; or between words like *bigness, activity, truth, fool, brute,* and *fame* and the Class 3 words *big, active, true, foolish, brutish,* and *famous*. Examples of Class 2 words contrasting with those of Class 3 are *brighten* versus *bright, enable* versus *able,* and *liberalize* versus *liberal*; while *happy* versus *happily, cheerful* versus *cheerfully,* and *social* versus *socially* illustrate an important contrastive pattern involving Class 3 and Class 4 words. In addition to these contrasts in the forms of words, contrasts signaled by morphological markers—for instance, between singular and plural (*boy/boys, man/men, child/children*), between present and past (*work/worked, sing/sang*), between degree of quality (*big/bigger/biggest*), and so forth—also furnish criteria for recognizing the four parts of speech as they occur in the speech stream.

In summary, then, Fries considers the identifying characteristics of the four form classes to be of two kinds, namely, formal contrasts in the shape of individual words and positional relationships among words in the sentence. He insists, however, that ultimately it is the arrangement of the words in the construction that furnishes the most reliable evidence of their structural use and class affiliation. Thus, in the sentence *The poorest are always with us*, the word *poorest* has the formal characteristics of a Class 3 word; but the marker *the* preceding the word supersedes the word form, so that in this particular utterance *poorest* as a functioning unit belongs to Class 1.

IMMEDIATE CONSTITUENT GRAMMAR

The recognition of form classes is only the first step in recognizing larger structures. In one of his last chapters, Fries turns his attention to the grouping of the speech units, CONSTITUENTS, that make up the structural patterns of utterances. Having identified what he calls "minimum free utterances" like *The concert was good* (which could be called a *basic sentence pattern* of English), he examines the way the separate constituents are grouped and fitted into larger structures in order for him to arrive at the complete structural meaning of any utterance. In the ordering of speech units, that is, in determining the interrelationships of the constituents of a sentence, Fries applies the principle of IMMEDIATE CONSTITUENT ANALYSIS (usually abbreviated IC) that has been widely used by structuralists as a technique of breaking up syntactic structures into successive components (or constituents) consisting of words or groups of words. This approach makes the basic assumption that in any given sentence some words are more closely related than others and views a sentence as being made up of two-part constructions on a series of levels (or layers). For instance, the sentence *The rebellious students walked to the dean's office* consists of two main parts—two immediate constituents—namely, *the rebellious students* and *walked to the dean's office*. Each part, in turn, consists of two parts, and each of these consists of two parts, until by cutting the sentence into smaller and smaller groupings, we reach the level of single words or morphemes, the ultimate constituents.

A complete IC analysis of the example sentence above would look something like this:

Step 1: The rebellious students | walked to the dean's office
Step 2: The | rebellious students | walked | to the dean's office
Step 3: The | rebellious | students | walked | to | the dean's office
Step 4: The | rebellious | students | walked | to | the | dean's office
Step 5: The | rebellious | students | walked | to | the | dean's | office[15]

These steps could also be represented diagramatically, as follows:

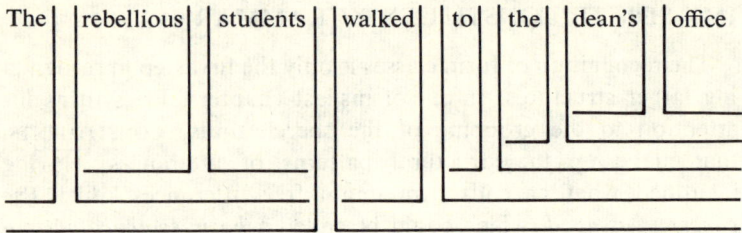

A basic method of ascertaining the IC's of any given construction is the test of substitutability of comparable items (word groups or single words) which can occur in similar environments. This procedure, illustrated in the following series of utterances, gives a rather clear picture of how a basic sentence pattern can be expanded into larger sentence constructions:

The	rebellious students	walked	to	the	dean's	office
The	rebels	walked	to		his	office
The	rebels	walked		there		
	They		walked			

The IC analysis approach and, generally speaking, the structural methodology illustrated by Fries' "discovery" procedures (based on noting and describing all the positions which the units of a given language can occupy) were generally regarded as the proper technique for syntactic analysis until about a decade or so ago. The advantages in the use of precise *formal* and *distributional* definitions of word classes based on observable and verifiable linguistic facts, as opposed to the rather vague *notional* definitions based primarily on meaning, were generally recognized. Furthermore, there was general agreement that IC analysis, strongly reminiscent of the traditional parsing of school grammars, was a much clearer procedure for showing the formal relationships between noun phrase and verb phrase and their constituents (the parts of speech that traditional grammar would describe as subject and predicate and their respective modifiers).

In the late 1950s and early 1960s this structurally based grammar, which came to be known as IMMEDIATE CONSTITUENT GRAMMAR, and the whole Fries framework in general, came under sharp attack.[16] For one thing, it was felt that IC analysis proved difficult to apply to some constructions—for instance, *Did the rebellious students walk to the dean's office?* where we are left wondering what the two main parts, the two IC's, would be. In addition, it was felt that IC analysis failed to explain many important relationships between basic and derived sentence structures, for example, the active–passive voice relationship, as in *John found a penny* versus *A penny was found by John*. Furthermore, there were objections that the Fries kind of analysis (and that of the structuralists in general) was based on a *finite* set of actual utterances recorded by the linguist—such as Fries' collection of telephone conversations—and that a descriptive grammar based on such a sentence inventory, technically known as a CORPUS, was scarcely more than the listing of its contents. The requirements of a grammar, the critics observed, should be that it contain general statements to account not merely for the sentences of the corpus but for the infinite number of other sentences that may have never occurred before and that a native speaker of a given language could conceivably produce, or "generate." A data-gathering grammar, a so-called TAXONOMIC GRAMMAR, in other words, is inadequate because it fails to take into account what the native speaker already knows about his language intuitively.

THE TRANSFORMATIONAL FRAMEWORK

Largely as a reaction against these shortcomings of structural linguistics, there emerged a new method of analysis in syntactical studies which received its most prominent and significant expression in a book by Noam Chomsky, Professor of Linguistics at M.I.T. Published in 1957, *Syntactic Structures*[17] is the seminal work of what has come to be known as TRANSFORMATIONAL-GENERATIVE GRAMMAR. Chomsky's aim is to "attempt to construct a formalized general theory of linguistic structures,"[18] a theory of grammar that will seek to explain how an infinite number of sentences can be produced from a limited number of basic structures by applying a variety of rules also limited in number so as to "generate" larger and more complex sentences. The requirements of such a theory, according to Chomsky, are to specify and predict all the sentences in a given language that a native speaker is able to understand and produce, even though they may have never been spoken or written before. Chomsky, as opposed to the structuralists, is neither interested in nor concerned with collecting samples of actual utterances and describing what people are observed to say (or write), for these data cannot even begin to exhaust all the possible sentences in the language (assuming that these utterances are, indeed, sentences), and such a sampling gives incomplete information about the structure of sentences in general.

The fundamental goal in the linguistic analysis of a language, which Chomsky defines as "a set (finite or infinite) of sentences, each finite in length and constructed out of a finite set of elements"[19] is to find a set of rules (which make up the grammar of the language) by which *all* the grammatical sentences and *only* the grammatical sentences of the language may be generated, and none of the ungrammatical ones. But what are the criteria for determining what is grammatical and what is not? And to what extent is grammar dependent on meaning? Chomsky's frequently quoted sentence *Colorless green ideas sleep furiously* is at once recognized by the native English speaker as grammatical, even though it is meaningless, while his "intuition" tells him that *Furiously sleep ideas green colorless* is both nonsensical and ungrammatical. In the same way, the native speaker of English would be aware of the ambiguity in the utterance *the shooting of the hunters*, which can mean that either (a) the hunters shot something (taking *hunters* as the subject) or (b) someone shot the hunters (taking *hunters* as the object).[20]

In the following pair of sentences

John is easy to please
John is eager to please

our intuitive understanding of English tells us that in spite of their apparent identity in terms of structural signals, these two sentences are, in reality, quite different. This can easily be shown by changing them from the active to the passive voice: *John is easily pleased* is acceptable to the native speaker of English, whereas **John is eagerly pleased* is not. (The asterisk preceding this sentence indicates that it is not acceptable.)

The implications of the foregoing are that (a) the notion "grammatical" cannot be identified with "meaningful" or "significant" in the sense in which the word *meaning* is generally understood and (b) the native speaker of a language has a set of rules stored in his mind, an "internal grammar," so to speak, which enables him to judge whether a given sentence is grammatical or not. It is this COMPETENCE, this intuitive knowledge of the language as a system (as opposed to the PERFORMANCE, that is, the actual use he makes of his language in a given situation) that enables the native speaker to produce and understand sentences which he may have never said or heard before. A theory of grammar, according to Chomsky, must also account for this intrinsic linguistic competence of the speaker.

Transformational-generative grammar takes the syntax of a language, that is, the arrangement of words in a sentence, as its starting point. This movement from sentence to sound represents a radical departure from the structuralist's approach of "from sound to sentence." Let us briefly examine the main outlines of this theory and see how it works. (Changes in some of the theoretical concepts and method of transformational grammar have been very rapid since their first statement in *Syntactic Structures*. Since it would be outside the scope of this brief introductory survey to discuss all of them, we shall limit our discussion mainly to Chomsky's initial exposition.)

Transformational analysis begins with the assumption that certain sentences are *basic* and that other sentences are *derived* from them by means of TRANSFORMATION RULES, or T-RULES. In other words, the core of grammar is made up of a relatively small number of basic sentence types (basic in the sense that they cannot be derived from any other sentences that underlie them), the foundation, as it were, upon which all sentence structures rest. These basic, elementary sentences of a language, also known as KERNEL SENTENCES, are "the stuff from which all else is made,"[21] the "all else" being all sentence structures derived from the kernels by a process of transformation and technically known as TRANSFORMS.

Basic sentence structures consist of two main parts, the *noun phrase* and the *verb phrase*, which function as subject and predicate, respectively. These sentence types, the shortest statements in the active voice—variously identified as between four and ten in number[22]—do not necessarily occur more frequently than other, more complex sentences. You may have little or no occasion to utter a sentence like *Birds sing*, but a sentence like *The singing of birds was heard in the distance* may not be unusual. Yet if we want to have a clear understanding of the structure of the more complex sentences, we must begin with the simple structure *Birds sing*.

In order to describe structural relationships as concisely as possible, the generative grammarian finds it convenient to use abstract terms, expressed by means of symbols, before translating them into lexical items. Thus the notion of the basic English sentence may be symbolized as follows:

$$S \rightarrow NP + VP$$

S stands for "sentence," NP for "noun phrase," VP for "verb phrase," and the arrow means "consists of," or—more in line with transformationalist terminology—"to be rewritten as." This information may also be represented on a *branching tree diagram* (or *derivational tree*), as follows:

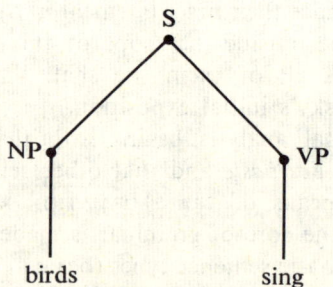

The dots in the tree are called *nodes*, and the lines that connect them are referred to as *branches*. Symbols not connected to lower nodes are known as *terminal symbols*; they make up the *terminal string*, as opposed to the *initial string*, which is S in this case, and the *intermediate strings*, which represent the various stages between the initial and terminal strings. (Symbols which can be read across in a line are referred to as strings.) Any node on a higher level is said to dominate a node on a lower level; thus, in our diagram the S node dominates the NP and VP nodes. The latter, in turn, may dominate other nodes, as can be seen in the following diagrammatic representation of the sentence *The man hit the ball*:[23]

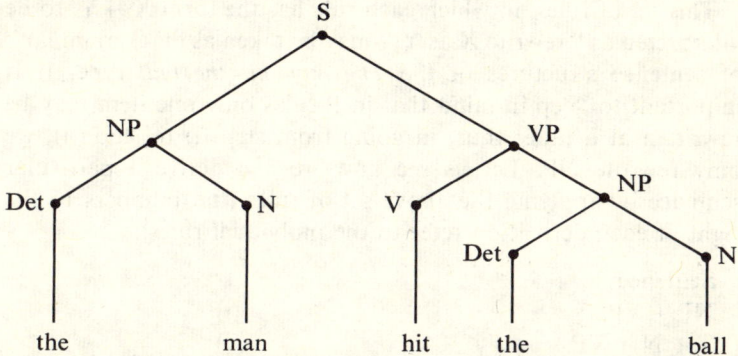

The first NP consists of the determiner (Det) *the* (sometimes symbolized as *Art* or *T*) and the noun (N) *man*; the VP consists of the verb (V) *hit* and the NP *the ball* which, in turn, dominates the nodes Det and N.

The derivation of this basic sentence type obeys a set of rules known as PHRASE STRUCTURE RULES (or simply P-rules). These rules specify how each symbol is replaced by one or more symbols (for instance, S by NP + VP, NP by Det + N, and so forth) until we reach the terminal string of symbols, that is, the level at which we turn to the lexicon and substitute morphemes for symbols. The following set of phrase structure rules is given by Chomsky to specify the derivation of the sentence *The man hit the ball* from its abstract representation.

    (i) Sentence → NP + VP
   (ii) NP → T + N
  (iii) VP → Verb + NP
  (iv) T → the
   (v) N → man, ball, *etc.*
  (vi) Verb → hit, took, *etc.*

At a later stage in his book, Chomsky introduces a new element into these rules, the *auxiliary* (Aux), and rewrites Verb as *Aux + V* (that is, auxiliary + main verb), since the element "Verb" may take different forms in other contexts. Thus *hit* may become *hits, have + hit, will + hit,* and so forth. The auxiliary class must specify the tense of the sentence (present or past) and may also include helping verbs that occur before the main verb.

This set of rules, in which each rule has the form X → Y, to be interpreted as "rewrite X as Y," may be taken as the "grammar" of sentence structures of the *The man hit the ball* type. It is important to keep in mind that in P-rules only one item may be rewritten at a time; thus, in going from step (i) to step (ii), we only rewrote NP. Let us see how we can derive a particular sentence by applying the above set of rules (the numbers to the right of each derivation refer to the individual rules).

Sentence	
NP + VP	(i)
T + N + VP	(ii)
T + N + Verb + NP	(iii)
the + N + Verb + NP	(iv)
the + man + Verb + NP	(v)
the + man + hit + NP	(vi)
the + man + hit + T + N	(ii)
the + man + hit + the + N	(iv)
the + man + hit + the + ball	(v)

The comparison of the successive lines in this derivation shows us clearly the order in which the rules were applied to construct the sentence. The *ordering* of rules, that is, the order in which they must be applied, is one of the fundamental concepts of this grammatical theory and must be strictly observed, lest unacceptable combinations result.

The sentence *The man hit the ball* is a terminal string generated by a set of six phrase structure rules, the "grammar" of that particular sentence. The tree diagram shown on page 97 is a graphic representation of the derivation of this string. Known also as a *phrase structure marker*, or simply *P-marker*, it is widely used by transformational-generative grammarians because it enables them to tell at a glance where the parts of the string come from. It is, in other words, a clear and explicit picture of the immediate constituent structure of a sentence.

The function of phrase structure rules is to produce the simple, basic sentences that underlie the more complex sentence structures encountered in daily language use. The way a given sentence is related to an underlying structure (or structures) is specified by the transformation rules. These rules, as the name indicates, apply specific transformations to the terminal strings produced by the P-rules and involve deletions, additions, and changes of order (permutations), as well as the linking of two or more basic sentences into one complex structure by the processes of *conjoining* and *embedding*, that is, coordination and subordination. Transformation rules are either *obligatory* or *optional*. Those applied to terminal strings of the phrase structure component to produce kernel sentences are obligatory, for instance, attaching suffixes to words ($en + eat \rightarrow eaten$)[24] or showing how tense combines with the verb (past + *have* $\rightarrow$ *had*). Optional transformations, on the other hand—for instance, the change from active to passive (*The ball was hit by the man*)—may or may not be applied in a particular case.

The relationship of a derived sentence to a basic sentence is ultimately determined by the rule we apply to the structure of the basic sentence. A classic example of a rule which illustrates this relationship is the *passive transformation*. Given a kernel string like

$$NP_1 + Aux + V + NP_2$$

that is, a noun phrase followed by an auxiliary (which specifies tense and may also include a helping verb), followed, in turn, by a verb (restricted to a transitive verb in this instance) which is followed by a second noun phrase, we may transform it into a passive string by rearranging these items and introducing three more, as follows:

$$NP_2 + Aux + be + en + V + by + NP_1$$

In order to arrive at this passive transform, we have (a) switched

Kernel P-Marker

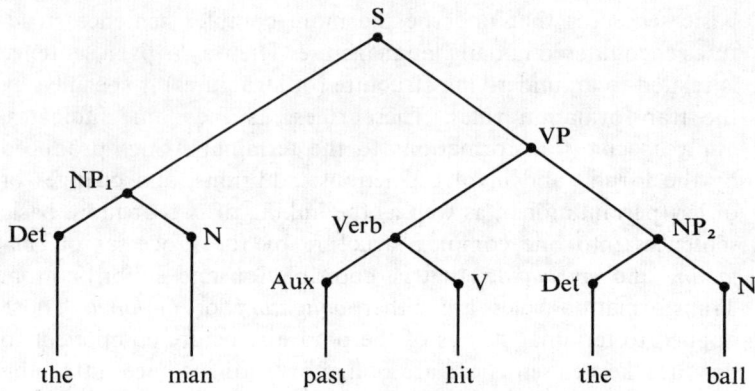

the two noun phrases around, (b) added *en* (the past participle morpheme, which combines with the verb) and *be* (to produce *was*) to the auxiliary, and (c) placed *by* before the second noun phrase (NP_1). By inserting appropriate words into the terminal kernel string we may come up with something like

the + man + past + hit + the + ball

which, in the passive, would produce the following string:

the + ball + past + be + en + hit + by + the + man

The concise statement of this passive transformation, the *T-passive rule*, reads as follows:

NP_1 + Aux + V + NP_2 ⇒ NP_2 + Aux + be + en + V + by + NP_1

The double arrow means "transformed into."

In terms of the P-markers that underlie both the kernel and the transform, this transformation could be diagramed as in Figure 10 above.

In similar fashion we can transform the sentence *The man hit*

Derived P-Marker

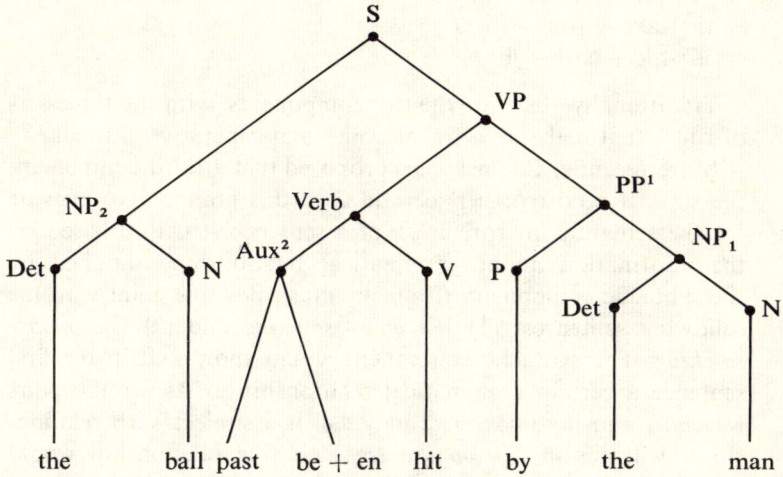

[1] PP stands for "prepositional phrase."
[2] The Aux *past* goes with *be* to form *was*, and the past participle morpheme *en* goes with *hit* to produce the past participle form *hit*. The *-en* suffix is deleted in this case.

the ball into a negative sentence (*The man didn't hit the ball*), a *yes–no* interrogative sentence (*Did the man hit the ball?*), a *wh-* interrogative sentence (*Who hit the ball?* or *What did the man hit?*), and so forth. We shall find that all of them are related to each other, since they derive from an identical underlying structure, namely *the + man + past + hit + the + ball*.

The phrase structure rules, including the lexical rules (for example, N → *man, boy, ball,* etc.), specify the underlying structures of the sentences of a language, while the transformation rules specify the changes wrought upon these structures. These two sets of rules are usually brought under the heading of the SYNTACTIC COMPONENT of the grammar. A third set of rules makes up the PHONOLOGICAL COMPONENT, which specifies the phonetic representation of each sentence. These rules, which are known as MORPHOPHONEMIC RULES, are stated in the same terms as the phrase structure rules (that is, "rewrite X as Y") and might include, for English, the following:[25]

(i) walk → /wɔk/
(ii) take + past → /tʊk/
(iii) hit + past → /hɪt/

Traditionally, these are the two components, with the three sets of rules, that make up a transformational-generative grammar.[26]

More recently, Chomsky has proposed that a third component, the SEMANTIC COMPONENT, be added to this grammar to provide for the semantic interpretation of a sentence structure based on the information about grammatical relationships supplied by the syntactic component. Chomsky illustrates this point with the following sentences: (1) *We enjoy smoking* and (2) *We oppose smoking*. The syntactic component would show that in the first sentence a certain grammatical relationship exists for the pairs *we–enjoy* and *we–smoke* (we may call it a subject–verb relationship), whereas in *We oppose smoking*, this relationship would only hold of the pair *we–oppose*, and not of the pair *we–smoke*. Making use of this information about grammatical relationships, the semantic component of the grammar would describe sentence 1 as a paraphrase of *We smoke and we enjoy it*, and show, at the same time, that sentence 2 cannot be paraphrased as *We smoke and we oppose it*.[27]

The central and fundamental part of a transformational grammar is its syntactic component, since both semantic and morphophonemic (phonological) rules require syntactic information for their proper application. Because, in a sense, these two sets of rules "interpret" the syntactically generated structure in a concrete representation, namely, a phonetic and semantic one, these components are also known as interpretive components. Thus, a grammar can ultimately be regarded as "a device for pairing phonetically represented signals with semantic interpretations, this pairing being mediated through a system of abstract structures generated by the syntactic component."[28]

Deep and Surface Structures

The distinction between kernel sentences generated by phrase structure rules and more complex sentences produced by means of transformations (*The man hit the ball* versus *The ball was hit by the man*), has led transformationalists to the insight that all sentences have a DEEP STRUCTURE and a SURFACE STRUCTURE. The deep structure of a sentence, the underlying terminal string of the phrase structure component contains all the information necessary to determine the semantic interpretation of a given sentence, while the surface structure can be considered as the "final product," that is, the syntactic and phonological representation of a sentence to which transformation rules have been applied. For instance, *The man hit the ball* is a surface structure, whereas *the + man + past + hit + the + ball* is a deep structure, since it has not yet undergone the obligatory transformation *past + hit → hit*.

The concept of deep and surface structures and how they are related to each other may become clear if we look at the pair of sentences given earlier.

(1) John is easy to please
(2) John is eager to please

On the surface, that is, in the surface structure, these sentences are identical. Yet when we transform them from active to passive, only sentence 1 turns out to be acceptable to the native speaker of English (see page 95). This is because they are quite different in the deep structure: *It is easy* and *Someone pleases John* underlie sentence 1, whereas sentence 2 is derived from *John is eager* and *John pleases somebody*. Similarly, the two interpretations of *Flying planes can be dangerous* (another frequently quoted example supplied by Chomsky) can be traced to the underlying deep structures (1) *Planes fly* and *Planes can be dangerous*, and (2) *Someone flies planes* and *Flying can be dangerous*. Grammatical ambiguities of this latter sort, which are left unresolved by immediate constituent analysis, may be cleared up by transformational techniques which show that apparently identical surface structures are different in meaning because they are derived from different deep structures.

As stated earlier, there have been a number of new developments in transformational analysis since its first exposition in *Syntactic Structures*. The theory presented in Chomsky's more recent writings,[29] as well as the theories of other researchers,[30] differs in many respects from its original version (for instance, the shift away from the concept of kernel sentences to that of deep and surface structures to designate the various stages in the process of generating sentences), although the changes involve methods of analysis rather than basic aims and objectives.

Summarizing our discussion, we could say that the transformationalist's aim, contrary to that of the structuralist, is to describe the speaker's intrinsic ability to generate any and all sentences in a given language. "A linguistic description of some natural language," says Postal, "is designed to provide a specification of the knowledge which speakers of that language have which differentiates them from nonspeakers."[31] Indeed, according to the transformational school of thought, one of the shortcomings of structural linguistics, with its insistence on observable and verifiable data, is, that it concentrates on the actual *performance* of the speaker (the *surface structure* of the utterance, we might say) and that it disregards, to a large extent, what the speaker intuitively knows about his language (or the *deep structure*). Rejecting traditional grammatical thought, in which such "intuitive knowledge" about language is implicit, the structuralist's goal is to show exclusively *how* language conveys meaning. In contrast, transformational theory insists on accounting for the speaker's linguistic *competence*, that is, for what he *knows about* rather than for what he *does* with his language. With the focus shifted to the "creative" aspect of language use (the speaker's ability to produce sentences never said or heard before), transformational analysis has placed traditional grammar back into proper perspective by reverting to the concerns, and even the specific doctrines, of traditional theory, for example, the question of the universal properties of languages.

We have seen how, within the last decade, a new and powerful school of linguistic thought has been developing as a reaction to what W. Nelson Francis called a "revolution in grammar." The term "transformational counterrevolution" may not be inappropriate to characterize this particular development in linguistics.

notes

1. *Quarterly Journal of Speech*, 40 (October 1954), 299–312.
2. *Ibid.*, p. 299.
3. *Ibid.*, p. 299.
4. *Ibid.* p. 299.
5. *Ibid.* p. 299.
6. Leonard Bloomfield, *Language*. New York: Holt, Rinehart and Winston, 1933, p. 5.
7. Few books on English grammar were written before the eighteenth century. Of historical interest is a grammar of English written in Latin by a geometry professor at Oxford, John Wallis (*Grammatica Linguae Anglicanae*, 1653), because it is here that the rule concerning the use of *shall* and *will* is enunciated for the first time.
8. For a good summary of the history of traditional grammar, see Francis P. Dinneen, *An Introduction to General Linguistics*. New York: Holt, Rinehart and Winston, 1967, chaps. 4 and 5, pp. 70–175.
9. *A New English Grammar*. Oxford: The Clarendon Press, 1891, vol. 1, p. 5.
10. On this point, see the article by Charles V. Hartung, "The Persistence of Tradition in Grammar," *Quarterly Journal of Speech*, 48 (April 1962), 174–186.
11. New York: Harcourt Brace Jovanovich, 1952.
12. *Ibid.*, Introduction, p. 7.
13. *Ibid.*, pp. 54–55.
14. *Ibid.*, p. 56.
15. Since syntactic constructions are concerned only with *free* morphemes, the ultimate constituents of any phrase are words. Further analysis, such as *students* into *student* and *-s* or *walked* into *walk* and *-ed*, would be a matter of morphology. It is, of course, perfectly possible to carry IC analysis to the morphological

level, for example, to show that the nominal group *the dean's office* or *the King of England's prerogative* has a bound morpheme as one of its constituents.
16. See, in particular, Robert B. Lees, "Transformation Grammars and the Fries Framework," in Harold B. Allen, ed., *Readings in Applied English Linguistics*, 2nd ed. New York: Appleton-Century-Crofts, 1964, pp. 137 ff.
17. The Hague: Mouton & Co.
18. *Syntactic Structures*, p. 5.
19. *Ibid.*, p. 13. What Chomsky means by this definition is that the number of sentences in a given language (which are constructed out of a morpheme inventory that is finite in size) is unlimited because no ceiling can be placed on their length, even though any particular sentence may be finite, that is, limited in length.
20. This ambiguity, incidentally, is of quite a different sort from Fries' *Ship sails today*, since it involves no absence of proper part-of-speech markers, and the ambiguity could not be cleared up by adding structural signals.
21. Paul Roberts, *English Syntax*. New York: Harcourt Brace Jovanovich, 1964, p. 1.
22. There seems to be some divergence of opinion among linguists regarding the number of these basic sentence patterns. Professor Owen Thomas, for instance, lists the following four types: (a) NP + be + Pred + (Adv), for example, *The student is good* (*always*) or *The man is my friend* or *The postman is here*, depending on whether the predicate is a noun phrase, an adjective, or an adverb of location; (b) NP + V_i [intransitive] + Ø + (Adv), for example, *The children play* (*noisily*); (c) NP + V_t [transitive] + NP + (Adv), for instance, *The teacher scolds the student* (*menacingly*) or *The members elected him president* or *The father gave his son a penny*; and (d) NP + V_c [copulative, except *to be*] + Comp [subjective complement] + (Adv), for example, *The professor looks angry* (*always*) or *The coffee tastes bitter* (*sometimes*) or *The sky seems clear* (*today*). See his *Transformational Grammar and the Teacher of English*. New York: Holt, Rinehart and Winston, 1965, p. 35 ff. The number of basic sentence structures given in textbooks on English grammar will ultimately depend on how detailed and complete the description of each sentence pattern is to be and how many different subclasses of verbs are to be distinguished. A system of ten basic sentence patterns is given by Paul Roberts, *English Sentences*. New York: Harcourt Brace Jovanovich, 1962, p. 30 ff.

23. From Chomsky's *Syntactic Structures*. The following discussion is based on material in this book, pp. 26–27.
24. It is customary in transformational analysis to use the *-en* suffix that appears in the past participle form of some strong verbs (*eaten, beaten, written*) as the symbol for the past participle in general, rather than the more frequent *-ed* ending of weak verbs. The use of the latter could be confused with the simple past tense.
25. From Chomsky, *op. cit.*, p. 32.
26. Besides Chomsky's original exposition of transformational theory in *Syntactic Structures*, this holds true of such widely known introductory texts as those of Emmon Bach, Andreas Koutsoudas, and Owen Thomas.
27. See Chomsky's Introduction (p. xii) in Paul Roberts, *English Syntax*, alternate ed. New York: Harcourt Brace Jovanovich, 1964. This book, incidentally, is a programed introduction to transformational grammar and may be most profitably used by the beginner.
28. Noam Chomsky, *Current Issues in Linguistic Theory*. The Hague: Mouton & Co., 1964.
29. See particularly his *Aspects of the Theory of Syntax*. Cambridge, Mass.: M.I.T. Press, 1965; *Current Issues* (see note 28); and *Topics in the Theory of Generative Grammar*. The Hague: Mouton & Co., 1966.
30. Literature on transformational theory is considerable, and much of it is scattered throughout scholarly journals. A recent text embodying latest research on the subject is Roderick A. Jacobs and Peter S. Rosenbaum, *English Transformational Grammar*. Waltham: Blaisdell, 1968.
31. Paul M. Postal, "Underlying and Superficial Linguistic Structure," in Janet A. Emig, James T. Fleming, and Helen M. Popp, eds., *Language and Learning*. New York: Harcourt Brace Jovanovich, 1966.

6
vocabulary: word formation

It is a generally accepted fact that English has the richest and most extensive vocabulary of any language in the world. The precise number of items in its word stock has never been determined;[1] indeed, it is unlikely that an accurate count could ever be made, if only because new words keep cropping up constantly as new objects, ideas, concepts, inventions, and discoveries require that new names be found to designate them.

In this chapter we are going to examine briefly, with special reference to English, the ways in which new words come into being, and the resources that languages have at their disposal for building up and replenishing their existing LEXICON.[2]

Basically, there are two ways of vocabulary building. One method consists of the creation of new words by utilizing the words and morphemes that are already available. This method of word formation consists of various processes, of which derivation and composition are the most common.[3] The other means by which new words may come about is borrowing from foreign sources. There is probably no natural language (as opposed to an artificially constructed language like Esperanto or Interlingua) that does not have the resources for the increase of its word stock, though some languages may show preference for one device over another. Thus, for instance, the process of word building by means of composition, that is, the putting together of two bases (generally free morphemes), is not frequent in French, while it is very freely used in languages like English and German. Compare, for instance, English *summit conference* and German *Gipfelkonferenz* with French *conférence au sommet* 'conference at the summit.'

DERIVATION

Native Resources

The process of DERIVATION already alluded to in a previous chapter (see derivational suffixes, Chapter 4, page 57) is one of the common methods of word formation. It is found in all Indo-European languages and, probably, most languages of the world. It consists of taking an existing base—either free or bound—and adding to it affixes—that is, prefixes or suffixes, or both. From the base form *cloud*, for instance, we can form the verb *becloud*, the adjectives *cloudy* and *cloudless*, and the abstract noun *cloudiness*. Many of the affixes used in modern English are survivals from Old English (OE), and some may indeed have been independent words at one time. Such is the case with the English suffix *-dom*, as in *freedom*, *kingdom*, and *martyrdom*, which represents OE *dom* 'statute, jurisdication,' or *-hood*, as in *childhood*, *parenthood*, and *priesthood*, which derives from OE *hād* 'quality, rank.' In addition to the *native* affixes, many English words are also made up of foreign elements that have come into the English lexicon as a result of certain historical circumstances surrounding the development of the language. While all languages borrow words from other languages, English seems to have borrowed a higher percentage of them than most, an estimated 75 percent.

Let us, first, consider some of the native *suffixes* that are still in use:

1. The adjectival suffix *-ly* (*manly*, *godly*, and *homely*) was an independent word at one time, since it goes back to OE *līc* 'body.'[4] Since the word was frequently used as a suffix with the meaning of 'having the body, shape, or appearance of,' the long /i/ eventually became short and *-līc* became simply *-ly*. Conversely, the suffix *-like*, in such recent formations as *gentlemanlike* and *homelike* represents a regular historical development of OE *līc*, which means that both suffixes are related, though there is certainly a difference in meaning between, say, *homely* and *homelike*.

2. The suffix *-y* (OE *-ig*) forms adjectives from nouns, as in *thirsty*, *bloody*, *greedy*, *fishy*, *jazzy*, *edgy*, *folksy*, *chummy*, and

some recent formations like *iffy* and *groovy*. It should not be confused with the common diminutive suffix *-y* (sometimes also spelled *-ie*), as in *birdie, Charlie, Billy, Kitty, Jackie,* and *Jeanie,* which imply smallness, affection, fondness, or familiarity.[5]

3. The suffix *-ish* (OE *-isc*) also converts nouns into adjectives (*childish, girlish,* and *foolish*) with the idea of 'in the nature of.' Originally, it implies nothing unfavorable (for example, OE *folcisc* 'folkish,' in the sense of 'popular'), but nowadays it often carries an unfavorable and even derogatory connotation, as in *bookish* and *old-maidish*. When added to an adjective, this suffix gives the general idea of 'somewhat,' as in *smallish, longish, thinnish,* and *reddish*. More recently, it has become a rather modish suffix meaning 'approximately,' as in *sixish, eight-thirtyish, fortyish*.

4. The suffix *-ful* forms adjectives, as in *wonderful* and *sinful*, as well as new nouns, as in *spoonful, mouthful,* and *handful*. Indeed, this suffix is so productive that it is freely added to words of foreign origin, as in *useful, peaceful, beautiful, grateful,* and many others.

5. The suffix *-less* (OE *-lēas*) also forms adjectives from nouns, as in *careless, hopeless, speechless, homeless,* and *childless*. Like the suffix *-ful*, this suffix is also frequently found with nonnative nouns, as in *useless, graceless, merciless,* and *pitiless*. It is related to the adjective *loose* and the verb *lose*.

6. The suffix *-ship* (OE *-scipe*) forms abstract nouns by denoting 'quality, condition, or state' (*friendship, fellowship*), 'rank or office' (*governorship, chairmanship*), 'status' (*lordship, ladyship*), and even 'ability or skill' (*leadership, penmanship*). The suffix competes with *-ness*, which is also used to form abstract nouns; it is used in new formations, such as the recent coinage, *brinkmanship* ('balancing on the brink of disaster').

7. The form *-ness* is one of the most productive suffixes for making abstract nouns from practically any adjective, as in *coolness, illness, manliness, girlishness, holiness, foolishness,* and countless others. It has largely replaced the native suffixes *-hood, -dom,* and *-th* (*health, filth*) in the formation of new abstract nouns. It is also commonly added to adjectives of foreign origin that end in *-ous* (ultimately from the Latin *-osus* 'having the characteristics of'), for example, *graciousness, consciousness,* and *covetousness*.

8. The so-called noun-agency suffix *-er* (OE *-ere*), meaning 'one who does something,' as in *baker, fisher, hunter, learner,* and *worker* and many family names (such as *Weaver, Miller,* and, of course, *Baker, Fisher* and *Hunter*). It is a very prolific suffix in modern English still and conveys meanings other than 'doer of an action.' Thus, it may denote instruments or things, as in *typewriter, eraser, slipper,* and *diner* (for *dining-car*). In *New Yorker, Londoner, Icelander* it denotes a resident of a certain place; it is also found in some colloquialisms like *fiver* 'five dollar bill,' or *breather* in the sense of 'breathing space.'

In words like *misnomer* 'wrong name or wrong use of term,' *disclaimer* 'denial or renunciation, as of a claim or title,' and *rejoinder* 'answer to a reply,' the *-er* suffix is not identical with the native *-er* ending of English. In this case it represents the infinitive ending of Old French, as in *mesnomer, desclamer,* and *rejoindre,* respectively.

An interesting variant form of English *-er* is the suffix *-ster,* as in *spinster* (originally meaning 'one who spins'), which goes back to OE *-estre* to form agent nouns of the feminine gender. This suffix also survives in family names like *Baxter* (OE *baecestre*), meaning 'baking-woman,' and *Webster* (OE *webbestre*) 'weaving-woman.' The corresponding masculine forms are, of course, *Baker* (OE *baecere*) and *Webb* or *Weber* (OE *webba*). The original connotation of 'femininity' having been lost, the ending *-ster* has been used to form new nouns like *teamster, roadster, gangster,* and *speedster,* as well as *youngster* and *oldster,* while the suffix *-stress* (made up of the suffixes *-ster* and *-ess,* the latter from French *-esse* and, ultimately, Greek *-issa*) came to be used to denote feminine agent, as in *seamstress* (rather than *seamster* from OE *seamestre*) and *songstress.*

Turning now to the native *prefixes,* we must note above all that they are far outnumbered by nonnative, especially Latin, ones. A glance at a list of such prefixes in a grammar book also concerned with the vocabulary of English will easily convince you of this fact.[6] Take, for instance, the negative prefix *un-* (OE *un-*), as in *unkind, unjust, unafraid, unclean, unbelievable, unfriendly, unruly.* It is in competition with three other prefixes that signify 'not,' namely *in-* (Latin), as in *ineligible, incorrect, invisible,* and *incredible*, as well as its variants *il-*, *im-*, and *ir-*, in *illegal, illegible, immature, immortal, irresponsible,* and *irrational; non-* (Latin and French), as in *nonconformist, noncombatant,* and *nondescript;* and *a-* or *an-* (Greek), as in *apathetic* 'indifferent, unmoved,' *atheist* 'unbeliever,' and *anonymous* 'unknown.' The native *un-* prefix is probably the commonest of them all, since it is freely used with both native and nonnative bases, for example, *unjust, unintelligible, unaffected, uneducated, unfilial,* and *ungracious,* while its nearest competitor, the Latin *in-*, is limited to words of French and Latin origin. It is often not easy to decide which is the appropriate prefix to use in a given case. Why say, for instance, *irresponsible* but *unresponsive*? After all, both the base *respons-* (actually made up of Latin *re-* 'back' and *spondere* 'to pledge') and the suffix *-ive* are of Latin-French origin, just as the suffix *-ible* is. Why not **irresponsive*? Since there is no hard and fast rule which determines the use of one or the other in cases like these, we must be governed by usage.

There is another *un-* prefix which is used with verbs only, for instance, *undo, undress, unbind, unfold, uncover,* and *unlock.* It expresses the contrary or reversal of an action. The separate origin of the two prefixes is not immediately apparent in English, but a comparison with modern German is quite instructive. English *un-*, meaning 'not,' is also *un-* in German, compare *unknown* versus *unibekannt, unconscious* versus *unbewusst,* and *unclean* versus *unreön,* whereas the verbal prefix *un-* is German *ent-*, as in *unveil* versus *enthüllen, unclothe* versus *entkleiden,* and *uncover* versus *entblssen.*

Other native prefixes include (1) *be-* as in *bemoan, bespeak* (for example, *His charity bespeaks a generous nature*), *becloud, befriend,* and *belittle* (this one is said to have been coined by Thomas Jefferson); it is used in various ways, as shown by these examples, and is still to some extent productive and often used merely as an intensifier, as in *bedeck* and *besmear.* In addition to *be-* are the prefixes (2) *for-*, expressing negation, privation, or prohibition when used with verbs, as in *forbid, forgo,* and *forswear,*[7] or merely adding an intensifying force to an adjective, as in *forlorn;* and (3) *mis-* 'amiss, wrong or wrongly,' as in *mistake, misunderstanding, misbehave, mishandle, misdeed,* and many others. In words like *mischief, misadventure,* and *misnomer* (that is, in words of French origin that have the sense of 'bad'), *mis-* is not a native prefix but ultimately comes from Latin *minus* 'less' by way of French *mes-*. (Compare French *mésaventure* and English *misadventure*.)

Some of these native prefixes are still occasionally pulled out of the lexicon to make new words, though some of them, like the prefix *for-*, may be said to have ceased to be a productive formative element in modern English.

Foreign Elements

It was stated earlier that a great many derivational affixes used in modern English are not native. In its earliest stage English made almost exclusive use of its own native resources for purposes of word building; however, as its speakers entered into contact with other cultures and civilizations, particularly the French and those of Greek and Roman antiquity, they enriched the native word stock by adopting thousands of words from these languages, either through the *spoken* tongue (in the case of French) or the *written* language (in the case of Greek and Latin). The widespread use of Latin prefixes has already been noted. Some of them, such as *re-* 'again, back,' as in *revert, resell, remodel, refurbish,* and *reread*, are not only very common but have become fully naturalized. Since Latin prefixes are very similar in meaning to native English prepositions and adverbs, we could, of course, replace them by the corresponding native function words. Thus, instead of *resell* we might say *again-sell* and for *remodel* something like *again-model*, using 'again' and 'back' as native prefixes. The word *againbite* for *remorse* is still used in a fourteenth-century work entitled *The Againbite of Inwit* 'The Remorse of Conscience' (published in 1340).

During the great revival of learning in Europe in the centuries that mark the transition from the medieval to the modern world, the period commonly known as the *Renaissance*, there was a wholesale importation not only of Latin but also of Greek terms. Both languages had, of course, already left some imprint on English as a result of cultural contact of the English people with Christianity in the sixth and seventh centuries. With the progress of science, new words, many of them quite common, are being coined from Greek roots (for example, *thermometer, telephone, drama,* and *sympathy*). The interesting fact about Greek elements in English is that for the most part *roots* rather than *words* have been borrowed from Greek and that these have been combined to express new ideas. For instance, from *phil-* 'love' and *anthropo-* 'man,' the words *philanthropy* 'love of man' and *philanthropist* 'lover of man, benefactor' have been created. These coinages also include two widely used and thoroughly naturalized Greek suffixes: *-y* (earlier *-ie*, ultimately from Greek *-ia* borrowed via the French suffix *-ie*) to denote abstract nouns (*philosophy, jealousy*), and the agent-noun suffix *-ist* (*scientist, moralist*).⁸

As a matter of fact, the Greek suffixes *-ist*, the corresponding verbal suffix *-ize* (compare *satirist–satirize, moralist–moralize*), as well as the ubiquitous *-ism* (attested as early as 1300 in the word *baptism*) have become virtually indispensable for the creation of NEOLOGISMS (Greek *neos* 'new' + *logia* 'speaking' + *ism*). Add to this list the prefixes *anti-, hyper-, pseudo-,* and *neo-*, and you have the principal elements for the expression of abstract thought, theories, doctrines and systems. As a verbal suffix *-ize* (from Greek *-izein* through French *-ise*) has become extremely popular and is responsible for such recent verb formations as *hospitalize, winterize, pressurize, slenderize, finalize, vietnamize,* and, even, *establishmentize*. It may be worth noting that the British still prefer the *-ise* spelling.

Sometimes a Greek root combines with a Latin one, as in *television* (from Greek *tele-* 'far' and Latin *visio* 'vision'), *sociology* (from Latin *socius* 'companion' and Greek *-logia* 'study, science'), or *automobile* (from Greek *auto-* 'self' and Latin *mobilis* 'movable'). These word formations are called HYBRIDS, since their constituent elements come from different languages. Hybrid forms are by no means limited to nouns, as shown by such verbs as *demoralize, decentralize, danationalize,* and *deodorize*, which contain the Latin prefix *de-* and the Greek suffix *-ize*.

With the influx of French words following the Norman Conquest of England in the eleventh century and their complete assimilation in the English lexicon, English also acquired a taste for using French derivative elements in combination with native bases for building new words. Thus, the French noun suffix *-age* (*voyage*) gives rise to words like *shortage, shrinkage, breakage,* and *leakage*; *-ment* (*movement*) gives such hybrid forms as *atonement* and *fulfillment*; *-ess* (*duchesse*) appears in *shepherdess* and *goddess*; the adjectival ending *-ous* (*gracious*) is extended to native bases like *wondrous* and *murderous*; and, what has probably become one of the most productive suffixes in modern English, the suffix *-able*, which can be tacked on to thousands of verbs to make adjectives, as in *laughable* (first attested in Shakespeare), *answerable, eatable, drinkable, understandable, washable*, and *nonshrinkable*.⁹

Another French derivative element that is worth mentioning because of its productiveness in modern English is the suffix *-ee* (also spelled *-é*). It conveys the idea of a person to whom something is done, as in *lessee, mortgagee* (as opposed to *lessor* and *mortgagor*), *trustee, payee, consignee, nominee, refugee, employee, trainee* and *draftee*. Originally a French participial ending in *-é* with passive force (for example, *employé* 'employed'), this sense is not always apparent in English (*consignee, refugee, trainee*), though in cases like *employee, nominee*, and *draftee* the passive value is very much in evidence. This suffix, which seems to have entered the language by way of legal terminology and has long since gone beyond the scope of the vocabulary of law, is but one more illustration of how formative elements coming from foreign sources have acquired full citizenship in English.

Before we turn to the process of word composition, a word about the creation of new words by means of PSEUDOSUFFIXES may be of interest. These word elements are called thus because they are not real suffixes but have somehow come to be felt as such in the popular mind. A classic example of such a pseudosuffix is *-burger* which has been subtracted from the word *hamburger* (formerly called *Hamburg steak*) and is now freely used to denote such culinary specialties as *cheeseburger, beefburger, fishburger*, and *pizzaburger*. Another word from which a pseudosuffix has been extrapolated is the word *cavalcade* 'parade of horsemen,' borrowed from French. While the actual suffix in this word is *-ade* as in *blockade*, new formations like *motorcade* 'procession of automobiles' and *aquacade* 'aquatic exhibition' clearly seem to indicate that there has been an erroneous interpretation of root and ending.

COMPOSITION

Unlike derivation, the process of COMPOSITION, or COMPOUNDING, involves the joining of two or more words, generally free bases, into a new lexical unit whose meaning is not necessarily the sum total of the concepts expressed by its component parts (for example, *hothouse, blackbird, railroad,* and *gentleman*). Word building by means of composition has been characteristic of the Germanic languages. This is well illustrated by modern German, which is capable of producing such crackjaws as *Donaudampfschiffartsgesellschaftskapitän* 'captain in the Danube steamship company.' Compounding was also freely used in Old English, but many native formations have been replaced by French or Latin terms, especially in the field of abstract concepts. For example, OE *mildheortnes* (literally 'mildheartedness') has been replaced by *mercy* or *compassion* (compare German *Mildherzigkeit*); OE *ofer-mōd* (literally 'over-mood') has been replaced by *arrogance* (compare German *Übermut*); and OE *mōd-craeft* (literally 'strength of mind') has been replaced by *courage, ability* (compare German *Mutkraft*). This does not mean, of course, that the formation of new words by compounding existing words is no longer productive in English. In fact, modern English has accumulated a great number of compounds and is producing new ones almost daily: *sit-in, teach-in, launching-pad, countdown,* and *blast-off*. The possibilities are almost limitless. Here are some of the more typical compound formations in English:

Compound nouns The most common ones are those in which two nouns are joined together, the first component qualifying the second one, as in *bookcase, notebook, keyhole, suntan, windmill, weekend, baseball, snowflake,* and countless others. These are also called PRIMARY COMPOUNDS because they are made up of two single free forms. This kind of compounding is very prolific in English and is perhaps the most typical.

The following are other frequent types of compound noun formations: adjective + noun (*bluegrass, blackbird, redcap, greenhouse*); noun + adverb (*fallout, check-up, mark-up, countdown*); adverb + noun or verb (*underpass, upkeep, outcome, downfall*); verb + adverb (*getaway, hideout, breakdown, knowhow*); and verb + noun (object) (*breakwater, cutthroat, crackjaw, daredevil, scarecrow*), as well as many family names like *Shakespeare, Kilroy, Lovejoy,* and *Drinkwater*. This latter type, unknown at an earlier stage of English, is said to have become quite productive under

French influence, where such compounds are frequent, for example, *passeport* 'passport,' *passetemps* 'pastime,' *porte-feuille* 'wallet' (compare English *portfolio*), *porte-cigarette* 'cigarette holder,' and *casse-noisette* 'nutcracker.' This last example, furthermore, illustrates an interesting point. Whenever the English noun object is placed before the verb, a combination of composition and derivation must be used to conform to the structure of the English language, which requires the object to follow the verb. Thus, a person who keeps house is a *housekeeper* rather than a *housekeep (along the lines of *cutthroat* and *daredevil*), someone who owns land is a *landowner*, and a gadget with which to crack nuts is a *nutcracker* and not a *cracknut (like *crackjaw* or *crackpot*).

Compound adjectives Many of them are formed by joining a *noun* with an *adjective* or *participle* (*bloodthirsty, penny-wise, heartbreaking, time-honored, peace-loving, old-fashioned, hand-picked*); an *adjective* or *adverb* with a *participle* (*low-flying, well-done, good-looking, narrow-minded, full-grown*); a *participle* with an *adverb* (*worn-out, washed-up*); and an *adjective* with another *adjective* (*light-green, dark-brown, red-hot*).

Compound verbs Since English nouns may be freely used as verbs, many compound nouns are also used as compound verbs, for example, *to skyrocket, to railroad,* and *to stockpile.* In addition, there are *adverb + verb* combinations, as in *outshine, overturn, update, undercut,* and *overcome.* But by far the most widely used compounds are verbal phrases consisting of a *verb + adverb* combination, as in *back down, build up, break down, let up, sit down, hold up, hand out, pay off, write up,* and many, many others. In accordance with the general principles of English stress patterns, compounds that consist of two separate parts are given only one primary stress, as in *bluegrass, hothouse, railroad* and *blackbird.* To put it in more technical terms, compounds are pronounced with *close juncture* (see Chapter 3, page 50). The primary stress has, in many instances, obscured the unstressed syllable (*gentleman* versus *gentle man*) to the point where the awareness of the constituent elements of a compound has been completely obliterated. Although the average English speaker may still be conscious of the component parts of the word *breakfast* as being *break* + *fast*,[10] the former compounds in modern English *lord* (OE *hlāf* + *weard* 'loaf-keeper'), *daisy* (OE *dæges* + *ēage* 'day's eye'), and *hussy* (OE *hūs* + *wīf* 'housewife') are no longer readily apparent.

A more complete discussion of the process of composition would also have to include the formation of compound *adverbs* (*overhead*) and compound *prepositions* (*underneath*), as well as formations made up of more than two elements, such as *sit-down strike*, *whodunit*, *happy-go-lucky*, *hand-to-mouth*, *matter-of-fact*, and *commander-in-chief*. Further information on these points is readily available in works devoted specifically to the English vocabulary, such as those of Sheard, Greenough-Kittredge, and Pyles listed in the bibliography.

BACK-FORMATION

Another source of word formation is called BACK-FORMATION. This process involves the creation of a new word from an existing one by cutting off a real or supposed suffix, as exemplified by the verb *edit*, derived from the noun *editor*. In a sense, back-formation is a kind of derivation in reverse and, like derivation, it usually involves the change of one part of speech to another. Typically, this process serves to make verbs out of existing nouns that give the appearance of ending with a known suffix, thereby implying the existence of a verbal base from which a given noun has been formed. Thus, the word *editor* looks like a noun formed on the verb *edit* to which the noun-agent suffix *-or* (as in *realtor*) has been added; actually, however, the *-or* ending is an integral part of the word and does not denote "agent," just as the *-er* in *butcher*, *butler*, and *peddler* has no connection with the English suffix *-er* in *baker*, *player* and *driver*.[11]

Examples of back-formations are *peddle* (*peddler*), *audit* (*auditor*), *cobble* (*cobbler*), *loaf* (*loafer*), *beg* (*beggar*),[12] *size* (*assize*, originally 'assembly'), and *swindle* (*swindler*). An interesting creation is the verb *grovel* from an old adverb *groveling* with the meaning of 'in an abjectly prostrate position,' which, despite the adverbial suffix *-ling* (the same as that in *headlong*), must have been felt as a present participle in *-ing*; hence the verb *to grovel*.

Other frequent back-formations include *donate* from *donation*, *orientate* from *orientation, intern* from *internment,* and colloquial and even slangy forms like *enthuse* from *enthusiasm, emote* from *emotion, orate* from *oration,* and *buttle* from *butler.*

SHORTENING

Another rather popular method of creating new words is the process known as SHORTENING, which involves the clipping off of an unstressed initial or final syllable, or syllables, of a word. Abbreviations thus created have often superseded the original longer form and a good many of them are fully accepted in the standard language. For instance, we go to the *zoo,* rather than to the *zoological gardens;* we ride a *bus* to go to work rather than an *omnibus* (Latin word which literally means 'for all'); and some of us try to avoid the fickle *mob* (from the Latin *mobile vulgus* 'fickle mass') as much as possible. An unmarried woman is a *miss* (from earlier *mistress);* a favorite pastime is a *hobby* (short for *hobby-horse);*[13] rock'n roll may be just a passing *fad* (from the French *fadaise* 'frivolity'); and a baseball devotee is known as a *fan,* rather than a *fanatic.*

Abbreviated forms used in lieu of full words occur frequently in the vocabulary of students, for example, *prof, lab, exam, trig, math, lit, gym,* and *Phys Ed,* though no one field of human activity seems to have any particular claim on them, as witnessed by forms like *piano, flu, cab, deb, mike,* and *bike.*

Among words shortened by clipping off the initial syllable, let us mention *wig (periwig), spite (despite), mend (amend), fence (defense), lone (alone), cute (acute), sample (example), fender (defender),* and *tend (attend).* Sometimes both the original long form and the shortened word exist side by side, usually with some difference in meaning; for instance, *mend* is not synonymous with *amend, lone* and *alone* are not usually interchangeable, and *cute* would hardly be used in connection with an *acute* attack of appendicitis.

Akin to the process of shortening is the use of initials as regular words, also called ACRONYMS, or ALPHABET WORDS. Such are *M.C.* (or *emcee*) for *master of ceremonies, C.B.* (or *seabee*) for *construction battalion, V.P.* (or *veep*) for *vice president, N.A.T.O.* (*Nato*) for *North Atlantic Treaty Organization, S.H.A.P.E.* (*Shape*) for *Supreme Headquarters Allied Powers Europe,* and

U.N.E.S.C.O. (*Unesco*) for *United Nations Educational and Scientific Organization*. An interesting instance of an acronym is the name "winne(r) circle" given to our local radio-station *WINA* here in Charlottesville. The use of initials of a phrase instead of the full phrase, such as *I.Q., I.O.U., C.I.O., P.O.W.*, and *V.I.P.* also belong under this heading.

BLENDING

The word-making process called BLENDING may be considered as a special kind of composition. But while compounds, as a rule, keep the elements of which they are made up intact, blends, also known as PORTMANTEAU or telescoped words, involve the combination of part of one word with part of another to form a single new word which may share or even combine their meanings. In what could be termed the classic type of blend, the two words coalesce about one or more letters they have in common, as in *don* 'put on' (from *do + on*), where the two elements are joined at the two *o*'s that overlap, or as in *motel* (from *motor + hotel*), where the two source words merge at the letters *ot*, which act as a link. Many words, however, are blended even though they do not have a common element, for instance *brunch* (*breakfast + lunch*), *flaunt* (*flout + vaunt*), *slide* (*slip + glide*), or *squash* (*squeeze + crash*).

Lewis Carroll has been credited with the creation of a number of portmanteau words, some of which are still in common use today, for example, *chortle* (*chuckle + snort*) and *galumphing* (*gallop + triumphing*). Many newspaper writers seem to be prolific "blenders": *smog* (*smoke + fog*), *smaze* (*smoke + haze*), *slanguage* (*slang + language*), *telecast* (*television + broadcast*), and many others. Some trade names are also blends: *Aspergum* (*aspirin + gum*), *Duralumin* (*durable + aluminum*), *Colorinse* (*colored + rinse*), and *Spam* (*spiced + ham*). Among geographical concepts made up of blends, one might mention *Amerindian* 'American Indian' and *Eurasian* 'belonging to Europe and Asia.' More recently, gas stations have been advertising *lubritection* (*lubrication + protection*) and at least one restaurant we know of is serving *broasted* (*broiled + roasted*) chicken.

An interesting instance of a pseudosuffix that owes its origin to blending is *-rama* in *cinerama* ('wide-screen motion picture'), a blend of *cinema* and *panorama* (from the Greek *pan* 'all' + *horama* 'view'). This -*rama* element has come to be regarded as a legitimate affix meaning 'big, wide, extensive' and is now being exploited in such new words as *colorama, autorama, bowlorama, futurama,* and *pizzarama.*

OTHER WORD CREATIONS

There are two other sources of words that must be briefly touched upon: (1) the use of proper names to designate new things, and (2) the part that individuals have played in the creation of a word, often out of thin air, as it were.

Concerning the conversions of proper nouns, we may note the names of scientists used to designate units of measurement, particularly in the field of electricity, such as *ohm* (after the German physicist Georg *Ohm*), *watt* (after the Scottish inventor James *Watt*), *volt* (after the Italian Alessandro *Volta*), *ampere* (after the Frenchman André-Marie *Ampère*), and *faraday* (after the English chemist and physicist Michael *Faraday*). Examples from other fields in which surnames have been turned into common nouns include such garments as *bloomers, bowler, mackintosh,* and *cardigan,* as well as miscellaneous words like *davenport, pullman, shrapnel, zeppelin,* and *sandwich.*

Personal names also lend themselves for use as verbs. Probably the best known examples are to *boycott* (also used as a noun), which commemorates the persecution of a certain Captain Boycott by the Irish Land League in 1880, and to *lynch,* after Captain William Lynch, a Virginian planter, who is supposed to have started the practice of capital punishment by mob action without trial. Both verbs have also passed from English into several European languages, for example, French *boycotter, lyncher,* Italian, *boicottare, linciare,* and German *boykottieren, lynchen.* More often than not the suffix -*ize* (see page 114) is added to the proper name, as in *pasteurize* (after the French bacteriologist Louis *Pasteur*), *macadamize* (after the Scottish engineer John *MacAdam*), *mesmerize* (after the Austrian physician F. A. *Mesmer*),[14] and *tantalize* (after the Greek mythological figure *Tantalus,* the son of Zeus, condemned to eternal hunger and thirst).

Place names have not escaped the tendency of turning proper names into common nouns either. Generally speaking, they are associated with the names of products first manufactured or sold in a given locality. Among names of fabrics, *calico* (from *Calicut* in India), *cashmere* (from *Kashmir*), *damask* (from *Damascus*), *madras* (from *Madras* in India), *gauze* (from *Gaza* in Palestine), and *jersey* (from the Isle of *Jersey*) come readily to mind. Many names of cheeses are also known by place names: *camembert, cheddar, edam, gorgonzola, limburger,* and *parmesan.* Further examples of this source of naming new things are *bourbon, champagne, sauterne, sherry* (from the Spanish town *Jerez de la Frontera*), *morocco, panama, suede* (the French name for *Sweden*), *tabasco,* and *tuxedo.*

Word creation is largely anonymous. No one knows for sure who first created a certain word, although occasionally somebody comes up with a new one that meets with general acceptance and favor. A case in point is *blurb,* invented by the American man of letters Gelett Burgess to designate the exaggerated and overly enthusiastic advertisements that publishers sometimes print on book jackets. Maury Maverick, a former congressman from Texas,[15] is credited with the word *gobbledygook* to denote the pompous and involved jargon of Washington officialdom (now extended to any bureaucratic jargon), while *globaloney* (actually a blend of *global* + *baloney*) is known to have been coined by Mrs. Clare Boothe Luce, with which she characterized some of the pronouncements of Washington "experts" on international affairs.

Some trade names like *Kodak, rayon, nylon,* and *dacron* may also be considered as outright coinages without reference to existing words, while names like *Jello, Kleenex, Windex,* and *Cutex* clearly suggest the words *jelly, clean, window,* and *cuticle* which underly them, with *ex* possibly representing "excellent." In this case Cutex, for instance, might mean something like "putting your cuticles in excellent shape."

The foregoing discussion points up the fact that the possibilities of word creation, whether by addition of affixes, by compounding, or by any of the other processes shown, are virtually infinite. Indeed, the making of new words goes on all the time, as evidenced by new formations and combinations found in the ad pages of last Sunday's paper. Some of these are quite short-lived, of course, and may never make the dictionary; but the ingenious human word mill keeps on grinding and sees to it that the vocabulary remains in step with the changes of a complex twentieth-century society.

notes

1. *The Oxford English Dictionary* of 1933 lists over 600,000 items.
2. The Greek word *lexicon* (from the base *lexis* 'word') may be defined as the total stock of morphemes of a language.
3. As morphological processes, *derivation* and *composition* should properly be treated under morphology. As sources of word building, however, there is ample justification to include them in a discussion of vocabulary.
4. The word originally applied to either a living or a dead body, though the latter connotation seems to have prevailed. It survives in the compound form *lich-gate* 'roofed gateway to a churchyard where a bier is placed to await the arrival of the clergyman,' as well as in *lich-house* 'mortuary' and the place-name *Litchfield* 'graveyard.' The related German word *Leiche* still means 'corpse.'
5. Diminutives are also formed by means of the suffixes *-ette* (*kitchenette*), *-kin* (*lambkin*), and *-let* (*leaflet*). English does not have many formations of this kind in comparison with some other languages—Russian, for instance.
6. See especially Paul Roberts, *Understanding English*. New York: Harper & Row, 1958, pp. 367–368.
7. Do not confuse this prefix with the prefix *fore-* in the meaning of 'beforehand,' as in *forestall*, *forewarn*, or *forecast*.
8. For a list of the most common Latin and Greek roots, see Roberts, *op. cit.*, pp. 368–375. Handy and authoritative guides for the use of Latin and Greek roots in English are the following: Rudolf F. Schaeffer, *Latin-English Derivative Dictionary* (Pamphlet 62) and, by the same author, *Greek-English Derivative Dictionary* (Pamphlet 70), both published by the American Classical League, Miami University, Oxford, Ohio, 1960 and 1963, respectively.
9. The *-ible* variant of this suffix is used only with roots that derive directly from Latin verbs, for example, *legible*, *edible*, and *divisible*.

The suffix *-able*, of course, is also used with nonnative roots, for example, *demandable, redeemable*.

10. That the word is felt as an inseparable lexical unit is confirmed by the fact that in the past tense we say "I breakfasted" rather than "I broke fast."
11. The word *butcher* comes from French *boucher*, originally 'one who kills and sells he-goats; *butler* is the French *bouteiller* 'cup bearer'; and *peddler*, also spelled *pedlar*, is probably a word of English origin with the original meaning of 'fish hawker.'
12. The word *beggar* is ultimately derived from the name of a medieval French mendicant order called the *Beghards*.
13. The idea of "horse" is still quite alive in the German word for 'hobby,' which is *Steckenpferd*.
14. This same Dr. Mesmer is said to have been immortalized by Wolfgang Amadeus Mozart in his opera *Così fan tutte*.
15. Not to be confused with the independent-minded ninteenth-century Texas rancher, Samuel Maverick, after whom the common noun *maverick* was coined.

7
vocabulary: borrowing from foreign sources

Word borrowing from foreign sources as a means of vocabulary building has already been alluded to. It was stated, in particular, that many English words are made up of foreign elements that have come into the English lexicon as a result of the particular cultural and socio-historical circumstances surrounding the development of the English language.

English, often called the world's greatest borrower, has indeed displayed remarkable powers of adaptation and assimilation by absorbing so many and such varied elements of vocabulary from diverse sources.

THE EARLIEST BORROWINGS

While the Anglo-Saxons (the collective name given to the Germanic invaders of Britain in the fifth century A.D.) were still wandering about the forests of northern Europe in the early centuries of the Christian era, such words as *street*, *wine*, and *cheese* (from the Latin *strata*, *vinum*, and *caseus*, respectively) had come into their language as a result of contact with Roman traders and soldiers. The first large-scale borrowing of foreign words, however, occurred around the end of the sixth century when Roman and Irish missionaries came to Britain to convert the pagan Anglo-Saxons to the Christian religion, bringing them into direct contact with the Latin of the Church. Lacking the words to designate the new concepts surrounding Christian doctrine and church usage, the new converts naturally adopted Latin words like *altar*, *mass*, *creed*, and *master*. Since the original language of the New Testament was Greek, many of the church words had previously been borrowed by Latin from Greek—for instance, *angel, bishop, devil, priest, monk*, and *school*, as well as the word *church* itself, which comes from the Greek *kyriakon*. The initial [k] sound of the Greek word is still reflected in the Scottish word *kirk*.[1]

The Christian missionaries established schools, and soon important centers of learning sprang up, especially in the northern part of England. It is here that the first great works of Old English literature were written, among them *Beowulf* (though it is likely that this poem, in oral form, antedates any Christian contacts).

DANISH ELEMENTS

About a century and a half after the arrival of the Christian missionaries, Britain was once again subjected to devastating raids by the Danish Vikings, the former neighbors of the Anglo-Saxons on the Continent. Coming across the North Sea, they destroyed everything in their way and would have conquered the whole island but for the heroic stand of the great West Saxon leader, King Alfred. Unable to drive out the Danes completely, he concluded a treaty with their leader which provided for the division of England. Drawing a line that ran roughly from northwest to southeast across the island, this arrangement created an English area in the southeast and a Danish one in the northeast. The latter was known as *Danelagh* or *Danelaw*. Since the two groups spoke kindred languages (Danish being a North Germanic and Anglo-Saxon, that is, Old English, a West Germanic dialect), the Danes gradually adopted English, however, not without carrying over into the new tongue their own words and pronunciation habits. It is often difficult to determine the linguistic contribution of the Danes to the language of the Anglo-Saxons, but many common, everyday words in modern English are clearly attributable to these Northmen—for instance, *fellow, husband, law, wrong, rotten* ("there is something rotten in Denmark"), and especially words that begin with a [sk] sound, as in *skip, skill, skull, skirt* (the corresponding Anglo-Saxon word being *shirt*), and *skin*. Possibly the most important borrowings were the pronominal forms *they, them*, and *their*, replacing the Old English plural forms *hie, heom,* and *heora* which were easily confused with the singular forms *he, him,* and *her*. The verb form *are* is also of Danish origin, replacing Old English *sind*.

Many English place-names are also of Danish origin, particularly those ending in *-thorp* 'village' and *-by* 'town.' The word *bylaw*, as a matter of fact, originally meant "the law of the town."

FRENCH INFLUENCE

For more than a century Anglo-Saxons and Danes lived side by side, merging in what was to become the English nation. But trouble was soon to beset England once again. In 1066 Duke William of Normandy crossed the English Channel and landed at Hastings with a huge army of Normans. These people were descendants of the Vikings who had settled on French soil in a region in northern France called Normandy about the same time that their Danish brethren had invaded England. Since the Normans had soon given up their native language in favor of French, the victorious William and his men brought the French language to England. For the next three centuries England was to become a country of two languages: the French of the Norman overloards—the ruling classes—and the English of the masses of the common people. Unlike their Danish predecessors, the Normans did not at first merge with the native population, for whose language and customs they cared little or nothing. French was used in the churches, the law courts, and the schools, and in every important political and business transaction. This separate existence of the two groups lasted for almost two centuries. Inevitably, however, the two had to merge, and the Norman rulers adopted English, so that by the middle of the fourteenth century it again became the language of the whole country. This was also the time of the poet Geoffrey Chaucer, who first elevated English to the ranks of the great literary languages of Europe and the world.

The victory of English over French was not won without a lasting mark of French influence on the English language: the introduction of thousands upon thousands of French words. These are of all sorts. They refer to government (*parliament, treaty,* and the word *government* itself); law (*justice, judge, court, prison, guarantee*); church (*sermon, parson, religion, baptism*); food and cooking (*bacon, cream, broil, fry, roast, toast, dinner,* and *supper,* as well as *beef, pork, veal,* and *mutton*—the cooked meats that come from the *ox, swine, calf,* and *sheep,* the names for which remained English because the animals were tended by Saxon peasants); household items (*curtain, chair, lamp, parlor*); leisure (*dance, music, chess, conversation*, and the word *leisure*); occupations and crafts (*carpenter, draper, mason, painter, tailor*); literature and science (*story, romance, poet, study, grammar, logic, surgeon, anatomy*); as well as thousands of ordinary, everyday words like *very* (from Old French *verai* 'true'), *nice, gentle, flower, cry, count, sure, plain,* and so forth.

Important as these additions to the English vocabulary were, the very core of the lexicon, the high-frequency words referring to the basic needs of everyday life (*father, mother, son, house, door, bread, live, eat, drink, come,* and *go*) remained English, and so did the essential structure of the language, which is today what it was in King Alfred's day, before the Norman Conquest—a basically Germanic structure.

In the centuries following the triumph of English, the language never ceased to grow. With the invention of printing, brought to England by William Caxton in the latter part of the fifteenth century, many new words were added, as people read and wrote in greater number than ever before. At the same time they also became interested in the old languages of Western civilization, with the result that many words of Latin and Greek origin found their way into the English word stock through translations of the great writers and poets of Greek and Roman antiquity. This period of "revival of learning," or *Renaissance*, supplied many of the "book" words or "learned" words, which make up the more literary and scientific portion of our vocabulary. The process of appropriating Greek and Latin words and roots, as was seen earlier, goes on relentlessly even today, for it is they which provide the ever-growing scientific terminology of our space age.

During the Renaissance many so-called "learned restorations" took place. There was a feeling among scholars that certain word forms borrowed from Latin through French were wrong and that they should be "reshaped" in accordance with their original Latin spelling. Thus the letter *b* was inserted in *debt* to show its derivation from Latin *debitum*, although the *b* had already been lost in Old French *dette*. In a similar fashion a *p* was introduced in *receipt* (French *recette*) to show its Latin heritage, *receptum*, and an *l* found its way into *fault* (French *faute*) to indicate that it was, indeed, related to Latin *fallere*. The restored consonant did not always affect pronunciation (as in *debt* and *receipt*); but in a number of words, it did come to be pronounced, as in *fault*, *vault*, and *assault*.

OTHER FOREIGN SOURCES

In addition to the Scandinavian French, and Greco-Latin elements that have left a deep enough mark on English to change its physiognomy with respect to what it was a thousand years ago, English has also borrowed a great many words from other languages. These loans are further witnesses of the commercial, political, military, and social contacts English-speaking people have had with the nations of the world in modern times, especially since the sixteenth century.

With the age of exploration, world trade, and colonial expansion, many new and strange products, inventions, fashions, and concepts were brought to England, together with the words that designate them. It is no coincidence that a large part of the musical and artistic vocabulary of English—to wit, *tempo, aria, alto, crescendo, piano, stanza, serenade, libretto,* and *adagio*—is of *Italian* origin, since the Italians made important contributions and innovations in the creative and performing arts. From Italy come too such terms of architecture and fine arts as *balcony, colonnade, corridor, mezzanine, fresco, chiaroscuro,* and *miniature*; while *traffic, risk, cash, deposit,* and *bank* (as well as *bankrupt*) reflect commercial relations between the two nations. *Burlesque, vogue, intrigue,* and *campaign* are also of Italian origin, despite their Gallic shape. Other examples taken at random include *partisan, sentinel, costume, pilot, carnival, escort, barrack, canteen, laundry, pants, studio, ghetto, piazza, concert, compliment,* and, of course, *broccoli, ravioli, macaroni,* and *spaghetti,* which are already plural nouns. The contribution from Italian, as you can see, is greater than is generally realized.[2]

At the time of Dutch maritime supremacy during the Middle Ages, England was engaged in important trade relations with the Netherlands. It is not surprising, then, that many nautical terms in English should be of *Dutch* origin, for instance, *buoy, deck, dock, hoist, moor, reef, skipper, yacht,* and *schooner,* as well as the interjection *ahoy*! The South African (Boer) War at the end of the nineteenth century led to the adoption of a few new Dutch words, such as *trek, spoor* 'trail' (compare German *Spur*), *boor*, and *commando* (which was originally from Portuguese).

International trade and the memory of the Invincible Armada are reflected in some *Spanish* loanwords like *armada, escapade, barricade, flotilla,* and *embargo*. However, Spanish, and to a lesser extent Portuguese, serves mainly as a carrier of words that ultimately come from the New World, such as *alligator, avocado, barracuda, cannibal, chocolate, tomato, potato, hurricane, maize, mulatto,* and *Negro*, to name but a few. Some of them, like *desperado, poncho, bronco, burro, patio, plaza, corral, rodeo, sombrero, bonanza,* and *aficionado*, appear unchanged. A borrowed word that deserves special mention is *cafeteria*, an American-Spanish term originally meaning "coffee shop." As it came to denote a self-service restaurant, it seems that the idea of self-service became identified with the ending *-teria*, giving rise to forms like *valeteria, marketeria, fruiteria, booketeria,* and *corseteria*.

German loanwords do not abound in English. *Swindler, plunder, carouse* (from German *gar austrinken* 'to drink up'), *halt, stroll, kindergarten,* and *poodle* are some of the most common ones, while some literary and philosophical terms, like *Gestalt, Weltanschauung,* and *Weltschmerz,* are used in their German form and may never become naturalized. On the other hand, many German words have been borrowed as *loan translations, that is, words brought into English through literal translation of their constituent parts*, as when we render the French phrase *raison d'être* as *reason for being* or *ça va sans dire* as *it goes without saying*. Such loan translations from German include *masterpiece* (*Meister + Stück*), *standpoint* (*Stand + Punkt*), *chain smoker* (*Ketten + Raucher*), *swan song* (*Schwanen + Gesang*), and Bernard Shaw's *superman* (*Über + Mensch*), in which he substituted the Latin prefix *super-* for the English *over-*.

Among other languages that have enriched the English vocabulary, let us briefly mention the following ones.

Contributions from *Russian* include *tsar, vodka, troika, bolshevik,* and *kulak*, as well as the suffix *-nik* of *sputnik*, which seems to be on the way to becoming quite productive, witness *beatnik, jazznik, peacenik,* and perhaps others we have not yet come across. From *Croatian* comes *cravat,* and *robot* comes from *Czech*.

The words borrowed from *Arabic* have come, as a rule, through other languages (often through Spanish, French, or Italian) and belong to a common stock of words appropriated from Arabic culture with which Western European civilizations came into contact during the Middle Ages. Here we find, first of all, terms relating to mathematics, astronomy, and science in general, for example, *almanac, algebra, alchemy, alcohol* (with the characteristic Arabic definite article *al*), *zero, zenith,* and *cipher.* Others suggest rare food and drink, such as *elixir, syrup,* and *sherbet* (the latter two being alternative forms of the same Arabic word, *sharāb*), or luxuries and amenities such as those reflected in *alcove, lute, divan, cotton, hashish, mattress, harem, carat,* and *hazard* (from *al-zār* ' the die '). The word *assassin,* which comes to us through Italian is, ultimately, derived from Arabic *hashāshīn* 'hashish-eaters,' who are said to have been a band of Moslem drug addicts who killed Christian leaders during the Crusades. The word *coffee,* which may take its name from the Ethiopian province of Kaffa, also comes from the Arabic, though it seems to have reached English by way of Turkish *qahveh.*

Direct loans from *Persian* include *bazaar, caravan* (and its shortened form *van*), *crimson, shah,* and *shawl.* Through Latin or Old French come the words *azure, taffeta, scarlet, tiger,* and *paradise;* while *candy, lemon, lilac, orange,* and *sugar* (ultimately from Sanskrit *çarkarā*) were brought to the West by the medieval Arabs. The English word *chess,* which was borrowed through Old French *esches,* ultimately goes back to Persian *shāh* ' king.' Taken over by the Arabs with the specific meaning of ' king at chess,' it gave rise to the expression *shāh māt* ' the king is dead,' the source of English *checkmate,* German *Schachmatt,* French *échec et mat,* and Italian *scacco matto.*

From the languages of *India* come *loot, pundit* (from Sanskrit *pandita* ' learned man '), *rajah, jungle, punch* (Hindi *panch* from Sanskrit *pañca* ' five,' referring to the number of ingredients in punch), *fakir* (from which we get the verb *to fake* and the noun *faker*), *coolie, bungalow, shampoo, thug, curry, monsoon, mandarin* (from the Sanskrit *mantrin* ' counselor' through Portuguese *mandarim*), *pagoda, veranda, dungaree,* and *pajama.* From the language of the Gypsies, an Indian dialect akin to Hindi, we get the popular word *pal.*

Among other loans from languages of the Far East, let us mention the *Chinese* words *tea, tycoon, typhoon, kow-tow, gung-ho,* and, possibly, *silk*: the *Japanese* words *kimono, samurai, geisha, harakiri,* and *sake* (the alcoholic beverage made from fermented rice); *atoll, tattoo,* and *taboo* from the *South Sea Islands*; and the useful *Australian* word *boomerang.*

Words from *African* languages mainly denote names of local flora and fauna, as well as names for certain customs: *gorilla, guinea, zebra, voodoo,* and its variant *hoodoo. Jazz* and *juke* are said to be Americanisms of African origin.[3]

To the *American Indian* languages we are indebted for words like *moccasin, totem, tomahawk, moose, skunk, hickory, toboggan, caucus,* and *papoose* 'North American Indian baby,' carried beyond the confines of the North American continent chiefly through the books of James Fenimore Cooper. As was stated earlier, many Indian words from Mexico and South America have entered the English vocabulary through Spanish.

Language historians are generally agreed that the hospitality of English to foreign words and the ease with which they have been absorbed is without parallel in linguistic history. Borrowing has been so important and extensive a source of new words that only about one fourth of the present English vocabulary is of Germanic origin, that is, from the language of the Anglo-Saxons. By far the greatest number of words adapted from a foreign source are derived, either directly or indirectly, from Latin. Yet, although approximately 75 percent of the words found in a modern English dictionary are loanwords, words of Old English origin are very frequent in spoken English (occurring about 50 or 60 percent of the time.) The nucleus of our vocabulary, it appears, is made up mainly of native elements. This native group of words is the one that people know best and use constantly in the daily affairs of life; it is, therefore, the group that we could least do without.

Borrowing, derivation, composition, back formation, blending, and other processes are, then, the major sources from which English has derived the great variety, richness, and cosmopolitan character of its vocabulary. To this list we may add one more source of vocabulary enrichment—the changes in the meaning of words that occur during the course of their history. This is treated in the next chapter.

notes

1. Except for Greek roots that occur in scientific terms, there has never been any direct borrowing from Greek to speak of. Most Greek words in English were first borrowed by the Romans, who then passed them on to other European languages, either directly or through French.
2. See Mario A. Pei, *What's in a Word.* New York: Hawthorn Books, 1968, pp. 54–66.
3. Thomas Pyles, *The Origins and Development of the English Language.* New York: Harcourt Brace Jovanovich, 1964, p. 350.

8
meaning and etymology

Language must have *meaning*. If this were not so, language would be merely a sequence of noises with no more significance than the parakeet's imitation of human speech. While linguistic forms, as was seen, are easily isolated, analyzed, and subject to objective description, their meaning is intimately bound up with man's mind, which is considerably more elusive and, in any event, does not lend itself to the same kind of direct observation that the speech signals or their written representation do. The study of meaning, then, is an inquiry into the relationship between mind and expression, with language serving as a device that correlates the speech signals with the extralinguistic world of ideas and concepts.

The branch of linguistics concerned with the meaning of words is technically known as SEMANTICS (from the Greek *semainein* 'to signify,' which, in turn, derives from *sēma* 'sign'). The term seems to have been first used by the French scholar Michel Bréal, who applied it to his study of the "intellectual causes which have influenced the transformation of our languages,"[1] specifically to the "laws" that govern changes of meaning. Bréal's work and that of his contemporaries was historically oriented and did not address itself to what has become one of the central issues of the study of meaning, namely the relationship between language and thought and between language and the world of experience. The question of "what is meaning" was not really probed until the publication of the now classic *The Meaning of Meaning* by C. K. Ogden and I. A. Richards,[2] in which the authors asserted that since meaning is a characteristic of all sign and symbol systems, it has a wider application than just to language and, hence, is not within the exclusive purview of the linguist. More especially,

Ogden and Richards focused attention upon the *psychological*, *philosophical*, and *logical* aspects of meaning, in addition to the *linguistic* one (the study of semantic systems of different languages and the changes of meaning). Their distinction between three components of meaning, the symbol (the word), the referent (the object or concept symbolized), and the thought or reference (the mental image of the referent), shown in the following diagram, has become widely known:

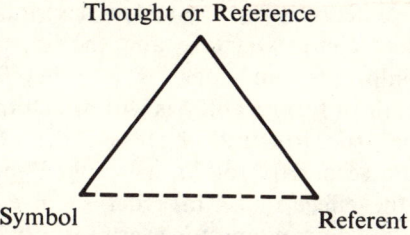

The relationship between the symbol, for example, the word *car*, and the object it symbolizes (the referent) is, as we know, wholly arbitrary and conventional; hence the broken line. On the other hand, the symbol (either spoken or written) is the representation of the mental picture we have of the referent (the car in our example), whether actually seen at the moment we utter the word or recalled from an earlier experience—a so-called memory picture. This triple symbol–mental-image–referent relationship brings into focus the nonlinguistic feature of the referent, as well as the fact that there is no one-to-one relationship between word and thing.

It has been suggested that a straightforward relationship like the one proposed by Ogden and Richards will normally work out for concrete referents like *table*, *chair*, *car*, *dog*, and *lamp*, but may be too restrictive in connection with abstract nouns like *freedom*, *faith*, *tolerance*, and *time*, descriptive adjectives like, *true*, *good*, and *fair*, and verbs. Therefore, abstract referents might be better described as SPHERES OF REFERENCE, rather than individual referents.³ A verb like *know* has a very large sphere of reference, especially if we compare it with the Romance languages and other Germanic languages which differentiate between knowing in the sense of 'being familiar with a fact' and 'being acqainted with someone or something,' for instance

German *wissen* and *kennen*, Dutch *weten* and *kennen*, French *savior* and *connaître*, Spanish *saber* and *conocer*, Italian *sapere* and *conoscere*, or Russian *znat'* and *umet'*.

Indeed, words can have wide ranges of meaning depending on the different sorts of environment in which they occur. That word meanings do not exist in isolation and may differ in the way they are used was already recognized by the ancient Stoic philosophers. "The meaning of a word is nothing else but the sum of the contexts in which the word occurs" states Paul Roberts,[4] thus voicing most linguists' preference for a contextual description of meaning.

Because of its complex nature and the appeal it makes to psychology, philosophy, and logic, which, they felt, lay outside the scientific rigor of formal analysis with which they approached linguistic studies, the structural linguists of the 1930s, 1940s, and 1950s assigned a secondary role to meaning. Hence Bloomfield's statement to the effect that "in order to give a scientifically accurate definition of meaning for every form of a language, we should have to have a scientifically accurate knowledge of everything in the speaker's world."[5] This has led some to claim that meaning had no place at all in Bloomfieldian analysis. Actually, Bloomfield's views on meaning have never been as radical as that;[6] he and his disciples relied primarily on the INTERNAL MEANING, which is based on the distribution and combination of linguistic units within the pattern of a given language, that is, on the observation and description of all positions which these units could occupy. This internal, or *distributional*, meaning is in sharp contrast to the EXTERNAL MEANING that introduces extralinguistic mental criteria in the analysis of language. With the recent advent of transformational-generative grammar and the shift of approach in linguistic analysis (see Chapter 5), concern with the "semantic component" of language has become important, since the transformational grammarian attempts to present in his analysis all that is implicit in the creativity and linguistic competence of the native speaker.

THE CONCEPTUALIZATION OF REALITY

"Every language is also a special way of looking at the world and interpreting experience. Concealed in the structure of each different language are a whole set of unconscious assumptions about the world and the life in it," said the late Harvard anthropologist, Clyde Kluckhohn.[7] This concept of language as the "mold of thought" was already underscored by the linguist-anthropologist Edward Sapir[8] and later developed by his pupil Benjamin Lee Whorf, who advanced the theory that the type of language habitually spoken conditions the thought processes and behavior of its speakers.[9] According to Whorf, then, the speaker is restricted in what he says or thinks by the limitations of his language. Thus, a speaker of English, Chinese, and Hopi (an American Indian language) would have very different sets of concepts because "language dissects nature in many different ways."[10] Whether or not we accept this scholar's thesis, it would certainly seem that we group and classify our experiences of the world around us in accordance with the patterns of our native tongue. An example in connection with the English verb *to know* has already been given to show that the conceptualization and segmentation of reality (the breaking up of the sphere of reference) varies from language to language. Here are a few more examples to illustrate this point:

1. English has one word for snow, whether it be falling snow, snow on the ground, snow drifts, wet snow, or snow packed hard on a ski slope. In Eskimo there is no such generic term; rather, there are several words for specific varieties of snow. It is quite obvious that in the culture of the Eskimos (using the word "culture" in the anthropological sense) snow is of great enough importance to split up the conceptual sphere that corresponds to one word and one thought in English into several distinct classes.

2. The Hopi language, Whorf tells us, has one noun, the word *masa'ytaka*, that encompasses every object and living being that flies, except for birds, which make up a different class denoted by another noun. Thus, an insect, airplane, aviator, and astronaut are signified by the same term, that which denotes the "flying class minus bird."[11] While the Hopi speaker seems to experience no difficulty about this state of affairs, such a class would be much too large and inclusive for an English speaker, just as our class for "snow" would be too general and vague for an Eskimo.

3. In Hungarian there is no word for "brother" or "sister" as such. Instead, there are two pairs of words which the speaker

uses to specify whether the brother and/or sister are older or younger than himself: *bátya* 'elder brother,' *öcs* 'younger brother,' *nővér* 'elder sister,' and *húg* 'younger sister.' In other words, the Hungarian equivalent of 'I have a brother' would have to be either *van egy bátyám* 'I have an elder brother' (literally 'there is an elder brother of mine') or *van egy öcsém* 'I have a younger brother.' Conversely, the word *testvér* corresponds to the concept of 'brother' and/or 'sister,' so that when a Hungarian speaker says *van egy testvérem*, we are left in the dark as to whether he has a brother or a sister, just as if one were to say "I have a sibling."

Differences in semantic categorization like those between Eskimo, Hopi, Hungarian, and English are not so readily evident when we compare the modern European languages, where there seems to be greater uniformity of thought pattern. This is undoubtedly because of their historical relationship (descent from a common Indo-European speech community) and the fact that they share, at least on the intellectual plane, a common Greco-Latin cultural heritage. Yet, even among these languages, there are some interesting differences that can be observed:

1. The concept to which the French *temps* refers is not the same as that which is reflected in English *time*, which is only a partial equivalent of the French term. The SEMANTIC FIELD (another expression for sphere of reference) of *temps* covers that of English *time, tense* (grammatical 'time'), and *weather* (for example, *Quel temps fait-il?* 'What's the weather like?'). Conversely, English *time* covers part of the French concept of *temps* and also French *heure* 'time of the day' (for example, *Quelle heure est-il?* 'What time is it?').

2. The German set of compound adverbs *hinein–herein, hinaus–heraus, hinunter–herunter,* and *hinauf–herauf*, in the meaning of *in* (*into*), *out, down,* and *up,* respectively, is of particular interest. The use of one or the other adverb of the pair depends on whether the action is directed toward or away from the speaker. For instance, *Kommen Sie herein* 'Come in,' but *Gehen Sie hinein* 'Go in'; *Kommen Sie heraus* 'Come out,' but *Gehen Sie hinaus* 'Go out'; *Kommen Sie herunter* 'Come down,' but *Gehen Sie hinunter* 'Go down'; *Kommen Sie herauf* 'Come up,' but *Gehen Sie hinauf* 'Go up.' This distinction of direction

with respect to the speaker is a unique feature in modern German.

3. Anyone who has ever studied Spanish remembers having struggled with the uses of *ser, estar,* and *haber* (meaning 'to be') and the rules that govern their use. Roughly speaking, the concept of location in Spanish is expressed by *estar* (*estoy en casa* 'I am at home'), that of permanent condition or identity by *ser* (*soy hombre* 'I am a man'), and the idea of 'there is' or 'there are' by *haber* (*hay un libro en la mesa* 'There is a book on the table'). Again, the meaning that Spanish speakers ascribe to these forms of the verb 'to be' correspond to a threefold segmentation of their experience.

Even if we do not go as far as Whorf does in claiming that our *Weltanschauung*, our way of viewing the world, is entirely determined by the structure of our language, the preceding examples would tend to show the extent to which our conception of reality depends on the classifications we make on the basis of the linguistic patterns of our mother tongue. It follows that the acquisition of a foreign language is not merely a matter of placing new labels on known concepts but presupposes that the learner also becomes familiar with a new *semantic system*, a new way of thinking and feeling. This is what makes total comprehension between people of different linguistic backgrounds so difficult, and sometimes even impossible, and this is why translation is so rarely able to render a thought faithfully. "*Traduttore, traditore*" ('The translator is a traitor') says the Italian proverb. There is, indeed, more to language than just its lexicon, as anyone knows who has ever attempted to render the various meanings of English *get* into a foreign language, for instance, *get a prize, get sick, get home, get someone to do something, get the meaning, get to Washington,* or *get caught in the rain.* And what about the uses of this verb in combination with an adverb, as in *get about, get away, get along, get down, get on, get through,* which thoroughly confuse the unsuspecting foreigner who struggles with our language.

CENTRAL AND TRANSFERRED MEANINGS

One of the central facts of semantics is that linguistic forms often have more than one meaning, that is, they can be used in more than one situation. Hence, each word may be looked upon as having a CENTRAL MEANING and a number of TRANSFERRED or MARGINAL MEANINGS. The central meaning of a word may be defined as that which the speakers consider to be the basic meaning, that which is ascribed to a form when it occurs alone and out of context. This is also the meaning that one is most likely to give when called upon to define a word. For instance, the word *lemon* invariably brings to mind the notion of a piece of fruit rather than that of a mechanically faulty automobile, unless the context in which it is used requires that we take the word in a transferred meaning. The information supplied by the context will ultimately determine whether the word *operation* is used in the sense of a 'surgical intervention,' a 'military expedition' (for example, Operation Overlord), a 'mathematical addition or subtraction,' or a 'financial transaction.'

Noncentral meanings of a word are identified as METAPHORS (from the Greek *meta* 'over' and *pherein* 'to carry'). A metaphor is a figure of speech in which a word or phrase primarily used for one thing is applied to another. It involves extending the application of a word to include a new referent or referents which resemble the original one. Metaphorical extensions like *foot of a hill, head of a pin, arm of a chair, neck of a bottle, shoulder of a road*, and *hands of a clock* are legion and are common to all languages. Without them language would probably be dull and matter-of-fact. They lend something colorful, lively, and picturesque to the exchange of ideas and are often more effective than more straightforward and prosaic expressions. Many metaphors have become so commonplace and so much a part of our language that we are no longer aware of the original figure that called them into existence, such as *daybreak*, *nightfall*, or expressions like *a horse of another color*.

The use of the same word in two or more different meanings is technically known as POLYSEMY ("multiple meaning," from the Greek *poly* 'many' and *sēma* 'sign'). For example, we may speak of a *table* in the sense of a "piece of furniture," as in *a book on the table*, or in the sense of "an arrangement of facts or figures," as in *a table in the book*. The question arises whether to consider *table* in both contexts as one word or two words. In a recent discussion on semantics, the Yale professor, Sydney M. Lamb,[12] proposes a distinction between LEXICAL WORD, or

LEXEME (an item of vocabulary), and SEMANTIC WORD, or SEMEME (an element of meaning of a given word). He then adds a third category, the MORPHOLOGICAL WORD, that is, the minimum linguistic unit that has independent existence (a *free* morpheme). According to this distinction, *table* and *tables* (the singular and plural) would be both two different morphological words, since the plural *-s* suffix cannot be used in isolation, and two forms of the same lexical word. At the same time, *table*$_1$ (*the book on the table*) and *table*$_2$ (*the table in the book*) are two semantic words, also corresponding to a single lexical word. In our previous example, the lexeme *operation* is connected with the sememes *operation*$_1$ (*eye operation*), *operation*$_2$ (*military operation*) *operation*$_3$ (*mathematical operation*), and *operation*$_4$ (*financial operation*).

Polysemy may also be accompanied by syntactic differences. In English especially, many words can be assigned to different parts of speech without changing their forms: the word *table* can be used as a noun, as a verb, and as an adjective. The FUNCTIONAL SHIFT from noun to verb is particularly favored in English, while languages like French and Spanish prefer to make nouns out of verbs, for example, French *rire* 'to laugh' and *le rire* 'laughter' (*le* being the definite article). Because of their different grammatical distribution, some linguists consider the words thus created as new words, rather than as a semantic extension of existing ones, and would classify functional shifts under the heading of word formation.

SYNONYMS, ANTONYMS, HOMONYMS, AND IDIOMS

When different words have the same, or nearly the same meaning, we call them SYNONYMS (from the Greek *syn* 'together' and *onoma* 'name'), for instance, *high* and *tall*. It is often argued, however, that true *synonyms* do not really exist since they always differ in some feature of meaning and, hence, cannot be used interchangeably in all contexts. This is true. Synonyms do not have identical spheres of reference. One could speak of *a high mountain* or *a tall mountain*, but *he is high* means something different from *he is tall*. The synonymy, even though never complete, is an important concept in the study of meaning. In a sense it could be considered the opposite of polysemy in that two or more lexemes may connect to the same sememe, whereas in polysemy two or more sememes connect to one and the same lexeme.

Words of opposite meaning, like *high* and *low*, *tall* and *short*, and *happy* and *sad*, are called ANTONYMS (from Greek *anti* 'opposite' and *onoma*). Those with identical spelling and pronunciation but with different meanings because of different historical origin, like *race* 'breed' and *race* 'competition,' or *seal* 'a sea mammal' and *seal* 'a wax impression on a letter,' are known as HOMONYMS (from the Greek *homos* 'the same' and *onoma*). Sometimes a distinction is made between homonyms and HOMOPHONES, that is, words that sound alike but are spelled differently, like English *scent*, *sent*, and *cent*, or *site*, *sight*, and *cite*, or French *sang* 'blood,' *sans* 'without,' *cent* 'one hundred,' and (*il*) *sent* 'he feels' (all pronounced /sã/).

There are certain combinations of words whose meaning cannot be determined from the individual meanings of their component parts. These are known as IDIOMS (from the Greek *idios* 'one's own'). An idiom, in other words, represents one unit of meaning, one *semantic unit*, which connects to a combination of lexemes, as in *hit the sack*, *let off the hook*, *beat a dead horse*, *run out of something*, *catch up with someone*, *be well off*, and countless others. Every language is full of constructions and turns of phrase peculiar to that particular language which cannot be literally translated into another. Many idioms may also be taken in a literal sense, in which case the string of words that make up an idiom will no longer represent one unit of meaning but several. The peculiar semantic structure of an idiom seems to be paralleled on the syntactic level also, for example, an idiom cannot normally be transformed into the passive voice.

CONNOTATION AND DENOTATION

The spoken or written word normally conjures up a number of associations in one's mind, both pleasant and unpleasant, in addition to the actual meaning it has for everyone who uses it. Semanticists, accordingly, distinguish between DENOTATIVE and CONNOTATIVE MEANINGS, the connotation of a word being the special supplementary values, as it were, that color our sphere of reference. Thus, a person who may have spent many long and painful hours in a hospital may have quite a different reaction upon hearing the word *hospital* from someone more fortunate who has never been sick or injured and thinks of a hospital simply as a huge brick building where people go to have an operation. Or someone may have learned a word, say the word *snake*, under rather terrifying circumstances, so that every time the word is mentioned, he goes through a traumatic experience. And what about the title of a piece of music that brings up a host of memories—a first kiss, perhaps, or, on the debit side of the ledger, a broken romance? True, these affective connotations, this personal aura associated with one's own experience in relation to words, have little or no communicative value. Yet, for the individual speaker they are just as real and valid as those that are more widely accepted, for instance, the adjective *fast* in *He is a fast worker*, which, according to the context, is widely accepted to mean that 'he has a technique of quickly getting to first base with the ladies.'

When we say, for example, "boys will be boys," we are not trying to advance a truism, a statement of fact, by equating the first *boys* with the second one. *Boys*$_1$ simply denotes 'a general class of young males,' while *boys*$_2$ invokes the connotations of the words that the speaker wishes to convey in this particular context—something like 'mischievous little rascals.' This kind of utterance shows the play upon two meanings of the same lexical item, one relating to an objectively verifiable reality, the other to supplementary values with which the speaker and/or hearer surround the word. Skillful propagandists, publicity agents, and demagogues have long made the most of these possibilities. These connotative aspects of meaning have been thoroughly studied by Professor S. I. Hayakawa, whose best-selling *Language in Thought and Action*[13] is widely used as a text in high-school and college courses on semantics.

The name of Hayakawa brings up the school of "general semantics," founded by the Polish mathematician and logician, Alfred Korzybski. In his influential and controversial *Science and Sanity*,[14] in which he sets forth the relationship between language, thought, and behavior, Korzybski states, among other things, that many of our social and personal problems are induced by "linguistic maladjustment," that is, the use of ambiguous multivalent terms so interwoven with emotions that our semantic reactions get hopelessly confused. He believed that through better awareness of the linguistic component of human thought and perception and the better use of critical judgment about the spoken and written word, many of our social and personal ills could be solved.[15] Although Korzybski's faith in the study of semantics as a cure for human ills may have been too idealistic, there is no denying that he and his followers have been most influential in awakening the layman's interest in and awareness of problems of meaning by pointing out that the world of reality consists of more than just a two-valued logic where things are either black or white.

CHANGE OF MEANING

As we have seen, words and phrases can have wide ranges of meaning, depending on the kind of context in which they occur. Whenever a word ceases to occur in a certain context and begins to show up in a new one, we have a *change in meaning*. This does not mean, of course, that SEMANTIC CHANGE must necessarily entail the disappearance of an older usage. Consider, for example, what has happened to the word *manuscript*. The word originally referred to 'that which is written by hand' (from the Latin *manū* 'by hand' and *scriptus* 'written'), but today refers also to material written on a typewriter, that is, a 'typescript.' (Editors would be very unhappy people if they were to receive manuscripts in the original sense of the word.) Or take the word *place*. Formerly it only referred to an open square in a village or town. Today, it covers a considerably wider range: we speak of *a place in a book*, and we can even *put someone in his place*. The meaning of these words has been EXTENDED, or WIDENED, while the original meaning has also been kept, as in *medieval manuscript* or *marketplace*. Some other examples taken at random are *citizen* (originally 'city-dweller'), *fellow* (originally 'associate'), *box* (originally 'boxwood'), and *junk* (originally sailor's slang for 'old rope').

A classic example of the LOSS OF MEANING may be seen in the words *ox*, *pig*, *sheep*, and *calf*, which, in Anglo-Saxon times, denoted not only the animals themselves but also their flesh. Today you would hardly ask the waiter to bring you "some pig." As a result of the Norman nobleman's habit of eating *beef*, *pork*, *mutton*, and *veal*, the English words may be said to have dropped out of the second context through borrowing from a foreign source. In the case of the word *bead*, which originally meant 'prayer' (OE *gebed*, compare modern German *Gebet*), the shift of meaning has entailed a total loss of the original meaning. The starting point is no doubt the expression *to count one's beads* 'to say one's prayers with a rosary.' During the Middle Ages the custom developed of saying one's prayers repeatedly and counting them by means of little balls of wood or ivory strung together on a rosary. These little balls came to be associated with the word *beads*, the only visible mark of someone 'counting his prayers,' and the meaning gradually shifted to these objects.

The meaning of a word can also become RESTRICTED. The word *fowl* (OE *fugol*) once referred to any bird, as the related German and Dutch words *Vogel* still do. By a narrowing of its sphere of reference, *fowl* is used in present-day English to refer only to a bird of the poultry kind. The word *bird*, which replaced it, comes from Old English *bridd* and was originally used mainly for the young of birds. Another example of restriction of meaning is illustrated by the verb *starve*. Old English *steorfan* meant 'to die,' not necessarily of hunger. Probably as a result competition with the verb *die*, borrowed from the Danish Vikings, with which it must have been used concurrently, the meaning of *starve* became specialized as it came to be associated with death from lack of food. Other examples of this process are *wife* (originally 'woman' and now restricted to a very special one) *deer* (originally 'animal'), *undertaker* (originally 'anyone who undertakes something'), *meat* (originally 'food'), *lesson* (originally 'reading'), and *liquor* (originally 'any liquid').

Closely connected with expansion and restriction of meaning is the change whereby a once concrete term has taken on an abstract meaning or, vice versa, an original abstraction has become concretized. An interesting example is the word *humor*, which in medieval medicine was thought to be one of the four fluids responsible for one's health and disposition that the body contained. Hence, it came to mean 'disposition,' 'temperament,' and 'mood,' thus shifting from a concrete to an abstract meaning. The abstract Latin word *fructūs* (derived from the verb *fruor* 'to enjoy') originally meant 'enjoyment,' but even in classical Latin, we find it frequently used in the sense of 'profit, income, fruit' (as in *the fruits of my labor*). By the time it developed into French *fruit*, it was already restricted to the enjoyment of tangible objects like apples, oranges, grapes, and pears. It reached English with this last meaning.

In the course of their history, words may rise or fall on the social scale by a process called PEJORATION (from Latin *pejor* 'worse') and AMELIORATION (from Latin *melior* 'better'). In the first instance, words that once had a favorable implication may 'degenerate' in meaning. Consider, for example, the words *boor, churl, knave,* and *hussy*. At one time, all of them were free from the unfavorable and opprobrious connotations they have today: a *boor* was simply a 'peasant,' a *churl* was a 'freeman,' a *knave* was a 'young man,' and a *hussy* was a respectable 'housewife.' The adjective *silly*, related to the noun *soul*, once meant 'blessed' and gradually shifted to mean 'good and innocent to the point of being foolish,' 'a blessed fool,' until finally the connotation of 'foolish' alone survived.

A *marshal* at one time was a 'stable boy,' and a *governor* was the steersman of a ship. The latter is now usually one that 'steers the ship of state,' while even a town marshal, probably the lowest rank of all 'marshals,' has nothing left of its original meaning. This amelioration or elevation of meaning is also found in some commonly used adjectives, like *fond, nice,* and *naughty*. Shakespeare still uses *fond* in the original sense of 'foolish'; *nice*, which ultimately derives from Latin *nescius* 'ignorant,' came to English from the Old French *niais* 'stupid' (still used in modern French with this meaning) but later acquired a pleasant connotation in modern English because of its use in expressions like "a nice point" and "a nice distinction"; *naughty* literally means 'naughtlike,' that is "worthless" and originally meant just that. As late as Shakespeare, it is used in the sense of "wicked," but nowadays it has weakened to a mild term of reproach.

Semantic changes have occurred all through the history of language; they are going on all the time. They may come about through a variety of factors, such as borrowing, changes in social attitudes and values, scientific and technical discoveries, names required for new objects and ideas, the creation of metaphors, and many other ways that semanticists have described.[16] The substitution of EUPHEMISMS (from Greek *euphemismos* 'use of a good or auspicious word for an evil or inauspicious one') for tabooed words and expressions is particularly common, especially when the taboos shock people's sense of decency and propriety. The word *toilet* at one time encompassed the whole process of dressing and grooming and is still so used in French, where this word comes from. It has fallen into disrepute because of a particular aspect of this process, and *toilet* is now replaced by *bathroom*, *restroom*, *powder-room*, and *ladies* (or *gentlemen's*) *lounge*. A *pregnant* woman is referred to as an *expectant mother* or a woman *in the family way*. It also seems more decorous to *perspire* rather than to *sweat*.

Taboos may also be due to fear or the desire to avoid naming something unpleasant in plain or blunt terms, as when people substitute the expressions *pass away* or *pass on* for the more specific *die*, or the word *mortician* for *undertaker*. Among taboos specifically induced by fear are the names of divine beings: we substitute *gosh* and *golly* for the name of *God*, or *gee whiz* and even *jiminy crickets* for that of *Jesus Christ*. In some primitive societies people believe that there is some mysterious connection between a thing and the spoken name for it and will not, therefore, name an enemy or some savage beast for fear that the mention of them will conjure up their appearance.

THE ORIGIN OF WORDS

The study of the historical phases through which the meaning of a word has passed (sometimes referred to as HISTORICAL or DIACHRONIC SEMANTICS to distinguish it from DESCRIPTIVE or SYNCHRONIC SEMANTICS, which expresses the semantic tendencies of a language at a particular time and the relations between language and thought) is closely connected with another historical study, the study of word origins, or ETYMOLOGY. Traditionally, etymology (from the Greek *etymos* 'true' and *logos* 'word') is concerned with tracing words to their earliest ascertainable form, as well as with the search for the original or "true" meaning of a word, as when modern English *knight* is traced to Old English *cnīht* 'youth, servant,' or the homophonous but semantically different words *flour* and *flower* to Old French *flour* 'flower,' which, in turn, goes back to the Latin *flōrem* of the same meaning. This is, essentially, the information that etymological dictionaries supply. There is, however, more to etymological studies than merely the search for the *etymon* (Greek word meaning 'literal sense'), the original form of a word, that is, its phonetic shape, from which its derivatives have evolved. In addition to ascertaining the earliest form of a word, the etymologist is also interested in finding out everything that happened to a word since its first occurrence in a given language, the whole history of the word in all its ramifications and relations to other languages. Just as knowing something about the background of a person helps us to understand him better, so the life history of a word makes its present meaning clearer. In a sense, then, the etymologist becomes a kind of linguistic detective, who probes into unrecorded history, customs, traditions, and ways of life of bygone days.

Consider, for instance, the English words *book* and *beech*. They derive from the same historical root that means 'beech tree.' The Old English *bōc*, as a matter of fact, meant both 'book' and 'beech tree.' The reason for this is interesting. Before the Germanic peoples adopted the Roman alphabet from the Christian missionaries around the seventh century, they scratched their RUNES (the name of the characters of their alphabet) on thin boards and shavings of beech wood; hence the relationship between *book* and *beech*. Consider also the noun *robe*: the word was borrowed from French *robe* 'dress,' but it ultimately goes back to the Old High German word *raup* 'spoil, booty' (modern German *Raub* 'theft'). This same word also survives in Spanish *ropa* 'clothing' and Italian *roba* 'things, goods, material,' which, like *thing* in English, is also used in an abstract sense. With his knowledge of social history the etymologist should be able to come up with a plausible explanation for this shift from 'spoil' and 'theft' to 'piece of clothing.' It might go something like this: since during the Middle Ages clothing was among the most precious possessions that could be stolen, *raup* came to connote the garment taken from the victim of a hold-up or murder, or from the slain on the battlefield. As the meaning of the word shifted more and more toward this connotation, the original idea of illegal acquisition gradually wore off.

A discussion of eytmology invariably brings up the concept of COGNATE FORMS (from the Latin *cum* 'with' and *gnatus* 'born'). These are a group of words in different languages that are derived from a common ancestor.[17] The cognates of English *son* are Dutch *zoon*, Swedish *son*, Danish *son*, German *Sohn*, and Russian *syn*. But cognates do not necessarily keep the same meaning, despite their common origin. English *knight* and German *Knecht* are almost opposite in meaning; the German word still means 'servant,' as did the Old English *cnīht* mentioned earlier. The same is true of English *knave* and German *Knabe* 'boy,' which derive from a Germanic form *cnapa* (OE *cnafa*) that had the same meaning as the modern German word. In the first instance, the English word moved up the social scale; in the second one it lost considerable prestige. The reasons for these semantic shifts are best left up to the etymologist.[18]

Not to be confused with cognates are the so-called DOUBLETS, that is, two or more words derived from the same native or foreign source at different periods of history. A case in point is the *frail–fragile* pair in English. Both words ultimately go back to Latin *fragilis* 'breakable'; *frail* was borrowed from French *frêle* and *fragilis* was taken directly from Latin. These two stages of development—(1) *frail*, the word in spoken use which has undergone all sound transformations that are normal in language, and (2) *fragile*, the word taken bodily from a written text or the lexicon with a minimum of adaptation—are commonly called POPULAR and LEARNED DEVELOPMENTS, respectively. Sometimes the same word develops differently in two different dialects of the same language. This happened with OE *scyrta*, which in the Midland dialect developed into *shirt*, while in the northern English dialects strongly influenced by Danish speech habits it became *skirt*: hence, the *shirt–skirt* doublet in modern standard English. Occasionally *triplets* are found, as in *sir*, *sire*, and *senior* (all going back to Latin *senior*, the comparative form of *senex* 'old, aged'), and also a rare instance of *quadruplets*, as in *gentle*, *genteel*, *gentile*, and *jaunty*, borrowed from the French *gentil* 'noble, kind' (also derived from Latin *gentilis*, an adjective related to *gens* 'clan, family').

A special kind of etymology is POPULAR or FOLK ETYMOLOGY. This method of explaining word histories is usually the result of an association in the popular mind of words that resemble each other in sound and perhaps in meaning, although there is no historical connection between them. In this category belong such words as English *crayfish* or *crawfish*, borrowed from Old French *crevice* (modern French *écrevisse*), which is not really a fish. Another example is *cockroach*, from the Spanish *cucaracha*, which shows the substitution of two familiar English morphemes of approximately similar sounds, though neither *cock* nor *roach* have anything to do with the insect. Popular etymology is also at the root of some misspellings. A case in point is the spelling *playwrite* for *playwright*, due to the association of playwrighting 'working up a play' (*-wright* being derived from *work*) with writing. Some amusing instances of popular etymology in French due to misunderstanding are the words *contredanse* 'quadrille' (literally 'counter-dance') which is a false interpretation of English *country dance*, and *l'âne salé* (literally 'the salted donkey') which purports to reproduce the English game of *Aunt Sally*.

Originally a purely historical study concerned with changes of meaning and the principles underlying such changes, semantics has come into its own as an important branch of linguistics. No longer regarded as being outside the competence of the linguist, something for the philosopher, logician, sociologist, and psychologist to grapple with, the study of meaning has become one of the central concerns of contemporary linguists, both here and abroad, as evidenced by the ever-growing literature in the field. For a progress report on this new discipline, which claims equality with other levels of language study, for an account of its past achievements, the problems that remain to be solved, as well as for suggestions for new lines of inquiry, the reading of Stephen Ullman's *Principles of Semantics* (see note 16 for details) will prove both stimulating and rewarding.

notes

1. First published in Paris in 1887 under the title of *Essai de Sémantique*. The English edition, entitled *Semantics: Studies in the Science of Meaning*, appeared in 1900 over the imprint of Henry Holt & Co., New York. The English version was reissued by Dover Publications, Inc., New York, in 1964. Our quotation is taken from the latter, p. 5.
2. Third ed., rev. New York: Harcourt Brace Jovanovich, 1930.
3. See especially Simeon Potter, *Modern Linguistics*. New York: W. W. Norton & Co., 1964, p. 143 ff. (originally published by Oxford University Press, 1957).
4. *Understanding English*. New York: Harper & Row, 1958, p. 361.
5. Leonard Bloomfield, *Language*. New York: Holt, Rinehart and Winston, 1933. p. 139.
6. See Charles C. Fries, "Meaning and Linguistic Analysis," *Language*, 30 (Part 1) (January–March 1954), 57–68.
7. *Mirror for Man*. Greenwich, Conn.: Fawcett Publications, 1967, p. 139 (originally published by McGraw-Hill, 1944).
8. Edward Sapir, *Language: An Introduction to the Study of Speech*. New York: Harcourt Brace Jovanovich, 1921, p. 22.
9. *Language, Thought and Reality: Selected Writings of Benjamin Lee Whorf*. Edited by John B. Carroll. Cambridge, Mass.: M.I.T. Press, 1956, p. 212.
10. *Ibid.*, p. 214.
11. *Ibid.*, p. 216.
12. "Lexicology and Semantics," in *Linguistics Today*. Edited by Archibald A. Hill. New York: Basic Books, 1969, p. 41.
13. Second ed. New York: Harcourt Brace Jovanovich, 1941.
14. *An Introduction to Non-Aristotelian Systems and General Semantics*. Lancaster, Pa.: Science Press, 1933.
15. For a short summary of the ideas advanced by Korzybski, consult S. I. Hayakawa, "Semantics," in *ETC: A Review of*

General Semantics, 9 (Summer 1952). Selected essays from this publication on various aspects of semantics appear in *Language, Meaning, and Maturity,* edited by S. I. Hayakawa. New York: Harper & Row, 1954.

16. A discussion of the various factors that have been suggested to account for semantic changes will be found in Stephen Ullman, *Semantics: An Introduction to the Science of Meaning.* Oxford: Basil Blackwell, 1962. pp. 193–235.

17. The term *cognate* is also used to designate a group of languages that go back to a common ancestor. Thus we can say that English, French, Russian, and Hindustani are cognate languages because they all stem from an Indo-European ancestor.

18. Actually, these shifts are not too difficult to account for. In medieval times *knight* was originally a youth who served the king or a nobleman as an arm-bearer. At a later period, when he went into battle on their behalf, the idea of 'servant' was lost and only the lofty connotation remained. The semantic change in *knave* would seem to point to a shift in the direction of general connotations like 'rascal' and 'urchin,' conceivably due to expressions like "A knave is a knave," paralleling our "Boys will be boys."

9
writing
and its relation to speech

Verba volant, scripta manent, "the spoken word flies away, the written word remains," says the Latin proverb. Writing is the graphic counterpart of speech. It records the spoken language, however imperfect this record may be. The immense social importance of the written word cannot be underestimated, despite the general agreement among linguists that speech is the more fundamental of the two language activities and therefore should be the primary object of their investigations. Yet it is writing that has made the record of human knowledge accessible to us; it is the key to the history of mankind.

There is no human society without language, but most of the 3000 or so languages of the world have never been written down. There are many cultures, in fact, which have just as fully developed languages as we do—that is, whose members are able to express all their thoughts and feelings—but have never achieved the remarkable feat of devising a system for recording them on paper, clay, stone, wood, leather, or any other material. For these people language exists only as something which is spoken. In these societies, as in all societies before people got around to recording their speech, knowledge and cultural traditions are transmitted by word of mouth. In all preliterate societies, whether present or past, it would seem that man's memory is much more heavily taxed than it is in our literate cultures, where there are so many memory aids at our disposal and the records of human knowledge available for consulation.

PICTOGRAPHS, IDEOGRAPHS, AND LOGOGRAPHS

Writing is a late development in the history of civilisation. All the available evidence suggests that it grew out of a stylized form of drawing. We began by representing a picturable object, either animate or inanimate. Gradually, the erstwhile object became unimportant because the number of picturable objects is necessarily limited, and the picture turned into a symbol that represented a spoken language form.

Written records are very recent in terms of man's cultural history. It seems unlikely that any complete system of writing was employed before approximately 3500 B.C. Prehistoric wall paintings like those found in the caves of Altamira in northern Spain or in the Dordogne in southern France are generally traced back to the later Paleolithic period (10,000 to 20,000 B.C.), but there is probably no connection between them and the known ancient systems of writing.[1]

The fascinating story of writing has been told and retold many times within the framework of the history of civilization. Much of it is still controversial. For instance, did the art of writing originate in one place, say, with the Sumerians, who left us the earliest written records, dating back to between 3000 and 4000 B.C.? Could it therefore be that all writing systems ultimately stem from their CUNEIFORM, or wedge-shaped, script (from the Latin *cuneus* 'wedge')? Or were different writing systems developed by different people in various parts of the world, some of them, possibly, contemporaneously? We seem to be as much in the dark about the *when* and the *where* of the origin of writing as we are about the origin of speech. It is only about *how* writing developed that we are somewhat better informed, although here too our records are incomplete, and we must rely on reconstruction and intelligent guesswork.

The earliest forms of writing are nonalphabetical. Man began by drawing or painting pictures of familiar objects on rocks or stone, or by scratching them on bone, ivory, or wood. Was it to satisfy his artistic urge? Did he do it for purposes of magic and ritual practices? Or was it to convey a message or story? We do not really know. There are those who think that the pictures left by prehistoric man are not meant to record important events or to communicate ideas.[2]

Alongside prehistoric picture writing, there are other ways of recording a message or communicating an idea. These include MNEMONIC (memory aid) DEVICES such as the knotted ropes, or *quipus*, of the ancient Incas, primarily used for keeping accounts; the *notched sticks* used by primitive peoples in many parts of the world even today; and the *wampum* of the Iroquois Indians, which consist of shells or beads strung together in such a manner as to show some important occurrence.

A system of pictorial representation in which pictures actually reproduce familiar objects can be considered as the most primitive way of representing and conveying thought. Many primitive peoples have used a simple picture or a whole series of pictures to communicate. The American Indians, the Australian natives, and some African tribes have all at some time scratched such messages on the bark of trees, animal skins, rocks, and other suitable material. This system, which has no connection with any linguistic form and hence can be understood by people speaking different languages, is generally termed picture writing, or PICTOGRAPHY. But as soon as a sequence of events, rather than a single event, is being portrayed, a picture is bound to go beyond the mere representation of concrete objects and come to be used to express an idea, much the same way that a traffic sign showing a picture of a girl and a boy stepping into the roadway conveys the idea of a school. The pictorial representation that purports to convey the idea associated with the object or objects depicted (as when the picture of the sun comes to mean "daylight" or "day") introduces an element of conventionalization into the system, so that gradually the picture turns into a *symbol* that stands directly for an idea. The picture is simplified and eventually may even lose all connection with the original picture, or at least may no longer be recognizable. At this point we have IDEOGRAPHIC WRITING. Two clasped hands standing for agreement are no longer a pictograph, that is, a picture symbol representing a definite object; they are an ideograph, that is, a picture symbol of an idea.

The pictographic-ideographic representation, which may reach a high level of system and convention, as in the writing of some North American Indians or that of the ancient Mayas and Aztecs of Central America, has normally no connection with any one language or linguistic form. If we accept the premise that the written word is the symbol of the spoken word, a premise enunciated by Aristotle, then the picto-ideographic devices cannot be called writing at all, since writing represents units of language (that is, sounds and forms) and is not directly related to meaning or ideas. In the transition from picture writing to "true" writing, there must, therefore, be an association of a conventional symbol with a linguistic form. Professor I. J. Gelb has called these descriptive-representational devices in the development of writing the stage of *semasiography* (from the Greek *sēmasía* 'meaning' and *graphē* 'writing'), in which "pictures convey the general meaning intended by the writer,"[3] as distinct from the stage called *phonography* (from the Greek *phonē* 'sound' and *graphē*), in which "writing expresses language."[4] Phonography, in turn, is divided into (1) *word-syllabic* writing systems, (2) *syllabic* writing systems, and (3) *alphabetic* writing systems.

The crucial question is how the transition from the essentially pictorial origin of writing to the representation of the sounds of language came about. It would seem that the representation of entire words long preceded the representation of syllables, which, in turn, preceded that of individual sounds. The linguistic units that were first symbolized in writing were words. A system of writing that uses a symbol for each word of the spoken chain is called LOGOGRAPHIC (from the Greek *logos* 'word'). The classic example of such a system is Chinese writing (often erroneously referred to as pictographic-ideographic, although its pictorial and ideographic origins are undeniable), in which each symbol, or *character*, represents a morpheme of the language. Since many, if not most, of the morphemes are monosyllabic, it may be said that each character corresponds to a syllable. However, the character, as a rule, has no phonetic value except insofar as the word it represents has a pronunciation.[5] A system like that of Chinese has the unquestionable advantage that it can be used over a wide area where mutually unintelligible languages are spoken (as is still the case in China today), since the characters indicate morphemes rather than sounds; hence they can be read by people of different linguistic backgrounds who are familiar with the written conventions. Our Arabic numerals and chemical symbols, among others, are good examples of logographs. Assuming he is familiar with the symbol 5, a Frenchman will read it as *cinq*, a German as *fünf*, a Spaniard as *cinco*, and a

Hungarian as *öt*. We say *five*. Similarly with the symbol H$_2$O. An English speaker reads it as *water*, a Spaniard as *agua*, a Hungarian as *víz*, a Russian as *voda*, while a Frenchman says *eau*. The disadvantage of a word-syllabic writing system is that one has to learn a symbol for each word, so to speak. It is estimated that one needs to have a command of about 4000 characters to be able to read modern literature in Chinese and that it would require at least 10,000 characters to become a sinologist (a specialist in Chinese studies).

SYLLABIC WRITING

The next step in the evolution of a true alphabet occurs when a character is assigned a purely phonetic value. This phonetic factor is already in evidence in some Chinese characters (see note 5 on loan characters and "phonetic compounds"). Words come to be used as syllabic signs, much as they are in a *rebus* (literally 'by things' from Latin *res*), which consists of pictures of objects that by the sound of their names suggest words or phrases, as in "4 sale" or "† ing" ("crossing"). In the ancient Egyptian carvings on temple walls and tombstones known as HIEROGLYPHICS (from the Greek *hieros* 'sacred' and *glyphein* 'to carve'), which date back to about 3000 B.C., the visual symbol for the sun was a circle with a dot in the middle. The spoken word for it was *re*. The sun symbol is often found in hieroglyphic inscriptions standing for the spoken syllable *re* as part of a word, rather than depicting the sun. If followed through to its logical conclusion, this use of the word sign with phonetic value, that is, as a syllable sign, would eventually result in what is commonly called a SYLLABARY, a system of written characters that represent spoken syllables rather than individual sounds. As it is, the ancient Egyptian system of hieroglyphics, as well as the more conventionalized forms of cursive writing that developed from it—the so-called *hieratic system* and its *demotic,* or "popular," offshoot—may be considered a combination of word and syllable writing. The Egyptians stopped just short of the final step of associating all their pictorial symbols with sounds or groups of sounds, which would have led to a fully syllabic alphabet.

In addition to the Chinese and Egyptian systems, the cuneiform writing of the Sumerians in Mesopotamia, probably antedating that of the Egyptians, as well as the Hittite hieroglyphic writing in use from about 1500 to 700 B.C., must be mentioned as major word-syllabic writing systems of ancient times.

It is customary to attribute the important breakthrough of assigning a single symbol to represent a sound or group of sounds, and thus of establishing a direct relationship between the spoken word and its written counterpart, to the Semitic peoples of Palestine and Syria. Adopting the Egyptian principle of using syllabic signs to write monosyllables without indicating vowel differences, they created a writing system that generally goes by the name of the *West Semitic Syllabary*. It is still a moot question, however, whether or not the Semitic symbols are derived from Egyptian hieroglyphics, although some symbols seem to show an unmistakable resemblance to the original Egyptian symbols. For instance, the ox head ⟨ox⟩ developed into the symbol ⟨K⟩ in West Semitic (reminiscent of the horns of an ox), which was later turned upside down by the Greeks in ⟨A⟩ ; hence the symbol for *A* as we know it.

In a syllabic writing system, as was stated earlier, each symbol represents a single syllable or syllable type. Since each symbol has a specific phonetic value, it is used in any word which contains a syllable with that particular value. In such a system, if applied to English, the word *family* would be written with three symbols standing for *fa, mi,* and *ly*, respectively, and the same symbols would be used whenever these syllables occurred in other words. The advantage of such a system over word-syllable writing is readily apparent. Instead of using hundreds or even thousands of symbols, the number is reduced to more manageable proportions (the so-called *Cherokee syllabary* devised early in the nineteenth century comprises about 85 syllabic symbols), although this system may still prove to be quite cumbersome if we consider that ideally each symbol must stand for a given syllable of the language. In practice, however, it seems that the early Semitic syllabaries do not fully represent all the syllables of the languages they portray. As a matter of fact, to this day the Arabic and Hebrew alphabets, which are direct descendants of the West Semitic Syllabary, do not normally represent vowel values.

Of the early syllabaries that were developed independently of the Semitic ones, the Japanese *kana* is still in use today. The Japanese adopted their system of writing from the Chinese about the fourth century A.D. Because of the radically different grammatical structure of these two languages (isolating versus agglutinative), the Chinese script was not really suited to express the grammatical morphemes of Japanese. Therefore, during the ensuing centuries some Chinese word signs were isolated and adapted as syllable signs for the specific purpose of representing these grammatical forms. Thus, while most independent root-words are still written with Chinese characters (known as the *kanji*), grammatical morphemes and loanwords are written in one of the two kana syllabaries, the *hiragana* and *katakana*, respectively. As an interesting sideline it might be mentioned that in the 1880s a society was founded under the name of *Romajikai* with the express aim of adapting the Roman alphabet to the Japanese language. This reform movement has received renewed impetus since the end of World War II. The Chinese-derived characters may not be best suited for a country which has become westernized in many of its cultural aspects, but people seem to hold on tenaciously to their writing habits. What the ultimate outcome of the Romanization of Japanese writing may be is anybody's guess.

But let us come back to Semitic syllable writing. The West Semitic Syllabary, which is a rather general name given to the various forms of writing used by the Phoenicians, ancient Hebrews, and other Semitic peoples, made use of a 22-syllable system patterned after the 24-syllable system of the ancient Egyptians. In use anywhere from 1500 B.C. on, this system, in which each character stands for both a consonant and the following vowel, is also sometimes referred to as the "Semitic or Phoenician alphabet," although it is a matter of controversy whether or not to call a syllabic writing system an "alphabet," since it is not "a system of signs expressing simple sounds of speech."[6]

The final and decisive step to an ALPHABETIC SYSTEM was taken by the Greeks, who came into contact with Semitic writing through trade relations with the ubiquitous and enterprising Phoenician seafarers in the Mediterranean basin, probably around the tenth century B.C. Having adopted the forms of the West

Semitic Syllabary, the Greeks assigned vowel values to certain syllable signs that represented Semitic consonants they did not have in their language. In this way they were able to reduce the value of the Semitic syllables to simple consonants and vowels. It is true that the Semitic system did occasionally employ special phonetic signs technically known as *matres lectionis* 'mothers of reading' to facilitate the reading of vowels, but the honor of first using vowel signs in a systematic way nevertheless belongs to the Greeks. As a matter of fact, the use of vowel marks in the modern Hebrew and Arabic alphabets, which are essentially consonantal writing systems, is said to be due to Greek influence.[7]

In order to adapt the Semitic system to their own use, the Greeks assigned the symbols for syllables beginning with consonantal sounds that were unknown in their language to specific vowel sounds. For example, the name of the first symbol of the West Semitic Syllabary was *'aleph*, which stood for a kind of glottal stop represented in writing by an apostrophe ('). Since the Greeks did not make use of this sound at the time the syllable symbols were borrowed, the symbol for *'aleph* was taken over as *alpha* to represent the sound [a]. In the same manner, Semitic *yodh* was used for Greek *iota*, Semitic *hē* for Greek *epsilon*, Semitic *wāw* for Greek *upsilon*, and so forth. The derivation of the Greek symbols from a Semitic prototype is even more evident when one considers the close correspondence of the names given to them. For instance, *alpha*, derives from *'aleph*, which meant "ox" in both Phoenician and Hebrew; similarly, Greek *bēta*, *delta*, *gamma*, and *lambda*, to name just a few, are derived from Semitic *beth* 'house,' *dāleth* 'door,' *gimel* 'camel,' and *lamed* 'whip' (presumably used on the camel).

THE ALPHABET; PHONEME-GRAPHEME CORRESPONDENCES

The Greek alphabet may be considered as the direct ancestor of all alphabetic scripts in use today that indicate vowels by separate signs. It would be outside the scope of this brief chapter to pursue the details of the spread of the alphabetic system throughout the civilized world. Suffice it to say that the Greek alphabet has been variously adapted, the most important variants being undoubtedly the *Roman alphabet* and the *Cyrillic alphabet*. The former, originally a 21-letter alphabet (the symbol *c*, derived from Greek *gamma*, standing for both the sounds of [k] and [g]), was adapted from a western form of the Greek alphabet, probably by way of the Etruscans, around the seventh century B.C. As is well known, the Roman alphabet is the most widely used not only by European nations but also by such diverse languages as Turkish, Swahili, Indonesian, and Vietnamese, which all have discarded earlier scripts in favor of the Latin alphabet. As for the Cyrillic alphabet, it is a direct adaptation to the Slavic languages devised by the Christian missionaries Saints Cyril and Methodius around the ninth century A.D. It is now used by those Slavic peoples who follow the Eastern Church—Russians, Ukrainians, Bulgars, and Serbs—as opposed to those Slavs—Poles, Czechs, Slovaks, Croatians, and Slovenes—who as Roman Catholics use the Roman alphabet. The Cyrillic alphabet has also been adapted to many of the indigenous non-Slavic languages of the Soviet Union and peripheral areas, such as the Mongolian Peoples' Republic.

Direct offshoots of the West Semitic Syllabary are the present-day Semitic alphabets and other alphabets whose users follow the Islamic faith, like Persian and Urdu. Many scripts of southern and southeastern Asia have remained to some extent syllabic, among them the so-called *devanāgari script*, the Sanskrit alphabet used in modern Hindi and other languages of India.

Alphabets are in almost universal use today. The advantage of a system that uses a relatively small number of symbols to represent the sound units of a language, rather than the morphemes or syllables, is quite obvious. This is what makes an alphabet the most easily adaptable system of writing. Ideally, of course, an alphabet should have one separate sign, one GRAPHEME, for each distinct sound or phoneme, but apart from special systems devised by phoneticians such as IPA (International Phonetic Alphabet), no such alphabet exists. The Roman alphabet is makeshift, at best, adapted as it is to the varying requirements of different languages.

The use of a single grapheme for each phoneme, that is, a one-to-one correspondence between graphemes and phonemes—what linguists call a perfect "fit"—is an ideal that few languages approximate. Finnish, Hungarian, and Turkish are often mentioned as the languages that come closest to such a one-to-one relationship, while English and French are generally cited as the prototypes of an irrational correspondence between phonology and writing system. The 26 graphemes of the English alphabet, for example, must serve to represent about 45 phonemes of the language. To do this, various devices must be resorted to, such as combining graphemes to represent a single phoneme, for instance *th* for /θ/ or /ð/, or assigning more than one phoneme to a single grapheme, as in *cent* versus *cool*, where *c* represents the phonemes /s/ and /k/, respectively. And what about the various phonemes represented by the *ough* letter combination in the amusing phrase *though the tough cough and hiccough plough me through* given by E. H. Sturtevant[8] to illustrate the "erratic" spellings of English? In addition, there are alternate representations of a single phoneme, as in *be, meet, eat, niece*, and *people*, in which the unitalicized letters all stand for /i/.

It is not quite fair, we feel, to consider English spelling utterly irregular and idiosyncratic. To begin with, many consonant graphemes have constant phonemic value, for example *b, d, f, v, m, l,* and *r*. (The "silent letters" in *debt* and *doubt* are due to excessive reverence for etymological spelling on the part of Renaissance scholars—see Chapter 7, page 128.) The use of *c* for the phonemes /s/ and /k/ also follows a regular pattern: When followed by a front vowel, as in *cinema, cent, juice,* and *cyanide*, this grapheme always stands for the sound of [s], whereas in all other combinations, for example, *cat, comb, cup, fact,* and *lucrative*, it represents the sound of [k]. The grapheme *k*, on the other hand, regularly occurs before *e* and *i* to represent the phoneme /k/, as in *keen, keep, kin,* and *king*; before *a, o,* and *u* it only occurs in words of foreign derivation, like *kayak, kangaroo, kosher, kowtow, kudos,* and *kulak*. In a language like Hungarian, on the other hand, the graphemes *c* and *k* always have a constant phonemic value; they stand for /ts/ and /k/, respectively, regardless of the phonetic context.

The English vowels present a far greater source of irregularity of grapheme-phoneme correspondence than do the consonants. The letter *a*, for instance, represents a different phoneme in each of the following words: *male, palm, hat, fall, many, alone*. Nevertheless, consider some of the regular patterns, for example, *beef, beetle, deer, deep, eel, fee, feeble, geese, heel, keen, leech, meek, peer, reel, seek, sleep,* and *teeth*, where the *ee* combination invariably stands for the phoneme /i/. Another example of regular patterning is the device of using a silent *e* after a consonant to make a phonemic distinction in the preceding vowel, as in the pairs *Mack–make, nap–nape, pal–pale, Sam–same, man–mane, fat–fate, pin–pine, rip–ripe, sit–site,* and many others. Indeed, this regularity is such that any native speaker encountering the form *lat* (a former monetary unit of Latvia) will automatically pronounce it /læt/, like *fat*. There are even a few words in English that represent a perfect grapheme-phoneme fit, like *flow, low, slow,* and *snow,* as well as other words ending in *-ow* (*bow, mow, row, sow, tow*) where this grapheme combination represents the diphthong [ow].

Just as phonemes have allophones, that is, positional variants, so graphemes have ALLOGRAPHS. For example, except for a handful of foreign words, the phoneme /k/ in Italian is represented by the letter *c* before the back vowels *a, o,* and *u,* as in *caro* 'dear,' *coro* 'chorus,' and *cura* 'care,' but is written *ch* before *i* and *e*, as in *chilo* 'kilo' and *cheto* 'quiet.' In the same way *c* and *qu* in Spanish may be considered allographs, since the latter occurs only before front vowels to represent the phoneme /k/, as in *quilo* and *quedo* (with the same meaning as the corresponding Italian words), while the former occurs in all other cases to represent the same phoneme.

A perfect correlation between grapheme and phoneme would probably be found in a language that is static, such as an artificially constructed language. But living speech changes from generation to generation, and the written symbols inevitably lag behind linguistic changes. English spelling of a thousand years ago was much more phonemic than it is today. For instance, the word *knight* (/najt/) now uses six graphemes to represent three phonemes, whereas in the Old English form *cniht* (pronounced /knixt/) each of the five letters stood for a phoneme. The English writing system is largely where it was at the time of Shakespeare because it has failed to keep pace with the important changes that the phonemic structure of the language has undergone in the last few hundred years. Yet it is probably far less "chaotic" than it might seem at first. As the graphic representation of what is undoubtedly the richest language on earth, it is well worth mastering. It might be argued, of course, that in this day and age, with all kinds of electronic devices to preserve and transmit the spoken word, the days of writing are numbered. Therefore, why spend so much time trying to learn a seemingly irrational spelling perfectly. "We may expect that at some time in the future ... mechanical devices for reproducing speech will supersede our present habits of writing and printing," wrote Leonard Bloomfield back in the 1930s.[9] But the day thus envisaged has not yet arrived, and in the meantime every effort is being made on the part of departments and ministries of education to foster literacy. Whatever the future of writing may be, it is still ahead of speech in transcending time and space.

notes

1. David Diringer, *The Alphabet: A Key to the History of Mankind.* New York: Philosophical Library, 1948, p. 20.
2. *Ibid.*, p. 22.
3. *The Study of Writing.* Chicago: University of Chicago Press, 1952, p. 191.
4. *Ibid.* p. 190.
5. There are some word symbols in the Chinese language that may be considered primarily phonetic in nature. In ancient Chinese we already find the use of so-called *loan characters*, that is, symbols for words with nonpicturable meanings that originally represented different but phonetically similar words whose meanings could be pictured. For example, the character depicting a wheat plant, pronounced /laj/, has also come to be used for the homonymous word meaning 'come.' Sometimes, in order to avoid ambiguity between the original word and the one for which the character has been borrowed, an additional character is added to show which of the homonyms should be read. These additional characters are called *classifiers*, and the thus enlarged character is known as a "phonetic compound." For example, the symbol for *ma* 'horse' and the symbol for *nü* 'woman' are combined to serve as the symbol for *ma* 'mother.' For further information on this point, see Yuen Ren Chao, *Mandarin Primer.* Cambridge, Mass.: Harvard University Press, 1948, pp. 60 ff.
6. Gelb, *op. cit.,* p. 166.
7. *Ibid.,* p. 197.
8. *An Introduction to Linguistic Science,* New Haven, Conn.: Yale University Press, 1947, p. 25.
9. *Language.* New York: Holt, Rinehart and Winston, 1933, p. 503.

10
regional and social speech variations

If language is to serve its purpose as a means of social cooperation and interaction, it must be based upon an agreement among the members of a social group as to the general meaning of its symbols and signaling devices. Since language is the strongest bond that links an individual to a particular social group, the individual speaker is not at liberty to make arbitrary changes in the language patterns he acquires from this group, which allow him to understand and be understood as a member of a speech community.

LANGUAGE, DIALECT, AND IDIOLECT

Language, on the other hand, does not exist outside its social context, and a greater or lesser degree of flexibility and adaptability within the system is necessary to meet the requirements of the great complexity and variability of life in society. It has often been said that no two people speak exactly alike, that each person has speech habits peculiar to himself as an individual—what linguists have come to call his IDIOLECT—and that even the same person changes his language during his lifetime, however slightly, in accordance with shifting social settings. As a child, the individual's vocabulary varies from that of his parents because his interests and environment vary from that of his elders; as a college student, he may use a different vocabulary and more "careful" grammatical constructions than the educationally less fortunate; as a member of a certain social group, he may use a vocabulary that is more in keeping with his own special requirements, and so forth. All of us, to be sure, use a more colloquial, and even slangy, language with friends and relatives than we do in more formal communication.

By the same token, within a larger community of speakers there are many subgroups which, though fully participating in the life of the community, have special speech habits involving sounds, meaning, vocabulary and sometimes even grammatical structure. As long as the community or social group remains united by ties which make mutual intelligibility indispensable, variations in speech, technically known as DIALECTS, will not be so considerable as to impair understanding. Let, however, the common bonds loosen up as a result of geographical, political, or social changes and the need decrease for a common means of linguistic communication. Gradually, parts of the group will grow independent of each other and a certain degree of lack of understanding will eventually be reached between two or more subgroups, so that one can no longer speak of one and the same language. This is how, in essence, the once more or less homogeneous Indo-European speech community broke up into diverging languages several thousands of years ago, eventually giving rise to such mutually unintelligible modern descendants as English, Russian, Irish, French, Greek, Albanian, Armenian, and Hindustani.

Consider the case of English. This historical continuation of the tongue of the sixth-century Anglo-Saxon invaders of England was once just another Germanic dialect spoken along the northern coastline of the European mainland—the homeland of the Angles and the Saxons. Within a couple of centuries, and because there were no common political institutions and no communications to check linguistic and social changes, the speech of the invaders and that of their erstwhile brethren on the mainland became so different as to constitute separate, mutually incomprehensible languages. The tongue of the English settlers who came to America was identical with the Elizabethan English (the language of Shakespeare) spoken by those who stayed behind in the mother country. And even though migration to America took place at a time when political, cultural, and religious bonds were considerably stronger than they were ten centuries earlier, communications across the Atlantic were still so difficult that British speech and the English of the American colonists soon began to diverge to the point where some people felt justified in speaking of an "American language," a designation that the late H. L. Mencken chose for the title to his classic account of American English.[1]

As it is, there were two powerful factors that prevented divergence of British and American English from reaching a point of mutual unintelligibility, namely printing and education. Most of the books in the early years of settlement came from England, and it must be assumed that the early settlers maintained strong intellectual and cultural ties with the homeland, unlike their Anglo-Saxon forefathers. It is very likely, on the other hand, that if John Smith and the Pilgrim Fathers had come to these shores a few centuries earlier—and, at any rate, before the invention of the printing press—there might, indeed, have developed an American language as different from English as, say, Spanish is from French.

It would seem, then, that the criterion of distinguishing between language and dialect is the degree of mutual intelligibility. So long as parts of a group of people merely develop certain linguistic peculiarities sufficient to give their language a characteristic stamp, without thereby completely breaking the fundamental uniformity of the language of the whole group, we refer to these speech variations as dialects of the same language. If, on the other hand, there occurs such a separation, either in time or space, that the speech of one group of people becomes incomprehensible to another group, we are justified in speaking of different languages.

The problem thus stated, however, is somewhat oversimplified. The borderline between language and dialect is difficult to establish and mutual comprehension does not always constitute a sufficient yardstick. This is particularly true in some areas of the world where the population has been settled for a long time and is far less mobile than in other parts, say, in the United States. In countries like Britain, France, Italy, or Germany, regional differences may be very pronounced and even surprising to the speaker of American English accustomed to traveling hundreds of miles without encountering major problems of mutual understanding. But if you cross Italy from north to south, you will find that speakers of the dialects of Piedmont (in the north) and Sicily (in the south) must communicate in standard Italian if they wish to understand each other, though they are hardly farther apart than the speakers of the Virginia Piedmont and the extreme north of Maine, who find no particular difficulty communicating with each other in their native dialects. To take an even more extreme example, a Chinese speaker of the Mandarin dialect (the speech of northern China and the capital city of Peking) must, in the absence of a standard Chinese language, employ the common system of written characters to make himself understood by a Cantonese speaker from the south.²

Regional differences are more often than not a reflex of historical developments. For instance, the boundary line which divides the areas of Swiss German [hus] 'house,' [min] 'mine,' and [bluəmə] 'flower' from standard German *Haus* [haws], *mein* [majn], and *Blume* [blumə], technically known as an ISOGLOSS (from Greek *iso-* 'equal' and *glossa* 'speech'), is determined by the fact that Swiss German dialects generally kept an older phonetic stage of a once common language, the Old High German of the Middle Ages, and did not undergo the changes that modern High German has.³

Objectively speaking, each city, town, and village has its own distinctive speech form and, as was said earlier, each individual has his characteristic speech features, his personal dialect or idiolect, which set him apart from other members of his group. What people actually speak, then, are personal dialects which, by virtue of similarity of pronunciation, vocabulary, and grammar can be considered as subdivisions of a language that a given social group holds in common. Borrowing a term from music, we might say that dialects are "variations on a theme," the theme being a particular linguistic system, such as the languages officially known as English, French, German, Russian, Hungarian. Turning our definition around, we could also say that a language is a collection of related dialects which have enough of their sound system, vocabulary, and grammatical patterns in common to permit their speakers to understand each other in the daily affairs of life. Viewed in this light, American English and British English are dialects of the same language.

What is commonly referred to as a "standard" or "national" language is *the* dialect which, in the course of the history of a particular speech community, has gained supremacy and social prestige over its "fellow" dialects for some reason that is almost invariably nonlinguistic. This PRESTIGE DIALECT is usually that of the social, cultural, and/or political center of a region. This is the case in many European countries, where the dialect of the capital city is considered the "accepted" standard by the population, as are Parisian French or London English although, historically, both are local dialects. The elevation of London speech to what is often called "Received Standard English" is quite illustrative of this process of sublimation of a regional speech form. When London became the political and cultural center of fifteenth-century England, the important affairs of the realm, particularly law, politics, and business, were conducted in London English. Consequently, the speech of the capital acquired social prestige to the point where it became fashionable (and important) for all those who wished to participate in the cultural and social activities of the center of English life to speak and write the English dialect of London. Similarly, the so-called *Francien* dialect of medieval France, spoken in and around Paris eventually triumphed over other dialects originally of equal social standing (for example, the dialect of Picardy in the northeast, which had a rich literature) and became standard French. Again, this happened not because of some inherent linguistic superiority, but because Paris became the capital of France. Thus Parisian French, which was used by the King, his court, and important men of letters, acquired social prestige.

DIALECT GEOGRAPHY

In the United States, where there is no *one* recognized center for the important political, business, and social affairs of the country, no *one* dialect of American English has become the accepted "official" or "standard" language. No single speech form is being foisted upon schoolchildren because it is the dialect of the capital, and no one is attempting to imitate the speech patterns of the President in office because there is a supposed social prestige attached to it. Attempts in the past to recognize, for instance, New England speech patterns as a standard worth imitating because of the long predominance of Boston and Cambridge as centers of intellectual and social life, or those of other cultural centers like New York and Philadelphia, have proved largely fruitless. Our standards of speech are mainly regional standards. However, before examining the question of a "standard" speech form as it relates to the American scene (which naturally implies that there are "nonstandard" forms as well), let us take a brief look at the regional dialect situation.

The study of language differences in a given speech area is known as LINGUISTIC or DIALECT GEOGRAPHY, or, simply, DIALECTOLOGY. Linguistic geography was developed in the late 1870s by the German scholar Georg Wenker, who hit upon the idea of asking thousands of schoolmasters throughout his country to translate a collection of sentences into their local dialect. With the well over forty thousand responses he received, he inaugurated the first *linguistic atlas*, a collection of maps on which he charted the local speech forms thus collected. The pattern for future dialect investigation, however, was set by a French scholar, Jules Gilliéron, who sent out a trained field-worker, Edmond Edmont, to interview speakers in about six hundred French communities. Armed with a questionnaire containing about 2000 words, phrases, and expressions that Gilliéron had carefully prepared, Edmont looked for representative "informants" in each community in order to elicit from them ways in which these questionnaire items would be rendered in the respective local dialects. He then transcribed in phonetic notation (there were no tape recorders available yet) what he heard. The result of this long and arduous labor was the *Atlas linguistique de France*, the linguistic atlas of France, published between 1902 and 1910. Each item is entered on a separate map of the area covered by the field-worker; for instance, there is a separate map for the word 'horse' as spoken in hundreds of French localities, another one for 'cat,' and so forth. Gilliéron's example was soon followed by an investigation of the dialects of Italy and southern Switzerland, which was undertaken by two of his pupils, Karl Jaberg and Jakob Jud. But while the French atlas had concentrated on the rural areas of France, the authors of the Italian atlas also included the speech of urban areas.

These dialect investigations provided the model for a monumental project, the *Linguistic Atlas of the United States and Canada*, which was started in 1930 under the general editorship of Professor Hans Kurath. The project is now directed by Raven I. McDavid, Jr., of the University of Chicago, with the assistance of many well-known linguistic scholars. To date, only one section, *The Linguistic Atlas of New England*, has been published. This covers the Atlantic Seaboard, that is, the area of original colonial settlement. In conjunction with the publication of the first volume of this Atlas in 1939 (the publication was completed in 1943), Kurath also published a *Handbook of the Linguistic Geography of New England*, giving information on methodology, phonetic notation, speech areas covered, the choice of informants, as well as an outline of dialect areas, and a history of original settlements. In the meantime, field records have been completed for other sections of the Atlas project, like the *North-Central States* and the *Upper Midwest*, and many special studies have appeared making use of Atlas findings.[4]

THE DIALECTS OF AMERICAN ENGLISH

Regional Variations

The principal sources of information about American dialects are the Atlas survey of the Eastern United States and the studies made on the speech of the Atlantic seaboard. It follows, then, that the clearest ascertainable dialect boundaries are found along this 1,000 or so mile stretch of coastal plain, where the first settlements were established. As shown on the map on page 173, evidence gathered from Atlantic seaboard records by Kurath and his associates has led to the recognition of three major dialect areas—*Northern*, *Midland*, and *Southern*, with various subdivisions in each area. These areas are distinctive in pronunciation, vocabulary, and grammar. For instance, the Midland speech area is usually subdivided into a *Northern Midland* and a *Southern Midland* region, the former comprising the Delaware, Susquehanna, and Upper Ohio Valleys, and Northern West Virginia, while the latter encompasses the Upper Potomac and Shenandoah Valleys, as well as the area to the southwest, that is, southern West Virginia.

Here are some random examples of typical regional speech features, both in pronunciation and word usage, that have come to light as a result of the research carried out within the framework of the Atlas project.

1. Throughout the northern and southern areas, speakers generally distinguish between /o/ and /ɔ/ in pairs like *hoarse* and *horse* or *mourning* and *morning*. In Midland speech, however, this distinction is not observed and the words are homophonous.[5]

2. Some sections of the eastern states, in particular the South

regional and social speech variations   173

The Speech Areas of the Eastern States

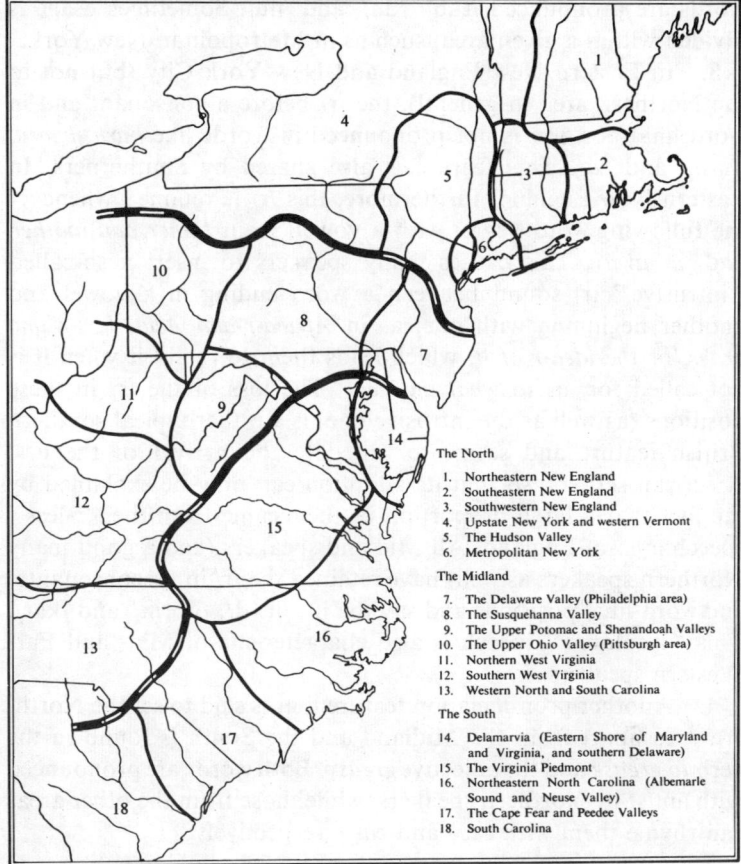

The North
1. Northeastern New England
2. Southeastern New England
3. Southwestern New England
4. Upstate New York and western Vermont
5. The Hudson Valley
6. Metropolitan New York

The Midland
7. The Delaware Valley (Philadelphia area)
8. The Susquehanna Valley
9. The Upper Potomac and Shenandoah Valleys
10. The Upper Ohio Valley (Pittsburgh area)
11. Northern West Virginia
12. Southern West Virginia
13. Western North and South Carolina

The South
14. Delamarvia (Eastern Shore of Maryland and Virginia, and southern Delaware)
15. The Virginia Piedmont
16. Northeastern North Carolina (Albemarle Sound and Neuse Valley)
17. The Cape Fear and Peedee Valleys
18. South Carolina

Adapted from Hans Kurath, *A Word Geography of the Eastern United States*. Copyright 1949 by the University of Michigan Press, Ann Arbor. Reprinted by permission of the publisher.

and South Midland, insert a [j] semivowel sound after /t/, /d/, and /n/ in words like *tube, due,* and *new,* while in the other areas these words are pronounced /tub/, /du/, and /nu/. Sometimes usage is divided within a given area, such as in Metropolitan New York.

3. In Eastern New England and New York City (but not in the Northern area in general), the /r/ before a consonant and in word final position is not pronounced in words like *burn, heard, warm,* and *car.* This feature is also shared by Southerners. In Eastern New England, furthermore, this /r/ is retained whenever the following word begins with a vowel, as in *father and mother* and *far away.* This causes many speakers to insert a so-called "intrusive" [r] sound between a word ending in a vowel and another beginning with one, as in *Africa-r-and Asia, law-r and order,* or *the idea-r of it,* which leads them to retain it when it is not called for, as in *what an idear.* The loss of the /r/ in these positions (as well as the intrusive one) is a rather typical southern British feature and seems to antedate the arrival of the first American settlers, so that its adoption can only be explained by the fact that a large proportion of them came from the "r-less" speech area of England. All Midland speakers (and a good many Northern speakers as well) have retained the /r/ in preconsonantal and word final positions and say /bɜ^n/, /hɜ^d/, /wɔrm/, and /kar/. This "r-colored" speech is also characteristic of Mid- and Far-Western speakers.

4. Another pronunciation feature that is said to set the Northern area apart from the Midland and the South is found in the verb *to grease* and the adjective *greasy.* Both words are pronounced with an /s/ by Northern speakers, while those from the other areas can rhyme them with *ease* and *easy,* respectively.[6]

5. Among typically Northern terms we could mention *pail* (referred to as *bucket* in Midland and Southern speech), *brook* 'small stream,' *comforter* 'thick quilt,' and *cherry pit* 'cherry seed'; typical of the Midland are *blinds* 'window shades,' *skillet* 'frying pan,' and *green beans* 'string beans' (*snap beans* in the South); while *fritters* and a *turn* of wood 'armful' are typical of the South where cows *low* instead of moo at feeding time.[7]

Regional variations in matters of pronunciation and vocabulary are much easier to organize and classify than are features of grammar. In his study of verb forms in the eastern United States,

E. Bagby Atwood recognizes that usage is rather sharply divided along social lines, more so than vocabulary and pronunciation.[8] Usage among cultivated speakers, however, is not entirely free from variant forms either, depending on the regions. Thus, a specifically Northern form is the past tense *dove*, whereas the Midland and Southern speakers show a preference for *dived*. Linguistic Atlas research has also shown that, on the whole, even nonstandard grammatical forms fall into a regional pattern similar to vocabulary and pronunciation features. For instance, while the standard past tense form *saw* is practically universal in educated speech, the form *I seen* (for *I saw*) occurs only sporadically in the Northern area (it is heard especially in the Metropolitan New York area), while it strongly predominates in the Midland region and is also common in the South. The form *I seed*, on the other hand, built on the regular past tense pattern of weak verbs, is rather typical of people of fair to poor education in South Midland and the South.

Dialectologists generally agree that the starting point of American dialects must be sought in the original colonial groupings: the New England settlement centering in Massachusetts, the Middle Atlantic settlement centering in Pennsylvania, and the Southern settlement centering in Virginia and the Carolinas. These, in turn, reflect the speech that the original settlers brought with them from different parts of England. Linguistic geographers have found, furthermore, that the pattern of the original settlements is also reflected in the spreading of dialects westward across the North American continent, though the farther West one goes the more dialects tend to overlap and blend into one another, so that dialect boundaries of major speech areas become difficult to define. It has been shown, for instance, that the speech of the educated Mid- and Far-Westerner derives, in the main, from that of western New England and Pennsylvania, thus disproving an earlier notion of a rather uniform "Midwestern" or "General American" type speech extending all the way from New Jersey to the Pacific Coast.

Social Variations

Traditionally, dialect studies have mainly concentrated on variations which correlate with geographical distribution. In addition to this "horizontal" dimension, investigations in connection with the Atlas project have opened up a new avenue of research by focusing attention on a "vertical" stratification of language, that is, speech which correlates with social and educational factors. It is rather obvious, even to the casual observer, that in a given locality, particularly in urban centers, the speech habits of some people or certain groups of people are more cultivated and that those of others are socially less desirable. These variations of speech, differing mainly in grammatical forms and sentence structure, reflect the degrees of schooling and the position that people occupy in society. These social or cultural speech levels, which, like regional varieties, gradually merge into each other, may be subsumed under two general headings, *standard* and *substandard*. STANDARD AMERICAN ENGLISH has been defined as that which is "naturally used by most college-educated people who fill positions of social, financial, and professional influence in the community."⁹ It follows then that SUBSTANDARD ENGLISH is the speech of the uneducated—either the illiterate or those whose schooling is very limited, that is, those who make up the unskilled labor force. (By standard English, as it applies to the American scene, we do not mean the kind of *Received Standard* of British English mentioned earlier but rather the regional cultivated American speech of such focal areas as Boston, New York City, Philadelphia, Richmond, Charleston, and the large urban centers in the West.)

Standard and substandard are relative terms, of course. A college education is by no means a necessary prerequisite for acquiring an acceptable command of standard English, nor does an educated speaker use the same language on all occasions. As a matter of fact, there are many people, usually speakers of the standard language, whose linguistic competence includes more than one social and sometimes even regional dialect which they turn on as the occasion demands. These speech levels are called functional varieties, or styles, and may be roughly grouped into *formal* and *familiar* writing or speaking. The familiar, or *colloquial*, variety itself exists in various degrees of familiarity or formality as, for example, informal conversation with relatives and friends, private correspondence, formal conversation (for example, with one's superior), and informal public address (such as many a campaign speech). Among the formal styles there is the language of a sermon, the formal public address (for example, the President's State of the Union Message), the scholarly paper, legal, scientific, and other expository writing, as well as literary prose and poetry.[10] These functional varieties exist both on the standard and substandard levels. For instance, the formal standard *it is I* becomes *it's me* in colloquial standard; *him and me grabbed us a bite to eat* is definitely colloquial substandard, while *between you and I* could be called formal substandard, which is in the nature of a *hypercorrection* or *hyperurbanism*. It arises when a speaker (and he need not be an uneducated one) overcorrects a feature which he believes to be substandard. (Having been told that *you and me* is incorrect when used as a subject and that he had better say *you and I*, the speaker avoids the use of *me* and substitutes *I* for it.)

The term "colloquial" does not, in and of itself, imply a cultural level and in no way designates a substandard form of English, as has been suggested on more than one occasion. By colloquial is simply meant a style of speech used mainly in conversation. Colloquial English can be just as standard as formal or literary English, or it can be substandard, as illustrated above. The literary artist accustomed to writing formal prose does not sink to a lower cultural level when he writes to his wife in a more informal style or engages in conversation with his friends. While in formal writing or speech he might say something like *The man to whom I was referring*, in colloquial English he is more likely to say *The man I was referring to*.

Special types of style are the jargon and slang of special groups within a particular community. Both terms are difficult to define and have meant different things to different people at different times.

JARGON now generally refers to the specialized and technical vocabulary of those engaged in a particular trade or profession or that of any other specialized group (such as a ski-club). It does not purport to be deliberately unintelligible and obscure to the non-initiated. It is "shop-talk." But because it consists of many words that are not familiar to the average speaker, the term *jargon* has often been used to designate unintelligible speech. The word itself is ultimately connected with the idea of "gurgling" and is defined in W. W. Skeat's *Concise Etymological Dictionary of the English Language*[11] as "a confused talk." In any event, jargon in its generally accepted meaning of "technical language" does not differ from the standard language and erstwhile highly technical terms easily pass into the general vocabulary of the average speaker (for example, all the new terms brought into general use by the space age).

SLANG has been called "one of those things that everybody can recognize and nobody can define."[12] But Stuart B. Flexner, coeditor of the *Dictionary of American Slang*[13] does define it as "the body of words and expressions frequently used by or intelligible to a rather large portion of the general American public, but not accepted as good, formal usage by the majority." The implications of this definition are (1) that slang is a substandard form of speech (but by no means always vulgar or impolite) and (2) that it is largely understood by all members of a social group. A slang term usually exists side by side with another, more general and "respectable" one, for instance *chick* and *girl*. Sometimes it may even become an accepted standard term, as has often happened throughout the history of a language. The term *hot dog* is a case in point. At one time it was used as a slang term for *sausage sandwich*, but it has driven its synonym out of use. Generally speaking, slang is characterized by newly coined words (*blurb*), existing words with new or extended meanings (*cool* 'great, excellent'), and colorful and even "wild" figures of speech (*the cat's pajamas* 'first-rate,' for example, a widely used expression of the 1930s and '40s). Slang seems to arise out of an attempt to find fresh, vigorous, and humorous expressions, as if "to escape the dull familiarity of standard words, to suggest an escape from the established routine of everyday life."[14] It comes and goes within a matter of years and even months, but if a slang term happens to catch on, it is elevated to respectability and becomes accepted as part of the standard vocabulary. On the other hand, some slang words manage to linger on for years and years without ever really becoming accepted. Terms like *dough* 'money,' *cop* 'policeman,' *nuts* 'crazy, insane,' *jalopy* 'automobile,' and *plastered* 'drunk' have not yet "made it" on the social ladder; yet we may expect them to be around for some time to come.

Slang may be nationwide, but it may also be restricted to a small group which purposely wishes to exclude outsiders. In this case it comes to be a sort of secret language which identifies those who belong to the group in question. This type of slang is now usually termed CANT and refers to the peculiar terms used especially by criminals, dope addicts, degenerates, and other undesirable elements who want to keep to themselves. Many slang terms in general use today betray their ultimate origin from the vocabulary of the element on the wrong side of the law, for example, *grand, take the rap, throw the book at, third degree,* and many others. Some terms have widened their meaning: *kick the habit* originally only meant to cure oneself of narcotics addiction, but lately has come to be applied to drinking and smoking habits as well. It would be inaccurate to say that slang is used by the less-educated people only. Everyone uses a slang word on occasion in the belief that it drives home a particular point quickly and explicitly—and also more personally—than a standard word would. Used with moderation and at the proper time and place, it lends expressiveness and something of a picturesque quality to our speech.

CONTACT LANGUAGES

Before bringing this brief sketch of regional and social speech variations to a close, we should make at least passing mention of an interesting variety of language variously called CONTACT, MAKESHIFT or, more commonly, PIDGIN LANGUAGES. These arise in response to certain situations that require some kind of immediate understanding between two groups whose languages are different. What happens essentially is that in a pidgin situation each speaker imitates the other's way of speaking with the result that there develops a sort of hybrid language which is native to no one. Imagine that you are trying hard to imitate the words and expressions you hear from a native speaker of Russian. Your imitation may be quite imperfect. Then, instead of correcting you and teaching you the sounds, sound combinations, and correct grammatical patterns of Russian, the speaker of this language replies to you in the same imperfect and broken way in which you attempted to speak his language. He may believe, as a matter of fact, that this is the best you can do and that unless he responds in "baby-talk" (the kind of "baby good girl," "baby not touch anything" talk) you would not understand him anyway. Both you and he are using a simplified version, a pidgin of Russian. In essence, this is how pidgin languages have arisen in the course of history among traders who wished to do business with people in far-away lands. Thus back in the seventeenth century arose *pidgin English* in the seaports of southern China, where British traders sought a compromise language between their own and the Chinese of the natives. (The word *pidgin* is said to be a garbled form of the English word *business* in the Cantonese Chinese dialect.) Instead of teaching them proper English—and because they assumed that the intellectually inferior natives were not capable of learning it anyway—the traders taught them a simplified variety of English which came to be restructured in accordance with Chinese syntactic patterns of the *no can do* type. For the most part, English words were used, with some concessions to native pronunciation, habits of thought, and sentence patterns.

There are as many pidgin varieties as there are places where a makeshift language has to be devised between people of different linguistic backgrounds who wish to communicate for business or any other purposes. Apart from the trade ports of China, there exist pidgins in the ports of Southeast Asia, the islands of the Pacific (Australia, New Guinea, the Melanesian Islands), the west coast of Africa, on the Indian subcontinent, and other far-flung corners of the earth. More recently, pidgin languages have arisen whenever American G.I.'s are stationed in foreign countries. Usually, however, our soldiers adapt their language to that of the native population, as in the case of *Korean Bamboo English*, which is a mixture of English, Japanese, and Korean, using English grammar in a greatly simplified form.[15]

In addition to the numerous varieties of pidgin English, there naturally exist pidgins of other languages as well, such as pidgin Malay of the former Dutch East Indies, the *Petit-Nègre*, a French pidgin spoken in French West Africa, the Portuguese pidgin of the West African coast, the Spanish pidgin of the Philippines, to name a few. Sometimes one such pidgin form not only survives the situation which called it into existence but actually becomes the everyday vehicle of communication of a speech community. This is the case of *Haitian (French) Creole, Melanesian (English) Pidgin*, and the *Afro-American Gullah*, which is spoken in the coastal areas of South Carolina and Georgia, where the erstwhile pidgin became the native language of a group of people, with its rules of phonology and grammar.[16]

To a linguist any language is of interest and worthy of study in its own right, whether it is a regional or social dialect, slang, pidgin, or creole. He knows that language is the common possession of all classes, the rich and the poor, the educated and the uneducated alike, and that, fundamentally, man seeks to establish some way of communicating with his fellow man. Linguistic geography has made an enormous contribution to our understanding and appreciation of both the geography and social dimensions of speech. Far from being "corrupted deviations" from a standard norm due to "ignorance" and "carelessness" on the part of common people, dialects are legitimate tools of human communication that reflect our environment and experiences. In spite of modern methods of communication, the general mobility of the population and other unifying forces (education, literature, central government, radio, TV) which may contribute to some standardization of speech, at least on the educated level, dialects show an astonishing degree of vitality. Speech features seem to remain firmly entrenched in the language of the people, and unless we become utterly dehumanized robots of some super state and mere statistics identified only by social security numbers, we may expect speech variations to be with us as long as our present social structure survives.

notes

1. *The American Language*, 4th ed. New York: Alfred A. Knopf, 1936 (originally published in 1919). This monumental work, to which its author added two supplements in 1945 and 1948, has recently been revised and abridged by Raven I. McDavid, Jr. (Knopf, 1963).

   During the early history of the young Republic voices were indeed raised both in state legislatures and in Congress to the effect that the name of the language spoken in the U.S. should officially be designated as the "American Language."

2. The Chinese mainland is divided into a number of major, mutually unintelligible, dialect groups, which are as far apart from each other as German is from English or Italian from French. Each major group, in turn, consists of numerous subgroups, within which speakers are able to communicate with comparative ease. The majority of Chinese speakers use some variety of Mandarin, which is on the way to becoming the official Chinese language, with the name of *kuo-yü* 'national language,' under the impetus of Mao-Tse-Tung, who has decreed that it be taught in schools throughout the country.

3. We conventionally call modern High German the standard German language used in literature, in schools, on the stage and, in general, by educated speakers. For a fuller explanation of the term, especially as it related to "Low German," see Chapter 11.

4. An excellent summary of the methods of linguistic geography, the work in progress on the Atlas project, and on dialect studies in the U.S., in general, will be found in chap. 9, "The Dialects of American English," written by Raven I. McDavid, Jr., in W. Nelson Francis, *The Structure of American English*, New York: The Ronald Press, 1958, pp. 480–543. Based on this chapter, the National Council of Teachers of English, Champaign, Illinois, published in 1963 a book on the regional varieties

of American English, authored by Jean Malmstrom and Annabel Ashley, for use primarily in secondary schools. Its title is *Dialects–U.S.A.*
A more recent introductory survey is that of Caroll E. Reed, *Dialects of American English*, Cleveland & New York: The World Publishing Co., 1967.

5. Homophonous words (from the Greek *homos* 'same' and *phonē* 'sound') are words that sound alike but are spelled differently, contrary to homonyms (from Greek *homos* and *onoma* 'name'), which are also spelled alike, as, for instance, *pole* and *Pole*.
6. For further data on pronunciation, consult Hans Kurath and Raven I. McDavid, Jr., *The Pronunciation of English in the Atlantic States*. Ann Arbor: University of Michigan Press, 1961.
7. The classic work on regional and local vocabulary along the Eastern Seabord is Hans Kurath's *A Word Geography of the Eastern United States*. Ann Arbor: The University of Michigan Press, 1949.
8. *A Survey of Verb Forms in the Eastern United States*. Ann Arbor: The University of Michigan Press, 1953.
9. W. Nelson Francis, *The English Language: An Introduction*. New York: W. W. Norton & Co., 1965, p. 246.
10. John S. Kenyon, "Cultural Levels and Functional Varieties," in *College English*, 10 (October 1958), pp. 31–36.
11. New and corrected impression. Oxford: Clarendon Press, 1927, p. 271
12. Paul Roberts, *Understanding English*. New York: Harper & Row, 1958, p. 342.
13. Compiled and edited by Harold Wentworth and Stuart Berg Flexner. New York: Thomas Y. Crowell, 1967, p. vi.
14. *Ibid.*, p. xi.
15. Jean Malmstrom, *Language in Society*. New York: Hayden Book Co., 1965.
16. For further details, see Robert A. Hall, Jr., *Pidgin and Creole Languages*. Ithaca, N. Y.: Cornell University Press, 1966.

11
languages in comparison

If you have had the good fortune of taking a European grand tour all the way from England to sunny Italy, with stopovers in the Scandinavian countries, Germany, the Netherlands, and France and a slight detour to Spain, you will have noticed striking resemblances among some of the languages spoken in these countries. The English-speaking waiter's *good morning* came out as *god morgon* in Swedish, as *god morgen* in Danish and Norwegian, as *goeden morgen* in Dutch, and as *guten Morgen* in German. The French hotel porter said *bon jour* to you, and in Italy you were greeted with *buon giorno*; the first part of the Spanish *buenos días* may have sounded quite familiar to you after your experience in France and Italy, but you will have been struck by the fact that French and Italian use a different word for "day." This is because the Spanish speakers long ago opted for the Latin word *dies*, whereas their Romance brethren to the east and south chose the Latin adjective *diurnus* 'daily,' which they eventually turned into a noun.

Hundreds of examples of these kinds of similarities could be easily found, and they would only serve to confirm the close linguistic ties within what are now called the *Germanic* and *Romance* groups of languages, thus betraying a common origin for each. In the case of the Romance group, we are in a particularly fortunate position, since we have a good knowledge of Latin, the language of which French, Italian, and Spanish are modern dialects. When we come to the Germanic group, which also developed from a single parent language, we are far less lucky, since we have no record of the parent language and can only assume that it was spoken contemporaneously with Sanskrit (or at least contemporaneously with a spoken variety of this literary language of the ancient inhabitants of northern India), Latin, and Greek, possibly in what is today both East and West Germany, as well as in Scandinavia.

In addition to the striking similarities within each group, these two major language groups also bear resemblances to one another. This is particularly true of English, which has incorporated a great many words from French as well as from Latin, the historical "ancestor" of the Romance languages. The English adverb *very*, as was seen in Chapter 7, is an adaptation of Old French *verai* 'true' (Modern French *vrai*). But resemblances between the Germanic and Romance groups, both in words that are not due to borrowings and in the way words are put together to form sentences, are by no means uncommon. Take the word *video*, for instance, with which you are no doubt familiar from television jargon (for instance, a program recorded on video tape). In Latin it is a verb form and means "I see." In Italian this form becomes *vedo*, and in Spanish it is *veo*. The English equivalent is an entirely different word. Yet there exists in English a word that shows an original kinship with the Latin word, namely, the word *wit*, though it has to do with knowledge and not with sight. But do we not normally acquire knowledge through sight? The ancient Hindus of northern India called their sacred books *Vedas*, that is, books of knowledge. In Greek, on the other hand, there is a word which resembles both English *wit* and Latin *video* and means "hear." Hearing is but another way of knowing. When we come to Russian, we find that the word for "see" is *vidyet'*, in which you will once again recognize the root of a word which must have existed in a hypothetical, unrecorded parent language, presumably with the meanings of "see," "hear," and "know."

It is the systematic study of these kinds of resemblances that led early nineteenth-century scholars to recognize the relationships among various languages of Europe and Asia, although during the centuries preceding the dawn of scientific linguistics, inquisitive minds had been speculating about the origins and affiliations of languages. Our earliest records of conscious awareness of matters linguistic come from ancient India and Greece. *Pāṇini's* fourth-century B.C. grammar of the Sanskrit language is the first known formal grammar of any language and is still considered to be the most authoritative analysis and description of classical Sanskrit. Quite independently of Pāṇini and other Hindu scholars, the Greeks worked out the grammatical concepts that have influenced our linguistic thinking until quite recently. But they were primarily philosophers and were more interested in speculating about the ultimate nature of language. Their debates about whether language is a phenomenon of supernatural origin (that is, God-given) or merely a matter of agreement among speakers are of interest because of subsequent discussions on this subject, eventually culminating in the clear underscoring by twentieth-century linguists of the conventional and arbitrary nature of language.

PRESCIENTIFIC LANGUAGE STUDIES

It is unfortunate that neither the Hindus nor the Greeks seem to have been particularly interested in the languages of other ancient peoples. Nowhere in their work do we find comparisons with other languages of antiquity. This lack of interest in other peoples' languages (except Greek, of course) also characterizes the Romans, who simply took over the theoretical and practical results of the Greek scholars, adapting them to their own needs, as they did with so many other creations of Greek intellectual life. Not that there was no awareness of foreign tongues in the Roman world; but, except for occasional references to the existence of other languages (for instance, the historian Livy's reference to *Etruscan*, the language of a once-flourishing civilization, or Cicero's mention of the use of interpreters in the city of Rome for "foreign" visitors from the Provinces who knew no Latin), the Romans left no descriptions of them. Such was their reverence for Greek that the resemblance of some Latin words to Greek words was taken as proof that Latin had descended from Greek, indeed, that Latin was a "corruption" of the language of Plato and Aristotle. In short, the Romans did not advance any knowledge about language except for organizing, synthesizing, and disseminating what they had copied from the Greeks. Their work on language is summarized in the treatises of first-century B.C. *Varro*, and especially in those of *Donatus* and *Priscian* in the fourth and sixth centuries A.D., respectively, which not only became the foundation of medieval grammatical theory but also were to influence the science of grammar for centuries to come.

Scholarship in medieval Western Europe was almost entirely confined to Latin. Greek had all but disappeared in the West. *Graecum est non legitur*, the forerunner of "it's Greek to me," became a stock phrase among scholars, and the study of language and grammar came to be identified with the study of Latin. Apart from restatements of Aristotelian speculations about the nature of language, it may be said that medieval philosophers and grammarians made no appreciable advances in linguistic thought. However, the concept of a "universal grammar," already implicit in Graeco-Roman thinking, received new expression by some thirteenth-century philosophers, particularly Roger Bacon, who declared that grammar was one and the same in all languages in its substance and that differences on the surface were due to accidental variations.[1] It was believed, in other words, that a universal grammar could be worked out independently of the structural diversity of languages but that it was within the province of the *philosopher* rather than the *grammarian* (whose exclusive job it was to teach grammar in school) to determine its theoretical principles. *Philosophus grammaticam invenit* 'the philosopher discovers grammar' is quite in line with scholastic philosophy, which viewed the phenomenon of language above all as an expression of logical argument.

The concept of a universal grammatical theory—based on the demands of logic—which would satisfy the structural essence of all languages found its most prominent representative in the well-known *Grammaire générale et raisonnée* (published in 1660) produced at the Parisian abbey of Port-Royal, a famous center of seventeenth-century French scholarship. This "philosophical grammar in the grand tradition,"[2] as it has been called, also served as a model for subsequent philosophical grammars, especially those of eighteenth-century rationalists like the Englishman James Harris, whose *Philosophical Inquiry Concerning Language and Universal Grammar* was published in 1751. The idea of language universals, largely rejected by nineteenth- and twentieth-century linguists impressed by the *diversity* rather than the *universality* of language structures, has, within the last decade or so, again become of increasing concern to linguistic scholars, who have particularly attempted to discover syntactic features common to all languages.³

Although linguistic thought during the medieval period was essentially a legacy of the Graeco-Roman past, not everyone followed the "line." There was one man in particular who had some original ideas on languages and their relationships. It was the great scholar and poet Dante who, in a treatise entitled *De vulgari eloquentia* 'about vernacular speech' (published in 1305), correctly identified Italian (as well presumably as Spanish and Portuguese), Provençal, and French as belonging to the same language group, since they had descended from a common ancestor, Latin. With his attempt at language comparison and explanation of language derivation based on the affirmative *yes* in these languages,[4] as well as his classification of Italian dialects (of which he distinguished fourteen), Dante may legitimately be considered as a precursor of modern linguistic thought. It is unfortunate that his ideas on language were not heeded by his contemporaries.

During the sixteenth and seventeenth centuries, when European horizons began to widen as a result of voyages of discovery and exploration to Asia, Africa, and the New World, scholars began to take notice of new and exotic languages, like the Aztec *Nahuatl* and other American Indian languages. Many grammars of both European and non-European languages appeared, though it does not seem to have occurred to their writers that the newly discovered languages were too diversified in structure to fit into the rigid mold of Graeco-Roman grammatical concepts. Side by side with grammars, surveys of the known languages also appeared, such as the Italian scholar J. J. Scaliger's treatise on the European languages (*Diatriba de Europaeorum linguis*) published in 1599, which is probably the first serious attempt at determining their affiliation. Scaliger recognizes four major groups based on their word for "God," namely, the *deus*- (Latin), *theos*- (Greek), *gott*- (Germanic), and *bog*- (Slavic) languages. These four groups (in addition to seven minor ones that he also recognizes) roughly correspond to present-day classifications of the languages of Europe but also comprise what are now considered to be subgroups of larger ones.[5]

With the rediscovery of Greek during the Renaissance, the study of Arabic and Hebrew (especially the latter, which was regarded as the oldest language and hence the parent of all others), and the increased interest in other languages, especially non-European ones, a large body of data became available. What was needed was a sound methodology to sift, organize, and interpret this knowledge. Though still operating within the framework of classical Graeco-Roman scholarship, seventeenth- and eighteenth-century scholars continued to explore hitherto unknown languages and to produce grammars. Further attempts at classifying languages culminated in the work of the German philosopher and mathematician *Leibniz*, whose proposed Eurasian language group may not be accurate in the light of our present knowledge, but who was nevertheless the first known scholar to propose a common prehistoric ancestor for the languages of this group.

THE DAWN OF SCIENTIFIC LINGUISTICS

The turning point that gave linguistic scholarship a completely new direction occurred toward the end of the eighteenth century with the disclosure of Sanskrit to the Western world. It was in 1786 that a British judge serving in India, *Sir William Jones*, who was a Sanskrit scholar in his own right, made the epoch-making statement before a learned society in London that the correspondences he had observed between Sanskrit on the one hand and Latin and Greek on the other, both in the roots of verbs and in their grammatical forms, could not be due to mere chance. He therefore concluded that these languages must have sprung from some common ancestor that might no longer be in existence. At the same time, Jones also suggested, though not as forcefully, that both Gothic (the earliest Germanic language on record) and Celtic also had a common origin with Sanskrit. Thus he gave the signal for comparative studies that were to mark a whole century of linguistic research, not that Sanskrit had been entirely unknown in Europe before Jones came on the linguistic scene. Back in the sixteenth century *Sassetti*, an Italian missionary who was ahead of his time, had already drawn attention to the similarities between some Italian numerals—particularly *sei* 'six,' *sette* 'seven,' *otto* 'eight,' and *nove* 'nine'—and their Sanskrit equivalents, *sás*, *saptá*, *aṣṭá*, and *náva*.

It was Sir William's theoretical statement about the relationship of Sanskrit to the known classical languages that laid the ground work for comparative historical studies. These studies led to the gradual revelation of the way in which many of the world's languages are related to one another, especially those that have come to be called the Indo-European languages because they cover a huge area that extends from northern India to western Europe. By advancing his hypothesis of a common source for Sanskrit, Latin, and Greek, Jones, in a sense, outlined the main concern of linguistic scholars for a whole century: to establish the linguistic unity of languages suspected of being related by tracing them to a "parent," or common, language. Three names, in particular, stand out as the pioneers of this new comparative methodology: *Rasmus Rask*, *Jacob Grimm*, and *Franz Bopp*. Through their individual contributions they rightfully earned for themselves general recognition as the founders of modern historical and comparative linguistics.

A prizewinning essay entitled "An Investigation Into the Origin of the Old Norse or Icelandic Language,"[6] submitted by Rask to the Danish Academy of Sciences in 1814, is generally considered to be the first landmark in scientific linguistic studies. In it the Danish scholar not only seeks to establish the derivation of Old Norse (the parent of modern Scandinavian languages) and its place within the larger scope of the Germanic languages, but he also shows how this language is related to other Indo-European languages, particularly Greek and Latin. In doing so, he draws attention to certain "letter" correspondences (today we would call them *sound* correspondences) in cognate words of identical or similar meaning. For instance, Rask finds that in Latin the *p* of *pater* corresponds to *f* in Old Norse *faðir* (English *father*) or that the Latin *p* in *piscis* is an *f* in Old Norse *fisk* (English *fish*). Similarly, the Latin *f* in *fagus* 'beech tree' corresponds to a *b* in Old Norse *bok* (English *book*), and the Latin *f* in *fero* appears as *b* in Old Norse *bära* (English *bear*, in the sense of "carry"). Insisting on the necessity of a regular system of phonetic correspondences (though he himself speaks of letters) between what he calls the "most essential, concrete, indispensable words ... especially when similarities in the inflectional system and in the general makeup of the languages correspond with them,"[7] Rask formulates the basic principles of the aims and methods of the systematic comparison of languages.

While Rask was concentrating on European languages only (at the time that he wrote his "Investigation," he was not yet acquainted with Sanskrit), his contemporary, the German scholar Franz Bopp, was approaching the problem of comparison from the point of view of Sanskrit. Under the influence of one of the founders of the German school of Romanticism, *Friedrich Schlegel*, and his celebrated treatise on the language and wisdom of the Indians,[8] in which Schlegel had urged the study of the grammatical structure of languages to determine their affiliation, Bopp set out to do in the field of morphology what his Danish colleague had done for comparative phonology. His book on the system of conjugation in Sanskrit[9] is a comparative study of Sanskrit, Greek, Latin, Persian, and Germanic verb inflections in which he not only attempts to show that in their earlier stages these languages have similar verb inflections but also seeks the ultimate origin of the inflectional elements of verbs. Bopp seems to have been obsessed with the idea that many verbs contain some form of the verb *to be*, that is, some form of the Sanskrit verbal roots *as* and *bhu* (two forms of the auxiliary) as, for instance, in the Latin *ibō* 'I will go,' which consists of three parts—namely, the root *i* 'go,' the verbal suffix *b* 'will' (Sanskrit *bhu*), and the personal ending *ō* 'I.' Although restricting himself to the study of the origins of the conjugational system, Bopp may be said to have taken the first step toward a truly comparative grammar of the Indo-European languages. He was to achieve this goal in his subsequent three-volume comparative grammar of Sanskrit, Zend, Greek, Latin, Lithuanian, Gothic, and German, published between 1833 and 1852.[10] In subsequent editions he added Old Slavic, Celtic, and Albanian to this list.

GRIMM'S "LAW"

The third great name of this period, and one of particular interest for students of Germanic languages, is Jacob Grimm, the elder of the Grimm brothers who have delighted millions of children and adults with their fairy tales. Building upon and expanding the information gained from Rask, Grimm published, between 1819 and 1837, a monumental German grammar[11] which, however, goes far beyond the scope of a grammar of the German language. In fact, the title is rather misleading, since it

192   introduction to the principles of language

is a comparative analysis of the sound and grammatical structures of the Germanic group of languages, that is, Gothic (the oldest one of the group on record), Dutch, English, Frisian,[12] German, and the Scandinavian languages (Icelandic, Danish, Swedish, and Norwegian). His systematic account of the regular correspondences of certain consonants in the Germanic and other Indo-European languages, like Sanskrit, Greek, and Latin, is still the best known of all such descriptions of sound correspondences within the Indo-European group. It has since come to be known as GRIMM'S LAW. Roughly speaking, it could be formulated as follows:

1. Where the Indo-European parent language has the *voiceless stops* [p], [t], and [k] as reflected in Greek and Latin, the Germanic cognates (represented by English, for example) have the *voiceless fricatives* [f], [θ], and [h]: Latin *pater*–English *father*; Latin *tres*–English *three*; Latin *cord(em)*–English *heart*; Latin *centum*–English *hundred*; and so forth.
2. Where the Indo-European parent language has the *voiced stops* [b], [d], and [g] (also preserved in Greek and Latin), the Germanic cognates have the *voiceless stops* [p], [t], and [k]: Latin *labium*–English *lip*; Latin *dent(em)*–English *tooth*; Latin *edo*–English *eat*; Latin *genus*–English *kin*; Latin *jugum*–English *yoke*; and so forth.
3. Where the Indo-European parent language has the aspirated *voiced stops* [bʰ], [dʰ], and [gʰ] (partially preserved in Sanskrit but turning into aspirated [pʰ], [tʰ], and [kʰ] there and into [f], [f], and [h] in Latin), the Germanic cognates have the *voiced stops* [b], [d], and [g]: Sanskrit *bhárami* (Latin *fero*)–English *bear*; Sanskrit *bhrāta* (Latin *frater*)–English *brother*; Sanskrit *dha*–English *do*; Sanskrit *rudhiras*–English *red*; Sanskrit *hansas* (where [gʰ] has become [h])–English *goose*; and so forth.

As we have seen, Rask had already established similar correspondences, but he applied them primarily to the Scandinavian languages. Grimm extended these principles to the Germanic languages in general. By studying the historical evolution of the Germanic consonant system, he focused attention on the systematic *shifts*—what he called the *Lautverschiebung*—that had occurred in this system with respect to other Indo-European languages. His "law" implies, in fact, that during a given period, generally thought to have lasted several centuries somewhere between 600 B.C. and 100 B.C., a regular sound shift took place throughout a group of prehistoric Indo-European speakers known as the Germanic group,[13] whereby [p]'s turned into [f]'s, [t]'s turned into [θ]'s, [k]'s into [h]'s, and so forth.

The causes of these changes are not known. It has been suggested that they may have been due to the contact of Germanic tribes with non-Germanic populations, that is, to a non-Germanic *substratum*.[14] Whatever the causes, the Germanic sound shift (also called the "first sound shift" for reasons that will presently become apparent) is probably the most distinctive of the features that set off the Germanic languages from their cognates in the Indo-European group of languages.

Grimm's comparative survey of the phonological and structural characteristics of the Germanic group of languages subsequently revealed another sound shift, this time within the so-called *West Germanic* subgroup.[15] This phonetic change is said to have occurred around the sixth century A.D., bringing about a division into the *Low Germanic* and *High Germanic* dialects, according to the elevation above sea level where each was spoken. The Low Germanic dialects (the ancestors of modern English, Frisian, Dutch, and Flemish), spoken in the lowlands along the seacoast, retained the consonant structure of common Germanic, as attested in Gothic; while the High Germanic dialects, spoken in the mountainous regions of central and southern Germany, Austria, and Switzerland, underwent a change in the pronunciation of certain consonants. This second, or High German, sound shift, as it is customarily referred to (*zweite Lautverschiebung* in Grimm's terminology), may be roughly summarized as follows:

1. In initial position, that is, at the beginning of a word, and after a consonant, the Germanic *voiceless stops* [p], [t], and [k] became the *voiceless affricates* [pf], [ts], and [kx]: English *pound*–German *Pfund*; English *apple*–German *Apfel*; English *tale*–German *Zahl*; English *heart*–German *Herz*; Old English *cū* (pronounced [ku])–Old High German *chō* (pronounced [kxo]);[16] Old English *cnēo* (pronounced [kneo]) 'knee'–Old High German *chniu*; and so forth.

2. When occurring between vowels or at the end of a word (preceded by a vowel), Germanic [p], [t], and [k] became the *voiceless fricatives* [f], [s], and [x]: English *ape*–German *Affe*; English *sleep*–German *Schlaf*; English *water*–German *Wasser*; English *foot*–German *Fuss*; English *make*–German *machen* (pronounced [maxən]); and so forth.

No one knows how long this second sound shift took, but it must have been completed by the eighth century. In any event, this cleavage within the West Germanic subbranch had been consummated by the time the first records in Old English and Old High German appeared.

Grimm's systematic exposition of these consonant correspondences between Germanic and other Indo-European languages set the tone of research in historical and comparative linguistics for future generations of scholars. As a result of a later supplement to his "law" to account for apparent exceptions in the regularity of correspondences, it became evident that sound change is not random and haphazard but follows certain patterns. Rask himself had already noted that in word-medial position the Latin [t], as in *pater*, showed up as a [ð] in Old Norse, as in *faðir*, rather than as the expected [θ], as in *þrir* 'three,' which corresponds to Latin *tres*. About half a century after Grimm's principles of sound correspondences had been laid down, the Danish scholar Karl Verner explained this and similar irregularities[17] by pointing out that the Indo-European [p], [t], and [k] became voiceless fricatives in this position only when the accent in the Indo-European root word (the accent having survived in Sanskrit) fell on the syllable immediately preceding the sound in question; otherwise, the consonant would be voiced. Thus, Old Norse *faðir* and Old English *fæder* are both quite regular in their correspondence with Sanskrit *pitá*. In the same way English *hundred* (rather than *hunthred*, which would correspond to Latin *centum*) represents a regular correspondence because of the place of the accent in Sanskrit *śatám*.[18]

This exception to the first sound shift, or VERNER'S LAW, as it has come to be known, may seem somewhat technical, but it is essential to an understanding of the developments in linguistic research in the latter part of the nineteenth century. By seeking a scientifically verifiable explanation for deviations in Grimm's law, Verner not only justified the claim of regularity in sound changes that this "law" had purported to establish, but he was also instrumental in setting the stage for a whole new school of linguistics in the 1870s, known as the Neo-Grammarians.

THE RECONSTRUCTION OF INDO-EUROPEAN

In the meantime the studies and systematic comparisons made by Rask, Grimm, and Bopp had cleared the way for a comprehensive comparative study of the Indo-European languages. In 1861 *August Schleicher*, one of the best methodologists of nineteenth-century historico-comparative linguistics, published his 'Compendium of the Comparative Grammar of the Indo-European Languages,'[19] in which he turned his attention particularly to the problem of *reconstructing* the Indo-European parent language. He even composed a short text in this hypothetical language and initiated the practice of marking reconstructed forms not attested in written documents with an asterisk (*).[20]

Let us see how such a reconstruction is arrived at. The methodology consists of putting side by side the earliest attested forms available for all languages that appear to be related and to reconstruct, on the basis of these forms, the unrecorded hypothetical form from which they must have developed. Two examples will illustrate this point.

1. The words that correspond to English *mother* appear in their *earliest* attested forms as follows:

Sanskrit	Iranian	Greek	Latin
matá	*mātar*	*mētēr*	*māter*
Irish	Armenian	English	Slavic
mathir	*mair*	*mōdor*	*mati* (gen. *matere*)

On the basis of the external resemblance of these forms to one another and their identical meaning, the conclusion seems inescapable that these are all divergent developments of an Indo-European root word presumed to have been something like **mātēr*.

2. Or take the following series of words, which all share the meaning "ten":

Sanskrit	Iranian	Greek	Latin
dā́śa	dasa	déka	decem

Irish	Armenian	Gothic	Slavic
deich	tasn	taíhun	deset

Comparison of these forms has led to the conclusion that the Indo-European numeral must have had the form *dékm̥.

In a similar fashion Schleicher and his fellow Indo-Europeanists have also been able to reconstruct grammatical forms. Here is an example involving two forms of the verb *to be*, the third persons singular and plural of the present tense.

	Sanskrit	Greek	Latin	Irish	Gothic	Slavic
'he is'	ásti	estí	est	is	ist	jestŭ
'they are'	sánti	eisí	sunt	it	sind	sǫtŭ

From this table it can be deduced that the third person singular form in Indo-European was marked by a final -*t* and that the third person plural ended in -*nt*.

THE GENEALOGY OF LANGUAGES

Schleicher was very much influenced by the Darwinian theory of evolution, which had revolutionized the biological sciences around the middle of the nineteenth century. He conceived of language as a living organism that develops in accordance with the biological laws of evolution, independently of man. Thus, a language is born, it lives for a time, and then it "gives birth" to another language, which eventually replaces it. The new language, in turn, undergoes the same life cycle, from birth to decay, that is characteristic of all creatures of nature. This concept of language led Schleicher to propose his "genealogical tree" theory, in which he likened the relationship between the Indo-European languages and the parent stock to a family tree. It is generally known by the German name of STAMMBAUM-THEORIE. Schleicher's genealogical model affords a convenient means of showing the historical relationships among the individual languages descended from the Indo-European parent language, although it is generally recognized that genetic relationships among languages cannot be charted the way one would chart a family pedigree. As R. H. Robins has pointed out,

> Languages do not sharply split at a given point in time corresponding to the division of a line in the tree; the splitting process begins subdialectally and proceeds through increasing dialectal divergence until the assumption of two or more distinct languages is warranted. This is a lengthy and gradual process, and the point at which each stage is reached must remain arbitrary.[21]

Schleicher's concept of language as a natural organism is no longer accepted by linguists. Languages are neither born nor do they decay; languages merely change. On the other hand, it is one of his great merits to have focused attention on the living languages at a time when the spotlight was turned on "dead" languages like ancient Sanskrit, Greek, and Latin, and the study of languages was strictly historical. Schleicher drew attention especially to Lithuanian, which because of its archaic structural features and the fact that it was a living language, offered even better possibilities for the reconstruction of Indo-European than did Sanskrit.

A similar proposal to study living languages had already been made by the great German philosopher and linguist *Wilhelm von Humboldt*, whose research in non-Indo-European languages, particularly his study of the *Kawi* language from the Island of Java,[22] opened up a whole new field of linguistic study. Humboldt, who is considered by some to be the greatest linguistic theoretician of the nineteenth century, was particularly interested in gathering and interpreting linguistic data taken from languages at a given point in time. Because of this *synchronic* approach to language study, as opposed to the essentially *diachronic* approach of his contemporaries, Humboldt may justly be considered a forerunner of modern descriptive linguistics. Among his many other contributions to linguistic theory, his typological classification of languages into isolating, agglutinative, and flexional languages (see Chapter 4, page 66ff.) and his study of the relationship between linguistic structure and patterns of thought have had lasting influence.[23]

While the work on the comparison of Indo-European languages was going on, there appeared a number of treatises concerned with individual branches of the Indo-European group. Under the influence of Grimm's grammar, *Friedrich Diez* began the publication of his grammar of the Romance languages in three volumes,[24] subsequently brought up-to-date by one of the greatest names in the field of Romance studies, *Wilhelm Meyer-Lübke*.[25] The advent of Romance philology, which had preceded Schleicher's work by about two decades, was of great help to comparativists because it made available abundant documentation on the ancestor of the Romance tongues, Latin, and made it possible to confirm reconstructed forms by those found in written texts.[26] For instance, the corresponding words for English *night* in the major Romance languages are French *nuit*, Italian *notte*, Spanish *noche*, Portuguese *noite*, Rumanian *noapte*, and Sardinian *notte*. If now, in accordance with normal sound changes, we postulate a Latin form *noctem*,[27] we shall find that it happens to be identical with the word found in written documents.

Other important comparative grammars of individual Indo-European languages were that of *Johann Kaspar Zeuss* on the Celtic languages, published in 1853 and entitled *Gramatica celtica* because it was written in Latin, and the four-volume work on the Slavic languages (*Vergleichende Grammatik der slavischen Sprachen*) by *Franz von Miklosich*, published in 1852–1876. Under the impetus of Humboldt, there also appeared, around the third quarter of the century, the first scientifically formulated studies of non-Indo-European languages, such as those of *W. H. Bleek* on the Bantu languages, *J. K. Bushmann* on the Malayo-Polynesian and some American Indian languages, *Mattis A. Castren* and *W. Schott* on the Ural-Altaic languages, and *K. R. Lepsius* on the Sino-Tibetan languages, to mention some of the most important ones.

THE NEO-GRAMMARIAN SCHOOL

The publication of Karl Verner's essay on the exception to the first sound shift opened up a new era of linguistic research, concerned with the application without-exception of phonological "laws" derived from the regular phonetic correspondences already observed by Rask and Grimm. Research on the various groups of the Indo-European family yielded ever-increasing evidence of a discernible pattern underlying sound change. Prompted by Verner's conviction that even exceptions to the rule are subject to rules, a group of young German scholars who have come to be known as the NEO-GRAMMARIANS set out to discover what these rules are. In the course of the mid- 1870s, this group, headed by *August Leskien, Karl Brugman,* and *Herman Osthoff,* formulated the theory that sound changes operate mechanically, in accordance with laws which admit of no exceptions, and that, furthermore, these laws have the same consistency as those of the physical sciences. Accordingly, in all the words of a given language or dialect, the same sound in the same phonetic context will have undergone the same change during a certain period of time. For instance, when it is found that the stressed long /ā/ of Old English *hām* changes to /ow/ in modern English *home,* the same development may be expected in other Old English words that have survived in modern English. Thus, Old English *bān, bāt, fām, hāl, rād,* and *stān* become in modern English *bone, boat, foam, whole, road,* and *stone.*

This thesis of the absolute regularity of phonetic "laws" was very much in keeping with the concept of the universality of natural laws that nineteenth-century scientists had developed as a result of advances in the natural sciences. Under bitter attack by various linguists who denied the cogency of these sound "laws" and insisted on the conscious role of the individual speaker in language change rather than the inevitability of change beyond the speaker's control, the Neo-Grammarians modified their stand. In particular, they recognized two factors that could account for anomalous developments and deviations from regular phonetic change: *loanwords* from other languages or dialects and *analogy.*

A good example of an apparent exception due to the influence of a borrowed word is modern English *kitchen,* Old English *cycena* [kykena]. The Latin word for it is *coquina,* and at first sight one might think that the English and Latin words are cognates. However, according to Grimm's Law, Latin [k] occurs as [h] in English, so that *kitchen* would appear to be an exception. Actually, the English word is a borrowing from Latin, and it is even possible to ascertain that it took place when the first sound shift had already run its course.

Analogy, or analogical creation, is an essentially psychological process in which there is interference with a sound change in a *analogy* — linguistic form from a related form with which it is subconsciously associated. It is a process, in other words, whereby a form is pulled out of its normal development to be brought into line with some existing pattern that, for some reason, has become particularly strong. Analogy may operate on all levels of language—phonology, morphology, syntax, and semantics. A few examples chosen at random will suffice to illustrate this process.

1. Consider the English word *grief*. It is a borrowing from Old French *grief*, an adjective meaning 'heavy, painful,' which, in turn, represents a development from the Vulgar Latin **grĕvis*, (which alone could have resulted in a diphthong in Old French) rather than the attested Latin form *gravis* with the same meaning (compare English *grave* 'serious'). The change from Latin *gravis* to **grĕvis* is said to have occurred by analogy with the Latin antonym *lĕvis* 'light.'
2. The English plural form *days* is an irregular historical development. The Old English form *dagas* (singular *dæg*) would have become something like **daws* (compare Old English *dagian*, which became Modern English *dawn*) had it gone through the normal sound change. However, at one point the ancestors of the speakers of Modern English rebuilt the plural *days* on the basis of the singular root *day*, by analogy with the numerous plural formations of the *boy–boys*, *girl–girls*, *table–tables*, type.
3. Analogical creation is also responsible for the kind of change that occurs when a child or untutored adult says **foots* for *feet*, **oxes* for *oxen*, **breaked* for *broke*, and **sticked* for *stuck*. The process involved is rather clear. On the analogy of countless regular formations like *hats*, *boxes*, *raked*, and *licked*, the speaker has brought *foot*, *ox*, *break*, and *stick* into line with what he considers to be the general pattern of plural and past tense formations. These kinds of creations have sometimes been represented by proportional formulas that purport to illustrate what may go on in the speaker's conscious or unconscious mind, as in the following example,

    box : boxes :: ox : ×
    lick : licked :: stick : ×

where × represents the new analogical formation.

The absolute regularity in the physiological mechanism of phonetic "laws," coupled with the new insights into the psychological process of analogy, completely revolutionized linguists' assumptions concerning the nature of human language. The hypothesis of regularity in language change has become a generally accepted postulate in twentieth-century linguistic thinking; hence, it is fair to state that the basic tenets of the Neo-Grammarian position are still regarded as a methodological requirement for historical linguistic research.[28]

THE REGULARITY OF LINGUISTIC CHANGE

Constant change both in time and space is a universal characteristic of any living language. Meanings, vocabulary, grammar, and, of course, sounds change. Nothing in language stands still until a particular language is no longer spoken. At that point it has become a "dead" language like classical Sanskrit, Greek, and Latin, which now exist only in written records. But although these languages no longer change in sound, grammar, and vocabulary, because they are no longer in the mouths of living people, in a sense Sanskrit, Greek and Latin, as well as other languages no longer spoken, never died. In the course of time, they were transformed, like the Latin of the Romans, which continues its existence in French, Spanish, Italian, Portuguese, Rumanian, and other Romance languages and dialects. Almost all the languages of Europe developed from a single parent language spoken some 5000 or so years ago.

How do changes come about? They follow a pattern, as we have seen, and do not, generally speaking, occur randomly. Since language is a system of oppositions in which the parts depend on one another, a change in one part of the system will normally trigger a change in another part. Thus when some final vowels in spoken Latin began to merge, so that subject and object could no longer be distinguished on the basis of word endings, a syntactic reorganization took place whereby the position of the subject and object with respect to the verb became fixed (subject–verb–object), as opposed to the rather loose word order of classical Latin (subject–object–verb; object–verb–subject; verb–object–subject, and so forth).

A shift in one sound may also trigger a whole chain reaction within the phonological system of a language. This can be illustrated in English by what is known as the GREAT VOWEL SHIFT, which affected all stressed long vowels in the Middle English (ME) period (that is, sometime between Chaucer and Shakespeare). Roughly speaking, all long vowels came to be pronounced with greater elevation of the tongue which means that except for those that could not be raised any further, namely /i/ and /u/, they were all raised in the same direction, toward a higher point of articulation. The process may be illustrated as follows:

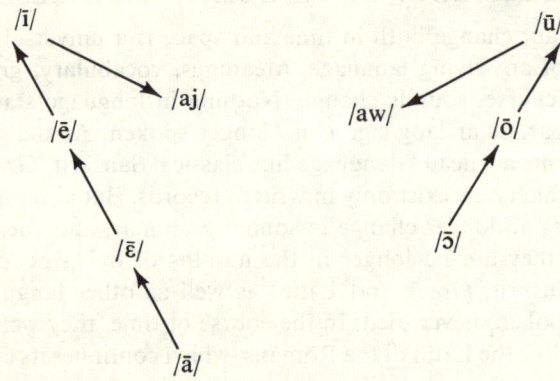

As ME /ā/ in /namə/ 'name' displaced ME /ɛ̄/ in /klɛn/ 'clean,' the latter, in turn, knocked out ME /ē/ in /med/, 'meed,' which moved into the area of ME /ī/ in /win/ 'wine.' Since the high front vowel could not move any higher without becoming consonantal, it broke up into the diphthong /aj/. The same shift also occurred in the back vowel series; ME /ɔ̄/ in /stɔnə/ 'stone' (which had already shifted to this sound from Old English /ā/ in *stāna*) moved into the position of ME /ō/ in /gos/ 'goose,' which, in turn, displaced ME /ū/ in /hus/ 'house.' The latter, paralleling the development of ME /ī/, also turned into a diphthong. Through subsequent shifts, ME /ā/ moved again, to /ē/, and ME /ɛ̄/ to /ī/. These changes did not, of course, take place in successive stages, as the arrows might suggest, but as part of a general vocalic movement that eventually resulted in the Modern English system of stressed vowels.

There is no easy explanation of the *causes* of such change.

Attempts to correlate sound change with, for instance, climate, way of life, or other environmental factors, or with racial mixture or the physiological structure of the speech organs, have remained unproven. The factor of prestige, that is, the imitation of the speech habits of people whom we happen to look up to, has also often been invoked, and so have imperfect hearing and reproduction of the older generation's speech by the younger generation. But whatever the underlying causes may be, linguistic and social factors are closely interrelated in the process of language change, which thus becomes an inevitable consequence of social cooperation and interaction.[29] Each generation that learns a language brings changes to it that are more or less significant. It is the sum total of these changes viewed in a historical perspective of scores of generations that has created a gulf between, say, French and Latin, though they represent one and the same language at two different stages of its history, much in the same way that a nonagenarian is the same person he was at the age of twenty except for the inevitable transformations brought about by the passing of years.

These then, in summary, were the major concerns of the great century of historical research: (1) the development of the comparative method, which led to the establishment of language relationships and the reconstruction of the Indo-European parent language, and (2) the study of how languages change. Thanks to the rigorous methodology worked out by nineteenth-century scholars, it became apparent that a number of diverse languages had, indeed, at one time been *one* language and that differences had come about through subsequent diverging developments. It would seem quite appropriate, therefore, that we should devote our last chapter to a discussion of the known language families of the world, particularly the Indo-European family, which to this day remains the one that has been the most thoroughly studied and reconstructed and has yielded the most information about linguistic change.

notes

1. R. H. Robins, *A Short History of Linguistics*. Bloomington: Indiana University Press, 1967, pp. 76–77.
2. John T. Waterman, *Perspectives in Linguistics*. Chicago: The University of Chicago Press, 1963, p. 12.
3. Parallels between the approach of the Port-Royal grammar and that of contemporary linguists have been drawn by Noam Chomsky, particularly with regard to the *deep structure* of languages, as opposed to variations in the *surface structure*. See his *Cartesian Linguistics*. New York: Harper & Row, 1966. For a discussion of specific universals in the fields of morphology and syntax, consult Joseph H. Greenberg, ed., *Universals of Language*. Cambridge, Mass.: M.I.T. Press, 1963.
4. The word is *sì* (from Latin *sic*) in Italian, *oc* (from Latin *hoc*) in *Provençal* (southern France), and *oïl* (from Latin *hoc ille*) in French (northern France). Hence the division of the two main linguistic areas of France, the *langue d'oïl*, northern French, and the *langue d'oc*, southern French.
5. Robins, *op. cit.*, p. 167.
6. *Undersögelse om det Gamle Nordiske eller Islandske Sprogs Oprindelse* (published in 1818).
7. Quoted in Waterman, *op. cit.*, p. 19.
8. *Ueber die Sprache und Weisheit der Indier* (published in 1808).
9. *Ueber das Conjugationssystem der Sanskritsprache* (published in 1816).
10. *Vergleichende Grammatik des Sanskrit, Zend, Griechischen, Litthauischen, Gothischen und Deutschen.*
11. *Deutsche Grammatik.*
12. Frisian, once the language of a Germanic tribe in northern Holland, is now limited to the Frisian Islands off the coast of the Netherlands and Germany. Of all the Germanic languages, Frisian is the most closely related to English.

13. For further information about this hypothetical speech community, see Chapter 12.
14. The technical term *substratum* is used to designate a population that takes over a new language, as a result either of conquest or of colonization, but keeps its old speech habits in learning the new language, thus modifying its sounds and, sometimes, its grammatical structure. The substratum factor has often been considered responsible for certain linguistic changes in the new language, and many scholars have insisted on its importance in phonetic evolution in particular. For example, it has been held that certain phonetic features in modern French, such as the passage of Latin /u/ in *luna* to French /y/ in *lune*, are due to the Gaulish substratum in the Latin brought to Gaul by Ceasar's legions.
15. It is customary to distinguish three subdivisions within the Germanic branch of Indo-European, namely the *Eastern* (represented by Gothic), the *Northern* (represented by Old Norse and its modern Scandinavian descendants), and the *Western* (represented by English, Frisian, Dutch, German, and their respective dialects). This split within unrecorded common Germanic seems to have occurred before the fourth century A.D., since it was an accomplished fact by the time the first document in a Germanic language appeared—Bishop Wulfila's fourth-century translation of the Bible.
16. The initial [k] sound has been restored in modern German. The fricative element still survives in some Swiss German dialects in which, for instance, the German word *Kuh* 'cow' is pronounced [kxuə], and even [xuə].
17. In an important essay published in 1875, entitled *Eine Ausnahme der erstein Lautverschiebung* ('An Exception to the First Consonant Shift').
18. The Indo-European [k] (which occurs in Greek and Latin) developed into a sibilant sound in Sanskrit (probably a palatal sibilant [š]). This same development also occurred in Iranian (*satem*), Slavic (*sto*), and Lithuanian (*šim̃tas*). The difference in treatment of the original velar stop has led to the division of Indo-European languages into a *centum* group and a *satem* group, corresponding to what must have been a prehistoric division into a western and an eastern branch.
19. *Compendium der vergleichenden Grammatik der indogermanischen Sprachen* (published in 1861–1862).
20. Linguists also use an asterisk to show that a form or construction is not acceptable.

21. Robins, *op. cit.*, p. 179.
22. *Ueber die Kawisprache auf der Insel Java* (published in 1836–1840).
23. His ideas on this subject are summed up in his monumental *Ueber die Verschiedenheit des menschlichen Sprachbaues und ihren Einfluss auf die geistige Entwicklung des Menschengeschlechtes* ('Concerning the Diversity of Linguistic Structure and Its Influence on the Intellectual Development of the Human Race'), first published in 1836 and reissued in 1949. Humboldt's theory of the relationship between language and thought was reformulated during this century by Benjamin Lee Whorf (see Chapter 8, page 137), while this insistence on the creative ability of the speaker has become one of the cornerstones of contemporary linguistic thought.
24. *Grammatik der romanischen Sprachen* (published in 1836–1843).
25. *Grammatik der romanischen Sprachen*, 3 volumes (published in 1890–1902).
26. The Neo-Latin, or Romance, languages derive not from classical Latin as it is recorded in the works of Cicero and Virgil but rather from the *spoken* Latin of generations of Romans. Like any other human speech, it underwent inevitable changes and transformations.
27. It is a convention among Romance linguists normally to derive Romance noun forms from the Latin *accusative* rather than the *nominative*; hence the form *noctem*, and not *nox*.
28. The validity of the concept of analogy as an alternative to exceptionless sound "laws" has recently been questioned. See Uriel Weinreich, William Labov, and Marvin Herzog, "Empirical Foundations for a Theory of Language Change," *Directions for Historical Linguistics,* edited by W. P. Lehmann and Yakov Malkiel. Austin: University of Texas Press, 1968, pp. 97–188.
29. See William Labov, "The Social Motivation of a Sound Change," *Word*, 19 (December 1963), 273–309.

12
indo-european and non-indo-european languages

INDO-EUROPEAN LANGUAGES

About five or six thousand years ago, as many scholars now think, somewhere in northern Europe, around the shores of the Baltic Sea, there lived a group of men who spoke a common tongue. As this group broke up and wandered off to such widespread places as Iceland and northern India, the members lost touch with one another. Their once common speech began to develop differences until, finally, a number of different speech forms emerged. How this occurred in every case we, of course, do not know, but the expansion must have begun in earliest historical times, since by the time people got around to recording an Indo-European tongue, the parent language had already changed radically. The oldest extant record of an Indo-European language that has come down to us is written in the language of the Vedas of ancient India, in so-called *Vedic Sanskrit*, and dates back to about 1500 to 2000 B.C.

Just who were these Indo-European speakers? By studying words that are common to a number of the languages presumed to belong to the Indo-European language group, we are able to get some idea of the culture these people may have had before their language broke up into separate tongues as a result of migrations many millennia ago. We may surmise that a word which occurs in a large number of the languages said to be descended from Indo-European must have designated an object or a concept with which these speakers were familiar. Common roots found in most of the Indo-European languages suggest that they were seminomadic, small-scale farmers. They kept domesticated animals like *dogs, cows, sheep, pigs,* and *horses,* and they used words having to do with the *plow*, *spade*, and *sickle*, and with *sowing*, *mowing*, and *grinding*. They used *arrows* and *axes* for tools and weapons, but it is interesting to note that we cannot find any word for *iron* (though we find roots for *gold*, *silver*, and even *ore*), which leads us to the conclusion that this metal must have been a later discovery. Words for *wheel*, *axle*, *yoke* seem to point to the use of a most efficient tool—the *wagon* or *cart*. Among the names of plants, we find the *birch*, *beech*, *oak*, *willow*, and *ash* trees and we also find terms for wild animals like the *bear*, the *wolf*, and the *fox*. On the other hand, Indo-European roots for *palm*, *olive*, *vice*, *laurel*, *tiger*, *elephant*, *lion*, and *leopard* are missing and it is essentially on the basis of this negative evidence surrounding the names of plants and animals that a temperate climate has been suggested as the original habitat of the Indo-Europeans, the more so, since they seem to have known both rain and snow.

There is also a large common Indo-European vocabulary for family relationships, the word for *daughter-in-law* being especially widespread in the descendant languages. This would seem to point to a patriarchal family structure founded on marriage—that is, a custom whereby the wife married into her husband's family, while the husband acquired no official relationship to his wife's family.

It is more than likely that prehistoric Indo-European swept away many earlier languages in Europe and Asia; by the same token, Indo-European languages did not survive everywhere and we do not really know how many of them may have become extinct in the course of history. From scraps of written records we know of at least two major branches that disappeared—*Hittite* and *Tocharian*.

Hittite, a language spoken by a people frequently referred to in the Bible (the Empire of the Hittites), is known through cuneiform inscriptions that probably date back to between the nineteenth and thirteenth centuries B.C. The texts in this language, discovered early this century in Turkey, clearly establish its Indo-European affiliation.

Tocharian, represented by fragmentary texts of a medical and religious nature, was also discovered early this century, as a result of explorations in Chinese Turkestan. It is said to have still been spoken in the seventh century A.D. Although the manuscripts found in a Buddhist monastery are not very copious, nevertheless, scholars have been able to determine an Indo-European parentage.

Of the eight surviving groups, the *Indo-Iranian* is the oldest for which we have written evidence. It consists of the *Indian* and *Iranian* subgroups. *Sanskrit*, the oldest surviving language of the Indo-European group and the oldest form of the languages of Northern India, survives in the sacred writings of Hinduism, the *Vedas*. This form of Sanskrit, one of the great liturgical languages of recorded history, is often called *Vedic Sanskrit*, to differentiate it from later *classical Sanskrit* of the great verse epics, the *Mahabharata* and *Ramayana*. The first known grammar of any language, you will remember, is a grammar of classical Sanskrit written by *Pāṇini* in the fourth century B.C. It is still used today by students of this language. Side by side with these literary forms, there also existed spoken varieties, just as there are spoken varieties of English along with the literary, written language. These languages are collectively called *Prākrits* and have survived in the modern vernaculars of millions of Indians who speak *Hindi*, the leading tongue of India, *Urdu*, the official language of *Pakistan*, *Bengali*, *Punjabi*, and *Mahrati*, to name some of the most important ones. What we call *Hindustani*, which is numerically the third of the world's languages, is really a combination of Urdu and Hindi, a kind of *lingua franca* used throughout Northern India.

An interesting spoken variety of the Indian languages is the language of the *Gypsies* (also called *Romany*), spoken in Northwestern India. Because of the wanderlust of these people, this language has spread to many lands, where it has been greatly influenced by the languages of the countries where the gypsies settled.

In its earlier form, called *Old Iranian*, the Iranian subgroup has come down to us in two varieties, *Old Persian* and *Avestan* or *Zend*. The former is known through cuneiform inscriptions dating back to the time of Darius and Xerxes (about sixth century B.C.), while the latter represents the language of the holy books of Zoroaster, the founder of the ancient religion of the Persians, who probably lived around the seventh century B.C. Avestan left no descendants. *Modern Persian*, whose vocabulary is strongly influenced by Arabic, is a development of old Persian through a Middle Persian stage known as *Pahlavi*. This tongue appears in history around the eighth century A.D. and is the vehicle of a rich literature.

Armenian, which is now recognized as an independent branch of Indo-European, is spoken by about four million people around the borderline of Asia and Europe, in the southern Caucasus mountains area, to be exact, between the Black and Caspian Seas. In addition, there are many settlements of Armenians who use their mother tongue in other parts of the world, including the United States. This language, first recorded in a Bible translation of the fifth century A.D., was formerly that of an independent country which is now a republic of the USSR.

Greek has had a continuous literary record from the eighth century B.C. down to this day. In ancient times, because of the influence of Greece in Asia Minor and the numerous Greek colonies along the shores of the Black Sea and the Mediterranean, Greek was subdivided into several important dialects. Among these, *Attic*, the language of Athens, and *Ionic*, the language of Homer, are the best known because of their distinguished literary history. With the great prestige that Athens came to assume as a result of political and literary supremacy, the Attic dialect developed into a common language, a *koiné*, which became the standard language of all Greeks and eventually displaced all other ancient dialects. *Modern Greek*, both the standard language and local dialects, derive from Attic. It is worth noting, however, that the development of a modern literary standard, properly "purified" with a considerable number of words from ancient Greek, is of comparatively recent vintage. This has led to a kind of double standard: a *literary* standard, which has also become the language of the upper classes, and a *colloquial* standard, which is the spoken language of the masses.

Albanian, like Armenian, is another small and isolated branch, spoken by about one and a half million people in Albania (on the east coast of the Adriatic Sea) and in some settlements of Greece, southern Italy, and North America. Its early literature, consisting mainly of folk-songs, dates from the seventeenth century. The vocabulary of Albanian shows a large number of words borrowed from Latin, Greek, Turkish, Slavic, and Italian.

A common ancestory closer to Indo-European is assumed for the *Balto-Slavic* group, although the relationship between the Baltic and Slavic languages is rather remote. In the first subgroup belong *Lithuanian*, *Lettish* (or *Latvian*), and *Prussian*, the latter still spoken in the seventeenth century before the state of Prussia became predominant in the German Empire. The Old Prussian language is now extinct. *Lithuanian*, an especially interesting language because, like Sanskrit and Classical Greek, it has preserved some archaic forms that are lost in related languages, as well as *Lettish*, are still spoken in the area of the formerly independent countries of Lithuania and Latvia. Both are now part of the Soviet Union.

The *Slavic* languages fall into three large groups:

1. *East Slavic*, which includes Russian, the official language of the USSR, *Ukrainian*, spoken in the Ukraine in southern Russia, and so-called *White-* or *Byelorussian*, spoken in a region to the North of the Ukraine, which comprises the cities of Minsk and Smolensk.
2. *West Slavic*, which consists of *Czech*, the official language of Czechoslovakia, *Slovak*, a variant of the former and an important minority language in this country, and *Polish*, the native tongue of about twenty-five million people and the language of a rich literature reaching back to the fourteenth century. It may be of interest to note that about three million Polish speakers and their descendants are located in the United States, mostly in the mining and industrial centers of Pennsylvania, Illinois, Ohio, and Michigan.
3. *South Slavic*, comprising *Bulgarian*, spoken in Bulgaria by about eight million people, *Serbo-Croatian*, the language of about twelve million Serbs and Croats who live chiefly in Yugoslavia, and *Slovenian*, spoken by about one and a half million people in the Alpine regions of the Slavic area and also the extreme northeast of Italy and the border districts of Austria.

The oldest Slavic dialect on record belongs to this last subgroup. It is represented by a translation of the Bible and goes by the name of *Old Bulgarian* or *Old Church Slavonic*, as it is sometimes called. In general, it can be said that the Slavic group is more homogeneous and far less differentiated than any other Indo-European group of languages.

Long before the start of the Christian era, *Celtic* languages were spoken over extensive parts of central and western Europe, Ireland, and Great Britain. They even reached into Asia Minor, as evidenced by the Apostle Paul's letter to the Galatians. The oldest Celtic language on record is *Gaulish*, spoken in Gaul (roughly what is France today) until it completely gave way to the Latin language brought to Gaul by the Roman conquerors. Except for a host of place and personal names, Gaulish disappeared by about the third century A.D.

The insular branch of Celtic in Ireland and Great Britain has partially survived in modern tongues like *Welsh*, the language of Wales, *Breton*, still spoken in Brittany (Northern France), where it was carried by fugitive Britons around the fifth and sixth centuries A.D., and *Scots-Gaelic* and *Irish*, which boasts of one of the richest literatures of the Middle Ages. Welsh, Breton, and the now extinct *Cornish*, once spoken in Cornwall, together form the *Brythonic* branch of Celtic, while the Gaelic of Ireland and Scotland and a variant called *Manx* (spoken by a few hundred people on the Isle of Man between northern Ireland and England) make up the *Goidelic* branch.

The oldest record of *Italic* is an inscription on a buckle dating back to the seventh century B.C., which reads *Manios medfhefhaked Numasioi* "Manius made me for Numerius." This group, which had made the Italian Peninsula its homeland, falls into two main divisions: *Latin-Faliscan* and *Oscan-Umbrian*. Latin, originally the dialect of the small district of Latium which comprised the city of Rome, is, historically and as a vehicle of a rich and important literature, the most important language of the whole group. With the extension of the political power of Rome, Latin became the everyday language of a vast Empire and lives on in the form of the Romance languages. These include the following.

1. *Italian* and its numerous dialects spoken all over Italy, including Sicily and the island of Corsica.
2. *Rhaeto-Romance*, a group of dialects spoken in eastern Switzerland and northeastern Italy.
3. *French*, the national and literary language of France, in

addition to being one of two languages of Belgium and one of the four of Switzerland. It is also an official language in many former colonies and is used as a second language in other parts of the world.

4. *Provençal*, once the language of medieval troubadours and the medium of a flourishing literature, nowadays hardly more than a name given to a group of local southern French speech forms.
5. *Catalan*, a language rather closely akin to Provençal and also spoken in parts of southwestern France, also native to inhabitants of Catalonia in northeastern Spain, though considerably encroached upon by Spanish, which is the official language.
6. *Spanish*, the language of Spain and most of the countries south of the Rio Grande. Roughly speaking, it is divided into two main varieties, *Castilian*, the dialect of northern Spain and its capital, Madrid, and *Andalusian*, the dialect of the south, which is also largely the basis of the speech of the American Spanish-speaking areas.
7. *Portuguese*, the language of Portugal and Brazil, originally an offshoot of the *Gallego* dialect of the province of Galicia in northwestern Spain.
8. *Sardinian*, spoken on the island of Sardinia by a little over a million people. It is of special interest to the student of Romance languages because of its archaic and conservative features, which make it closest to Latin of all Romance varieties.
9. *Rumanian*, with about twenty million speakers who live, for the most part, on Rumanian soil. It is the smallest of the national Romance languages.
10. *Dalmatian*, once spoken on the coast of Dalmatia and the island of Veglia in the Adriatic. With the rather violent death of the last speaker of the language on this island (he died in a mine explosion), it became extinct.

English, German, Dutch, Swedish, Danish, Norwegian, and *Icelandic* make up the roster of the national languages of the *Germanic* group. Unfortunately, the speakers of what has come to be called *Primitive Germanic* have left no written records, so that any information about this branch of Indo-European must be reconstructed just like the parent language. From the time the first written records of the different Germanic languages appear, there is ample evidence of three distinct subgroups, the Eastern, the Northern, and the Western.

The only *East Germanic* language of which we have any remains is *Gothic*. What we do have is also the earliest literary monument in a Germanic language—a fragmentary translation of the Bible by Bishop Ulfilas in the fourth century A.D. This branch is now extinct.

Runic inscriptions found in Scandinavia, dating back to the third century A.D., attest to the existence of a language we call *Old Norse* or *Old Icelandic*. Subsequently, this language broke up into separate languages, of which *Icelandic, Norwegian, Swedish,* and *Danish* are the modern representatives, constituting the *North Germanic* branch. In the Middle Ages, Icelandic produced a flourishing literature, of which the songs of the Edda are important monuments of world literature. It may be of interest to mention that until fairly recently the Norwegian official and literary language (which had died out in the Middle Ages) was a form of Danish called *Riksmaal*, which was first used at the time of the political unification of Norway and Denmark in the late fourteenth century. This language, however, has been giving way to a truly standard national Norwegian, the *Landsmaal* or *Nynorsk*, which is based on indigenous Norwegian dialects.

The *West Germanic* languages are conventionally divided into *High* and *Low*, according to the different altitudes above sea level where these languages are spoken. The basis of this classification, as was seen in our discussion of "Grimm's law" (page 193), is the divergent treatment of consonants, whereby, for instance, Low German *t* appears as *z* (pronounced *ts*) in High German. Roughly speaking, *English*; *Frisian*, spoken in the Frisian islands off the coasts of the Netherlands and Germany; *Dutch*, the national language of Holland and the closest relative of English among national languages; *Flemish*, spoken in the Belgian provinces of Flanders; and *Plattdeutsch*, a dialect spoken in northern Germany, all belong to the *Low German* division of West Germanic, thus setting themselves apart from *High German*, the official and literary language of Germany and its many dialects in Austria and Switzerland.

Indo-European tongues are spoken today by about one half of the world's people. The rest of the earth's population, the other half, speak languages that, for the most part, can also be grouped into families.

NON-INDO-EUROPEAN LANGUAGES

As far as historical studies, description, and classification are concerned, the *Semito-Hamitic* group of languages is a close runner-up to the Indo-European family. Languages of this group are spoken by about 125 million people throughout Africa, north of the Sahara desert, in the Nile Valley as far as the Equator, on the Arabian Peninsula, in Iraq, Syria, Israel, and Jordan. The group as a whole is composed of *Semitic* and *Hamitic*, which have a number of features in common, pointing to a possible common ancestry.

The *Semitic* tongues are thus called because it is believed that the people speaking Semitic languages owe their existence to Noah's eldest son *Shem*, while the Hamitic speakers are said to descend from *Ham*, the second son.

Until the fourth century B.C. *Akkadian*, a Semitic language written in cuneiform characters, was the language of the Babylonian Empire. After the fall of Babylon, it was displaced by other related languages, particularly *Aramaic*, the language of Christ. Akkadian is sometimes classified as *East Semitic*, while *West Semitic* includes Aramaic, as well as *Canaanite*, known from a few inscriptions dating back to 1400 B.C.; *Moabite*, whose speakers are mentioned in Genesis; *Phoenician*, the language of an enterprising seafaring people whose alphabet is ultimately the source of most writing systems in use today; *Hebrew*, once one of the great liturgical languages and recently revived as the national language of Israel; *Arabic*, the vehicle of a great religion and a world language of prime importance; and, finally, *Ethiopic*, the name given to the various languages of Ethiopia, of which *Amharic* is the most important. Within historical times many of the ancient Semitic languages disappeared and only Hebrew, Arabic, and a modernized version of the ancient Aramaic, called *Syriac*, survived, the latter still used by Christians who live among Arabic-speaking Moslems in the Near East.

Among the Hamitic languages, historically the best-known

member is the *ancient Egyptian* of the Pharaohs. Its oldest records, written in hieroglyphic characters, date back to about 3000 B.C. and represent an important milestone in the history of ancient civilizations. Thanks to the famous Rosetta Stone, found in 1799, which bears parallel texts in Greek and in ancient Egyptian hieroglyphic and demotic characters, it was possible to decipher and interpret this mysterious Egyptian writing. With the Roman conquest of Egypt and, particularly, the intrusion of Arabic-speaking Moslems around the seventh century A.D., the language of this once-great civilization became partially extinct, though its direct modern descendant, *Coptic*, continued to be spoken by Egyptian Christians until the sixteenth century. Coptic is still being used in church services by African Christians who belong to the Coptic Church.

Akin to the Coptic are the *Berber* languages of North Africa, concentrated mainly between Tripoli and Algiers. These are subdivided into various dialects, such as *Tuareg*, spoken by the Bedouins in the Sahara Desert, *Shluh*, the language of southern Morocco, and *Kabyl*, spoken in the mountains of Algiers and Tunis. In the eastern corner of Africa and in parts of Ethiopia, another group of dialects, the *Cushitic*, is spoken by a few million people. All these languages have, so far, heroically held their own in the face of stiff competition from Arabic.

Attempts to establish a genetic relationship between Hamito-Semitic and Indo-European have not been wanting but no cogent evidence has yet been produced to prove it. The grammatical structure of Indo-European, which is based on word endings to show sentence relationship, is in strong contrast with Semitic structure, which is based on roots consisting of three consonants, in between which vowels are inserted to show grammatical function (see Chapter 4, page 59). Basic vocabulary correlation between English *foot*, German *Fuss*, Latin *ped-*, Greek *pod-*, and Sanskrit *pad-* is also in contrast with Arabic *rijl* and Hebrew *regel*.

The languages of the rest of Africa, south of the Sahara Desert, estimated to run into eight hundred in number, fall into three distinct groups: *Sudanese-Guinean*, *Bantu*, and *Hottentot-Bushman*.

The languages of the *Sudanese* branch, covering most of Central Africa north of the Equator, are very numerous. By far the most important language of this group is *Hausa*, spoken by about fifteen million people in parts of the Sudan and Nigeria, because it serves as a language of trade and communication over a wide area. Among the languages of Africa, it is rivaled only by *Swahili*, the chief representative of the *Bantu* group, which covers parts of Central, East, and most of South Africa. Great as the diversity among languages of the Sudanese group is, the members of the Bantu group, comprising over fifty million speakers, are fairly homogeneous. Besides Swahili (from the Arabic *sahil* 'coast,' because it was originally the language of the people on the island of Zanzibar and the East African coast), some of the better-known languages of this group are *Zulu* and *Ruanda*, spoken in Tanganyika, *Duala* spoken in the Congo, and *Herero*, the language of a fierce, warlike tribe of the same name who live in southern Africa.

In the sparsely populated Kalahari Desert of southwestern Africa, about 250 thousand people speak languages that belong to the *Hottentot-Bushman* group. Their speech is characterized by so-called clicks, that is, sounds produced by drawing the breath into the mouth, clicking the tongue, and smacking the lips. The name of one of the languages that uses such clicks is conventionally spelled *Xhosa*, where the *xh* is used to represent these sounds.

Off the southeastern coast of Africa lies the island of Madagascar, the westernmost territory of the *Malayo-Polynesian* group of languages. Spoken by well over one hundred million people almost exclusively on islands in the Indian and Pacific Oceans, these languages extend from Formosa in the north to New Zealand in the south and to Easter Island, off the coast of Chile, in the east. This area, which is almost as extensive as the one covered by Indo-European languages, includes such well-known places as Hawaii, the Philippines, Indonesia, Malaya, and New Zealand. It does not, however, cover the continent of Australia and the island of New Guinea, except for some coastal areas. Despite the great distances separating these languages, their kinship is recognizable: compare, for instance, the word 'nine' which is *siwa* in Indonesia, *tsiwa* in Fiji, *iwa* in Hawaii and New Zealand, *iva* in Samoa, and *sivi* in Madagascar.

The Malayo-Polynesian languages are customarily divided into four subfamilies, corresponding primarily to geographical rather than linguistic divisions. These are *Indonesian, Melanesian, Micronesian,* and *Polynesian.* The -*nesian* ending, which appears in all the names, means 'pertaining to islands' and comes from the Greek *nesos,* meaning 'island.' Thus, these names really mean 'Indian islands' (thus called because of extensive colonization from India), 'black islands,' 'small islands' and 'many islands,' respectively. The leading tongue of the Indonesian subgroup (and leading among Malayo-Polynesian tongues) is *Malay,* which, with eighty million speakers, ranks among the thirteen major languages of the world. Under the name of *Bahasa Indonesian,* it has become, in a revised and highly standardized form, the official language of the Republic of Indonesia. Among the other languages of the Polynesian group, are *Maori* of New Zealand, *Tahitian, Hawaiian,* and *Samoan.* All these languages are characterized by a paucity of consonant sounds. Who has not heard of *aloha, hula, ukulele,* and *luau,* contributed to the English vocabulary by the fiftieth state of the Union?

The best known among the Melanesian languages are probably those of the *Fiji Islands,* but just like the Micronesian languages, they are all unwritten. It is estimated that over a hundred languages belong to these two subgroups.

Since mention was made of Australia and New Guinea, a word about the languages spoken in these areas may be in order. The languages of the original inhabitants of these areas do not appear to be related to the Malayo-Polynesian family. Native *Australian* languages, spoken by about fifty thousand natives, number about two hundred. They have been divided into a northern and southern group, although their mutual relationships is far from determined. In any event, both the languages and the natives who speak them are steadily vanishing.

The languages of New Guinea, known as the *Papuan* languages, are also not well known. Their exact number has never been accurately determined, estimates ranging from about eighty to one hundred and thirty. There seems to exist no connection between these languages and the Malayo-Polynesian or the Australian types.

In southern India there are about 100 million speakers whose languages belong to the *Dravidian* family. Considered as aboriginal, there are reasons to believe that Dravidian formerly covered a much larger area of India and may have been native to most, if not all, of India before the invasion of Indo-European speakers, who now occupy the northern half of the Indian subcontinent. Among the chief languages of the Dravidian group are *Tamil*, which possesses a rich literature, and *Telugu*.

The *Sino-Tibetan* languages of southeastern Asia, which extend over China, Tibet, Burma, and the greater part of Thailand (formerly Siam), are second only to Indo-European in number of speakers. This group of languages, with a total of about 800 million speakers, is subdivided into *Chinese*, or *Sinitic* (to use a more generic term, since there is no *one* Chinese language), *Tibeto-Burmese*, and *Thai* (or *Siamese*). The characteristic feature that these languages share is their essential monosyllabism (see Chapter 4, page 70). A further noteworthy feature of this group of languages is the use of a series of tone levels (high, low, rising and falling pitch) to differentiate between words otherwise identical in pronunciation.

Chinese, which is not only the most important but also the oldest language of this group in terms of historical records that reach back to at least 1500 B.C., is divided into a large number of dialects which are often mutually unintelligible. The majority of speakers speak some variety of *Mandarin*, the main dialect of northern China and the capital city of Peking. It is now taught in schools throughout the country and is on the way to become the official language of the Peoples' Republic of China. Meanwhile, *Cantonese*, the most important dialect of southern China, is still spoken by an important segment of the population as a native language and is also the language of trade in the great commercial centers of the south. It is spoken by about sixty million people (in contrast to 500 million speakers of Mandarin Chinese). Of the other Sinitic languages the *Wu* dialects of the Shanghai region, the *Hakka* dialect of the Meihsien region, and the *Min* dialects of the Fukien region, with about fifty million speakers each, deserve mention. It is only through their logographic writing system that all literate Chinese are able to communicate with each other, at least on paper.

Among the languages related to the *Thai* subgroup, we must mention *Vietnamese*, although this relationship has been disputed, some scholars preferring to place this language into a separate *Austro-Asiatic* group, while others link it up with the *Mon-Khmer* languages of Indo-China and Cambodia. In this connection, we should note that the first record in Vietnamese (fifteenth century A.D.) is written in Chinese characters, which were largely replaced by the Roman alphabet by the seventeenth century. Like the Chinese languages, Vietnamese is also a monosyllabic language and uses a set of seven tone levels to differentiate the meaning of otherwise identical words.

If you were to look at a *Japanese* newspaper, you might jump to the conclusion that this language must not be too different from Chinese. The fact of the matter is that there is probably as much difference between Japanese and Chinese as there is between English and Chinese. To be sure, both languages have a link as far as their writing system is concerned, since Japanese has used Chinese characters ever since they were brought to Japan by Chinese missionaries around the seventh century A.D. But this is where the similarity ends. While Chinese is essentially a monosyllabic language and relies, in its sentence structure, exclusively on word order, Japanese uses endings and variations in the shape of words to show grammatical relationships.

Japanese is a largely "island-locked" language spoken by about one hundred million people and is one of the important languages of the Far East, as a result of Japan's dominant political and economic role in that area. Its relationship with other languages of Asia is still a matter of conjecture, though a link with Korean, because of similarity of grammatical structure, has been repeatedly suggested. Like Japanese, the vocabulary of *Korean* has been heavily influenced by Chinese (the name *Korea* ultimately goes back to the Chinese *kao-li* 'lofty (and) beautiful') and it was even written in Chinese characters until the fifteenth century, when a special Korean alphabet was invented, based on that of Sanskrit. A possible relationship to the Altaic family (see below) has also been suggested.

Another unclassified and isolated language in this area of the world is *Ainu*, spoken by about twenty thousand white-skinned inhabitants of Hokkaido, the northernmost island of Japan. The Ainus seem to be remnants of the aboriginal people who lived on the islands before the arrival of the Japanese. The word *ainu* means 'man' and may be related to the word *inyu*, which appears with the same meaning in several American Indian languages.

It is estimated that about sixty million people speak *Uralic* and

Altaic languages, whose geographical extent stretches from the shores of the Pacific all the way across the plains of northern and central Asia to central and northern Europe. The names of these two language groups derive from two important mountain ranges, the *Urals*, between European and Asiatic Russia, and the *Altai Mountains* of central Asia. Since there is considerable disagreement as to a basic Ural-Altaic unity, these languages are now considered to constitute two separate and unrelated families. The *Uralic*, or *Finno-Ugric*, group includes mainly European languages such as *Finnish*, the national language of Finland; *Estonian*, once the language of an independent Estonia in northeastern Europe and now a republic of the USSR; *Lapp*, spoken by about thirty thousand people in Lapland, the northernmost regions of Finland, Norway, and Sweden; and *Hungarian*, or *Magyar*, the national language of Hungary. Some of the languages spoken in Siberia (in the Ural mountain area), which are subsumed under the general name of *Samoyedic* (from the name of one of the languages of this group, called *Samoyed*), are related to the languages of the Finno-Ugric group.

The *Altaic* family has been traditionally divided into *Turkic*, including *Turkish*, the national language of Turkey, and related languages like the tongues of the *Tatars*, *Turkomans*, and *Kirghiz* of east-European Russia, Southern Siberia, and west-central Asia; *Mongol*, largely confined to Mongolia, where it is spoken by about three million people; and *Manchu*, or *Tungus*, spoken in the area of the former eastern Asian state of Manchukuo, which includes present-day Manchuria. The number of speakers of Manchu-Tungus languages is estimated at less than one million, and this number is constantly diminishing in view of the encroachment of Chinese. Of the Uralic and Altaic languages, Finnish, Turkish, and Hungarian are the best-known national languages.

A possible relationship between the Altaic and *Eskimo-Aleutian* languages has been suggested, although the connection has not yet been clearly demonstrated. This group of languages extends from the Aleutian Islands and Alaska along the Arctic coast of North America and the shores of Hudson Bay to Labrador and Greenland. The most striking feature of these languages is that a single word may express a thought that we in English express by a phrase or a sentence, for instance, Eskimo *takusariartorumagaluarnerpa* 'do you think he really intends to go look after it?'[1]

Turning now to the Americas, we find numerous aboriginal languages with an estimated one hundred or more different linguistic groups, each comprising many separate languages. In many instances these languages, spoken by Indians in North, Central, and South America (hence the name *American Indian* or *Amerindian* languages) have only a few thousand, or even a few hundred speakers left. Though these languages (well over a thousand of them) show certain similar features, a common kinship has, to date, not been established. Many of the original Indian languages on the North American continent have long since perished and many others are destined to vanish without ever being recorded. However, thanks to the efforts of some of the great linguists and anthropologists of the twentieth century, some Amerindian languages have been well studied, so that we at least have an idea of what they look like. It was found, for instance, that a language like the *Oneida* of the Iroquian Indians, once concentrated in upstate New York, also expresses a complete sentence thought by what appears to be a single word, for instance, *gnaglaslizaks* 'I search for a village.'[2] Of the estimated twenty-five Amerindian families in North America, the best known are *Algonkian*, *Iroquois*, *Athapaskan*, *Chinook*, and *Sioux*.

The American Indian languages south of the Rio Grande seem to enjoy greater vitality than those in the United States or Canada. The *Aztec* or *Nahuatl* tongue is still spoken by nearly a million people in northern and central Mexico. South of the Aztecs we find the *Mayas* of Guatemala and Yucatán, a people who once had a highly developed and flourishing civilization. The Mexican and Central American Indian languages have also been grouped into about twenty different families.

The number of South American Indian languages, ranging from the *Carib* languages of the Antilles to the *Araucanian* in Chile, has been set at nearly eight hundred, divided into possibly as many as seventy distinct groups. Undoubtedly, many of these languages have become extinct, but others are very much alive and widely spoken throughout South America. Chief among them is *Quechua*, spoken by about six million Indians of Ecuador, Peru, and

Bolivia, and once the language of the great empire of the Incas. Another language is *Tupi-Guaraní*, still the dominant language of the Republic of Paraguay, although Spanish is the official language of the country. The very name Paraguay, as a matter of fact, is a Tupi-Guaraní word meaning 'parrot river.' Araucanian, spoken by the native Indian population of Chile and the Argentine pampas, is also one of the major Amerindian groups of the South-American continent. All in all, there are probably over eight million people who still speak Indian languages.

The term *Caucasian* applies to languages spoken in the Caucasian area of the Soviet Union, between the Black and the Caspian Seas, that are neither Indo-European nor Turkic. *Azerbaijani*, the language of the Azerbaijan Soviet Socialist Republic, falls into this group. These languages comprise about five million speakers, of whom about one and a half million speak *Georgian*, by far the best-known language of the group. It has a literary tradition that goes back to a fifth-century Bible translation and an alphabet of its own, while most of the languages of this group have no written representation and exist only as speech.

Recently the Caucasian languages have been connected with one of the linguistic curios of Europe, *Basque*, a non-Indo-European language isolated in the midst of an Indo-European language area. At present, it is spoken by about one million people on both the French and Spanish sides of the northern Pyrenees mountains. For a long time it was thought that Basque, or *Euskara*, as its speakers call it, was the descendant of an ancient Iberian tongue which was once spoken throughout the Iberian Peninsula and parts of southern France before the arrival of Indo-European speakers around the first millenium B.C. Structural similarities, however, have led some modern scholars to see a kinship between Basque and the languages of the Caucasus, while others have attempted to link it up with Semito-Hamitic and also *Etruscan*, once the language of a flourishing civilization in central Italy before it was completely displaced by Latin.

Basque enjoys the reputation of being a very difficult language to learn. There is even a legend to the effect that at one time the devil himself tried unsuccessfully to learn the language so that he could tempt the Euskars.

Our classification of the world's languages is by no means exhaustive; it is intended to suggest the diversity of human tongues. It is possible that behind these complex linguistic divisions there is some prehistoric speech to which all languages go back ultimately. In the light of our present knowledge, the probability of such interrelationship among the world's languages seems remote.

notes

1. Adapted from Louis H. Gray, *Foundations of Language*. New York: Macmillan, 1939, p. 374.
2. See Chapter 4, p. 71.

a selected bibliography

The following list of works is meant to serve as a guide for students who wish to have further information on some specific point or wish to pursue the study of linguistics on a more advanced level. Not all the titles mentioned in the notes are repeated here.

GENERAL INTRODUCTIONS

Black, Max, *The Labyrinth of Language*. New York: The New American Library, 1969.

Bloch, Bernard, and George L. Trager, *Outline of Linguistic Analysis*. Baltimore: Linguistic Society of America, 1942.

Bloomfield, Leonard, *Language*. New York: Holt, Rinehart and Winston, 1933.

Bolinger, Dwight, *Aspects of Language*. New York: Harcourt Brace Jovanovich, 1968.

Carroll, John B., *The Study of Language: A Survey of Linguistics and Related Disciplines in America*. Cambridge, Mass.: Harvard University Press, 1953.

Chao, Yen Ren, *Language and Symbolic Systems*. Cambridge: At the University Press, 1968.

De Saussure, Ferdinand, *Course in General Linguistics,* trans. by Wade Baskin. New York: The Philosophical Library, 1959.

Dinneen, Francis P., *An Introduction to General Linguistics*. New York: Holt, Rinehart and Winston, 1967.

Gleason, H. A., Jr., *An Introduction to Description Linguistics,* rev. ed. New York: Holt, Rinehart and Winston, 1961.

Gray, Louis H., *Foundations of Language*. New York: Macmillan, 1939.

Greenberg, Joseph H., *Anthropological Linguistics: An Introduction*. New York: Random House, 1968.

Hall, Robert A., Jr., *Introductory Linguistics*. Philadelphia: Chilton, 1964.

Hockett, Charles, *A Course in Modern Linguistics.* New York: Macmillan, 1958.

Hughes, John P., *The Science of Language.* New York: Random House, 1962.

Jespersen, Otto, *Language, Its Nature, Development and Origin.* London: Allen & Unwin, 1922.

Langacker, Ronald, *Language and Its Structure: Some Fundamental Linguistic Concepts.* New York: Harcourt Brace Jovanovich, 1968.

Lyons, John, *Introduction to Theoretical Linguistics.* Cambridge: At the University Press, 1968.

Pei, Mario A., *Invitation to Linguistics—A Basic Introduction to the Science of Language.* New York: Doubleday, 1965.

Potter, Simeon, *Modern Linguistics,* rev. ed. Oxford: Oxford University Press, 1967.

Pyles, Thomas and John Algeo, *English: An Introduction to Language.* New York: Harcourt Brace Jovanovich, 1970.

Robins, R. H., *General Linguistics: An Introductory Survey.* London: Longmans, 1964.

Sapir, Edward, *Language: An Introduction to the Study of Speech.* New York: Harcourt Brace Jovanovich, 1921.

Sturtevant, Edgar H., *An Introduction to Linguistic Science.* New Haven: Yale University Press, 1947.

ANTHOLOGIES AND COLLECTIONS OF ESSAYS

Allen, Harold B., ed., *Readings in Applied English Linguistics,* 2nd ed. New York: Appleton-Century-Crofts, 1964.

Anderson, Wallace L., and Norman C. Stageberg, eds., *Introductory Readings on Language,* rev. ed. New York: Holt, Rinehart and Winston, 1966.

Dean, Leonard F., and Kenneth G. Wilson, eds., *Essays on Language and Usage,* 2nd ed. New York: Oxford University Press, 1963.

Fodor, Jerry A., and Jerrold J. Katz, eds., *The Structure of Language: Readings in the Philosophy of Language.* Englewood Cliffs, N. J.: Prentice-Hall, 1964.

Greenberg, Joseph, H., *Essays in Linguistics.* Chicago: University of Chicago Press, 1957.

Greenberg, Joseph, H., ed., *Universals of Language,* 2nd ed. Cambridge, Mass.: M.I.T. Press, 1966.

Hamp, Eric P., *et al.,* eds., *Readings in Linguistics II.* Chicago: University of Chicago Press, 1966.

Hill, Archibald, A. ed., *Linguistics Today.* New York: Basic Books, 1969.

Hogins, Burl J., and Robert E. Yarber, eds., *Language: An Introductory Reader*. New York: Harper & Row, 1969.

Joos, Martin, ed., *Readings in Linguistics I*, 4th ed. Chicago: University of Chicago Press, 1966.

Kerr, Elizabeth M., and Ralph M. Aderman, eds., *Aspects of American English*. New York: Harcourt Brace Jovanovich, 1963.

Laird, Charlton, and Robert M. Gorrell, eds., *English as Language: Backgrounds, Development, Usage*. New York: Harcourt Brace Javanovich, 1961.

Lass, Roger, ed., *Approaches to English Historical Linguistics*. New York: Holt, Rinehart and Winston, 1969.

Rycenga, John A., and Joseph Schwartz, eds., *Perspectives on Language*. New York: The Ronald Press, 1963.

Wilson, Graham, ed., *A Linguistics Reader*. New York: Harper & Row, 1967.

PHONETICS AND PHONOLOGY

Bronstein, Arthur J., *The Pronunciation of American English*. New York: Appleton-Century-Crofts, 1960.

Chomsky, Noam, and Morris Halle, *The Sound Patterns of English*. New York: Harper & Row, 1969.

Heffner, R.-M. S., *General Phonetics*. Madison: The University of Wisconsin Press, 1949.

Jones, Daniel, *An Outline of English Phonetics*, 9th ed. Cambridge: W. Heffer & Sons, 1964.

Malmberg, Bertil, *Phonetics*, trans. by Lily M. Parker. New York: Dover, 1963.

Pike, Kenneth L., *The Intonation of American English*. Ann Arbor: University of Michigan Press, 1945.

Pike, Kenneth L., *Phonemics: A Technique for Reducing Languages to Writing*. Ann Arbor: University of Michigan Press, 1947.

Thomas, Charles K., *An Introduction to the Phonetics of American English*, 2nd ed. New York: The Ronald Press, 1958.

Wise, Claude M., *Applied Phonetics*. Englewood Cliffs, N. J.: Prentice-Hall, 1957.

GRAMMATICAL STRUCTURE

Bach, Emmon, *An Introduction to Transformational Grammars*. New York: Holt, Rinehart and Winston, 1964.

Chomsky, Noam, *Syntactic Structures*. The Hague: Mouton & Co., 1957.

Chomsky, Noam, *Current Issues in Linguistic Theory*. The Hague: Mouton & Co., 1964.

Chomsky, Noam, *Aspects of the Theory of Syntax*. Cambridge, Mass.: M.I.T. Press, 1965.

Chomsky, Noam, *Topics in the Theory of Generative Grammar*. The Hague: Mouton & Co., 1966.

Francis, W. Nelson, *The Structure of American English*. New York: The Ronald Press, 1958.

Fries, Charles C., *The Structure of English*. New York: Harcourt Brace Jovanovich, 1952.

Gleason, H. A., Jr., *Linguistics and English Grammar*. New York: Holt, Rinehart and Winston, 1965.

Hill, Archibald A., *Introduction to Linguistic Structures: From Sound to Sentence in English*. New York: Harcourt Brace Jovanovich, 1958.

Jacobs, Roderick A., and Peter S. Rosenbaum, *English Transformational Grammar*. Waltham, Mass.: Blaisdell, 1968.

Koutsoudas, Andreas, *Writing Transformational Grammars: An Introduction*. New York: McGraw-Hill, 1966.

Langendoen, Terence D., *The Study of Syntax: The Generative-Transformational Approach to the Structure of American English*. New York: Holt, Rinehart and Winston, 1969.

Roberts, Paul, *Patterns of English*. New York: Harcourt Brace Jovanovich, 1956.

Roberts, Paul, *Understanding English*. New York: Harper & Row, 1958.

Roberts, Paul, *English Sentences*. New York: Harcourt Brace Jovanovich, 1962.

Roberts, Paul, *English Syntax*, alternate ed. New York: Harcourt Brace Jovanovich, 1964.

Roberts, Paul, *Modern Grammar*. New York: Harcourt Brace Jovanovich, 1967.

Sledd, James, *A Short Introduction to English Grammar*. Chicago: Scott, Foresman, 1959.

Stageberg, Norman C., *An Introductory English Grammar*. New York: Holt, Rinehart and Winston, 1965.

Thomas, Owen, *Transformational Grammar and the Teacher of English*. New York: Holt, Rinehart and Winston, 1965.

Trager, George L., and Henry Lee Smith, Jr., *An Outline of English Structure*. Norman: The University of Oklahoma Press, 1951.

Whitehall, Harold, *Structural Essentials of English*. New York: Harcourt Brace Jovanovich, 1956.

VOCABULARY, MEANING, AND ETYMOLOGY

Bréal, Michel, *Semantics: Studies in the Science of Meaning*, trans. by Mrs. Henry Cust. New York: Dover, 1964.

Carnap, Rudolf, *Introduction to Semantics.* Cambridge, Mass.: Harvard University Press, 1948.

Chase, Stuart, *The Tyranny of Words.* New York: Harcourt Brace Jovanovich, 1938.

Chase, Stuart, *Power of Words.* New York: Harcourt Brace Jovanovich, 1954.

Greenough, James B., and George L. Kittredge, *Words and Their Ways in English Speech.* New York: Macmillan, 1961.

Hayakawa, S. I., ed., *The Use and Misuse of Language.* New York: Fawcett, 1962.

Hayakawa, S. I., *Language in Thought and Action,* 2nd ed. New York: Harcourt Brace Jovanovich, 1963.

Korzybski, Alfred, *Science and Sanity: An Introduction to Non-Aristotelian Systems and General Semantics.* Lancaster, Pa.: Science Press, 1933.

Langer, Susanne K., *Philosophy in a New Key.* Cambridge, Mass.: Harvard University Press, 1942.

Lee, Irving J., *Handling Barriers to Communication.* New York: Harper & Row, 1957.

Malkiel, Yakov, "Etymology and General Linguistics," *Word,* 18, nos. 1–2 (April–August, 1962), 198–219.

Ogden C. K., and I. A. Richards, *The Meaning of Meaning,* 3rd ed., rev. New York: Harcourt Brace Jovanovich, 1930.

Osgood, Charles E., G. J. Suci, and P. H. Tannenbaum, *The Measurement of Meaning.* Urbana, Ill.: University of Illinois Press, 1957.

Partridge, Eric, *Origins.* New York: Macmillan, 1958.

Pei, Mario A., *What's in a Word?* New York: Hawthorn, 1968.

Pyles, Thomas, *Words and Ways of American English.* New York: Random House, 1952.

Quine, Willard van Orman, *Word and Object.* Cambridge, Mass.: M.I.T. Press, 1960.

Ross, Alan, S. C., *Etymology: With Especial Reference to English.* London: Deutsch, 1958.

Sheard, J. A., *The Words of English.* New York: W. W. Norton, 1966.

Skinner, B. F., *Verbal Behavior.* New York: Appleton-Century-Crofts, 1957.

Stern, Gustaf, *Meaning and Change of Meaning.* Bloomington: Indiana University Press, 1931.

Ullmann, Stephen, *Semantics: An Introduction to the Science of Meaning.* Oxford: Blackwell, 1962.

Weekley, Ernest, *The Romance of Words,* reprint of rev. ed. (1949). New York: Dover, 1961.

Whorf, Benjamin Lee, *Language, Thought, and Reality*, John B. Carroll, ed. Cambridge, Mass.: M.I.T. Press, 1965.

WRITING

Gelb, I. J., *The Study of Writing: The Foundations of Grammatology*. Chicago: University of Chicago Press, 1952.

Diringer, David, *The Alphabet: A Key to the History of Mankind*. New York: Philosophical Library, 1948.

Diringer, David, *Writing* (Ancient Peoples and Places Series). New York: Praeger, 1962.

Pulgram, Ernst, "Phone and Grapheme: A Parallel," *Words*, 7, No. 1 (April 1951), 15–20.

REGIONAL AND SOCIAL SPEECH VARIATIONS

Atwood, E. Bagby, *A Survey of Verb Forms in the Eastern United States*. Ann Arbor: University of Michigan Press, 1953.

Bram, Joseph, *Language and Society*. New York: Random House, 1955.

Hall, Robert A., Jr., *Pidgin and Creole Languages*. Ithaca, N.Y.: Cornell University Press, 1966.

Jespersen, Otto, *Mankind, Nation and Individual From a Linguistic Point of View*. Bloomington: Indiana University Press (Midland Book), 1964.

Joos, Martin, *The Five Clocks*. Bloomington: Indiana University Press, 1962.

Kurath, Hans, et al., *Handbook of the Linguistic Geography of New England*. Washington, D.C.: American Council of Learned Societies, 1939.

Kurath, Hans, *A Word Geography of the Eastern United States*. Ann Arbor: University of Michigan Press, 1949.

Kurath, Hans, and Raven I. McDavid, Jr., *The Pronunciation of English in the Atlantic States*. Ann Arbor: University of Michigan Press, 1961.

Labov, William, *The Social Stratification of English in New York City*. Washington, D.C.: Center for Applied Linguistics, 1966.

Malmstrom, Jean, and Annabel Ashley, *Dialects—U.S.A*. Champaign, Ill.: National Council of Teachers of English, 1963.

Marckwardt, Albert H., *American English*. New York: Oxford University Press, 1958.

McDavid, Raven I., Jr., "The Dialects of American English," in *The Structure of American English*, by W. Nelson Francis. New York: Ronald Press, 1958.

McDavid, Raven I., Jr., ed., *The American Language*, by H. L. Mencken, abridged ed. New York: Knopf, 1963.
McDavid, Raven I., Jr., "American Social Dialects," *College English*, 26, No. 4 (January 1965) 10–16.
McDavid, Raven I., Jr., "Sense and Nonsense About American Dialects," *PMLA*, 81, No. 2 (May 1966) 7–17.
Mencken, H. L., *The American Language*, 4th ed. New York: Knopf, 1936. Supplement I, 1946. Supplement II, 1948.
Reed, Carroll E., *Dialects of American English*. Cleveland: World Publishing Co., 1967.
Stewart, William A., "Sociolinguistic Factors in the History of American Negro Dialects," *The Florida Linguistic Reporter*, 5, No. 2 (Spring 1967) 1–4.
Stewart, William A., "Continuity and Change in American Negro Dialects," *The Florida Linguistic Reporter*, 6, No. 2 (Spring 1968).

HISTORY OF LANGUAGE

Alexander, Henry, *The Story of Our Language*, rev. ed. New York: Doubleday, 1962.
Baugh, Albert C., *A History of the English Language*, 2nd ed. New York: Appleton-Century-Crofts, 1957.
Bloomfield, Morton W., and Leonard Newmark, *A Linguistic Introduction to the History of English*. New York: Knopf, 1963.
Diamond, D. S., *The History and Origin of Language*. New York: Philosophical Society, 1959.
Elcock, W. D., *The Romance Languages*. London: Faber, 1960.
Francis, W. Nelson, *The English Language*. New York: W. W. Norton, 1963.
Goad, Harold, *Language in History*. Harmondsworth, Middlesex: Penguin, 1958.
Hoenigswald, Henry M., *Language Change and Linguistic Reconstruction*. Chicago: University of Chicago Press, 1960.
Jespersen, Otto, *Growth and Structure of the English Language*, 9th ed. New York: Doubleday (Anchor Books), 1956.
King, Robert D., *Historical Linguistics and Generative Grammar*. Englewood Cliffs, N. J.: Prentice-Hall, 1969.
Lehmann, Winfred P., *Historical Linguistics: An Introduction*. New York: Holt, Rinehart and Winston, 1962.
Pedersen, Holger, *The Discovery of Language: Linguistic Science in the Nineteenth Century*, trans. by John Webster Spargo. Bloomington: Indiana University Press, 1962.
Pei, Mario A., *The Family of Words*. New York: Harper & Row, 1962.

Pyles, Thomas, *The Origin and Development of the English Language.* New York: Harcourt Brace Jovanovich, 1964.

Révész, G., *The Origin and Prehistory of Language*, trans. by J. Butler. New York: Philosophical Library, 1956.

Robertson, Stuart, *The Development of Modern English*, 2nd ed., rev. by Frederic G. Cassidy. Englewood Cliffs, N.J.: Prentice-Hall, 1954.

Robins, R. H., *A Short History of Linguistics.* Bloomington: Indiana University Press, 1967.

Stevick, Robert D., *English and Its History: The Evolution of a Language.* New York: Allyn and Bacon, 1968.

Sturtevant, Edgar H., *Linguistic Change.* Chicago: University of Chicago Press, 1917.

Waterman, John T., *Perspective in Linguistics*, 2nd ed., Chicago: University of Chicago Press, 1970.

LANGUAGES OF THE WORD

Bender, Harold H., *The Home of the Indo-Europeans.* Princeton, N.J.: Princeton University Press, 1922.

Meillet, A., and Marcel Cohen, *Les langues de monde*, new ed., 2 vols. Paris: Champion, 1952.

Muller, Siegfried H., *The World's Living Languages.* New York: Ungar, 1964.

Pei, Mario A., *The World's Chief Languages*, 4th ed. (formerly *Languages for War and Peace*). New York: Vanni, 1960.

index

abbreviated forms, *see* shortening
aboriginal peoples, 7
acoustics, 27
acronyms, 119–120
active-passive relationship, 93–94, 99, 103
adjectives, 41, 57, 60, 70, 110, 112, 117
adverbs, 60, 113, 138
affixes, 57–58, 60, 64–65, 68–69, 74, 109, 113
   derivational versus inflectional, 57–58
affricates, 29–30, 192–193
African languages, 132
agglutinative languages, 67–69, 71
agreement, 75n.
Ainu, 220
airstream, *see* breathstream
Akkadian, 215
Albanian, 210
Algonkian, 222
allograph, 163
allomorph, 61–66, 75n.
allophone, 43–45, 62
alphabet, 32, 34–35, 148, 158–161
alphabet words, *see* acronyms
Altaic languages, 221
alveolar stop, 62
ambiguity, 94, 106n.
American English, 32–33, 40, 169, 172–179
American Indian languages, 22, 48, 70, 132, 138, 222–223
American language, 167–168
Amerind, *see* American Indian languages
Amharic, 215
analogical creation, *see* analogy
analogy, 199–200, 206n.
analytic languages, *see* isolating languages
Ancient Egyptian, 157, 216
Ancient Greek, 20, 59, 67–68
Anglo-Saxons, 125–127, 132

antonyms, 142
appositive, 49
Arabic, 29, 45, 59, 76n., 131, 215
Aramaic, 215
Araucanian, 222
Aristotelian philosophy, 80
Armenian, 210
articles, 18, 54, 60–61
articulators, *see* speech, organs of
articulatory phonetics, *see* phonetics
aspiration, 34, 44
Athapaskan, 222
Attic dialect, 210
Atwood, E. Bagby, 175
audition, 25
auditory impression, 27
Australian languages, 132, 218
Austro-Asiatic languages, 219
auxiliary verb, 60–61, 68, 98
Avestan, *see* Zend
Azerbaijani, 224
Aztec language, *see* Nahuatl
Aztecs, 155

back-formation, 118–119
Bacon, Roger, 187
Bahasa Indonesian, *see* Malay
Balto-Slavic languages, 211
Bantu languages, 48, 58, 216–217
base, 56–61, 64, 68–71, 74–75n., 109, 112, 124n.
Basque, 224
Bengali, 209
Berber languages, 216
binary opposition, 46
Bleek, W. H., 198
blending, 120–121
Bloomfield, Leonard, 21–22, 56, 82, 136
Boas, Franz, 21
Bopp, Franz, 190–191
borrowing, 108–109, 125–133, 145
Bow-Wow theory, 4, 7
branching-tree diagram, 96–97

Bréal, Michel, 134
breathstream, 28–29, 32, 35–37, 45
Breton, 212
British English, 32, 169
Brugman, Karl, 199
Bulgarian, 211
Burgess, Gelett, 122
Burmese, 49
Bushmann, J. K., 198
Byelorussian, 211

Campbell, George, 80
Canaanite, 215
cant, 179
Cantonese, 169, 219
cardinal vowels, 39–40
    relation to English vowels, 40
Carib languages, 222
Carroll, Lewis, 84, 120
Castren, Mattis A., 198
Catalan, 213
Caucasian languages, 224
Caxton, William, 128
Celtic languages, 189, 212
centum languages, 205n.
Chaucer, Geoffrey, 127
Chinese, 67, 70, 76n., 132, 219
Chinese characters, 156
Chinook, 222
Chomsky, Noam, 93–103, 204n.
Class 1, 2, 3, 4 words, 86–91
classifiers, 165n.
clause terminal, *see* terminal contour
clicks, 217
close juncture, 50, 117
cognate word, 149
colloquialism, 111, 176–177
communication, 2–6, 12, 19–20, 24, 50
    vocal versus nonvocal, 2–3
commutation test, 46
comparative grammar, 191
comparative linguistics, 20
competence, 11n., 95, 104
complementary distribution, 43
composition, 108, 115–118, 123n.
compounds, 54, 56, 74, 116–117, 138
conceptual sphere, 136
conjoining, 99
conjugation, 60, 91
conjunction, 60
connotation, 110
    See also meaning, connotative versus denotative
consonantlike sounds, 32, 33, 37
consonants, 28, 35–38, 59, 61–62, 65
    syllabic, 42
    table of, 38
constituents, 91, 106n.

contact languages, *see* pidgin languages
Contact theory, 6
content word, 60–61
contentive, *see* content word
continuants, 29
contoid, *see* consonants
contrastive analysis, 20
Cooper, James Fenimore, 132
coordination, *see* conjoining
Coptic, 216
Cornish, 212
corpus, 93
creole languages, 180
Croatian, 130
cuneiform script, 154
Cushitic, 216
Czech, 47, 130, 211

Dalmatian, 213
Danelagh, 126
Danish, 9, 126–127, 184, 214
Dante, 188
Darwinian theory, 3, 196
"dead" languages, 20
declension, 60, 81
deep structure, 102–104, 204n.
derivation, 9, 65, 74–75, 108–115, 123n.
derivational tree, *see* branching-tree diagram
derivatives, 58–60
derived P-marker, 101
descriptive grammar, 82–83
descriptive linguistics, 20–21, 93, 104, 197
determiners, 97
devanāgari script, 161
diachronic linguistics, *see* historical linguistics
dialect boundary, 169, 175
dialect geography, 171
dialectologist, 175
dialects, 167–170
    of American English, 172–179
    West Germanic, 193–194
Diamond, D. S., 5
Diez, Friedrich, 198
Ding-Dong theory, 4
diphthongs, 31–32, 41–42
discovery procedures, 84–90
distinctive features, 34, 43–47
distinctive sound unit, *see* phoneme
distribution, 43, 65
distributional meaning, 136
Donatus, 186
doublets, 149
Dravidian languages, 218–219
dual number, 71, 76n.

Duala, 217
Dutch, 129–130, 184, 214

echoic word, *see* sound-imitative words
echoism, *see* sounds, imitation of
Edmont, Edmond, 171
Elizabethan English, 167
embedding, 99
English, 214
English grammar, 81, 83, 105n.
Eskimo, 8, 70, 136, 222
Eskimo-Aleutian languages, 221–222
Esperanto, 109
Estonian, 221
Ethiopic, 215
Etruscan, 186, 224
etymologist, 148
etymology, 147–148
  See also words, origin of
etymon, 148
euphemism, 147
European languages, 32, 68, 188
Euskara, *see* Basque

figure of speech, *see* metaphor
Finnish, 67, 69, 161, 221
Finno-Ugric languages, *see* Uralic languages
flap, 32
Flemish, 214
Flexner, Stuart B., 178
folk etymology, 149
foreign language learning, 139
form class, 57–58, 67, 72, 86–92
formal marker, *see* structural signal
Francis, W. Nelson, 78
French, 9, 11n., 13, 15–18, 30, 39, 45, 76n., 109, 112–117, 126–128, 140, 184, 203, 211
fricatives, 29–30, 192–193
Fries, Charles C., 83
Fries framework, 83–93
Frisian, 204n., 214
function word, 60–61, 88–90, 113
functional shift, 141
functional variety, *see* speech, levels of
functor, *see* function word
future tense, 58, 76n.

Gaulish, 212
General Semantics, School of, 143
gender, 67, 76n.
generative grammar, *see* transformational-generative grammar
Georgian, 224

German, 13, 15–18, 39, 76n., 109, 112, 116, 130, 138, 169, 184, 191
  High versus Low, 193, 214
Germanic languages, 59, 68, 116, 135, 184, 190–193, 213–214
gestural communication, 2–5, 9
Gilliéron, Jules, 171
Gleason, Henry A., 36, 63
glide sounds, *see* semivowels
glottal stop, 29
glottis, 28, 35, 37
Goad, Harold, 2
Goldberg, Isaac, 2
Gothic, 189, 193, 214
grammar, 78–86, 93–95
  definition and meaning of, 78–79, 102
  history of, 80–82, 105n.
  as "linguistic etiquette," 79
  rules of, 12, 81, 94
  scientific approach to, 81–82
  theory of, 93–95
  tradition in, 78–86, 104
  universality of, 187
    See also comparative; descriptive; immediate constituent; philosophical; prescriptive; taxonomic; transformational-generative grammars
grammarians, 12, 72, 80–82, 98
grammatical arrangement, *see* syntax
grammatical class, *see* form class
grapheme-phoneme correspondence, 161–163
Great Vowel Shift, 202
Greek, 80–81, 113, 125–126, 185–190, 196, 201, 210
Greenberg, Joseph H., 72
Greenough, James B., 118
Grimm, Jacob, 190–191, 194
Grimm's Law, 191–194
Gullah dialect, 180
Gypsy language, 131, 209

Haitian Creole, 180
Hakka dialect, 219
Harris, James, 187
Hausa, 216
Hawaiian, 218
Hayakawa, S. I., 143
Hebrew, 7–9, 76n., 215
helping verb, *see* auxiliary verb
Herero, 217
Herodotus, 7
Hill, Archibald, 18
Hindi, 131, 161, 209
Hindustani, 209
historical linguistics, 20
Hittite, 157, 208

Hockett, Charles, 59
homo sapiens, 3
homonyms, 142
homophones, 142, 182n.
Hopi, 136
Hottentot-Bushman languages, 48, 216–217
Humboldt, Wilhelm von, 197, 206n.
Hungarian, 15–16, 18, 39, 47, 67, 69, 136, 161–162, 221
hybrid forms, 114
hypercorrection, 177
hyperurbanism, *see* hypercorrection

IC analysis, *see* immediate constituent analysis
Icelandic, 214
Ideographs, *see* writing, pictographic-ideographic
idiolect, 166, 169
idioms, 142
Ilocano, 59
immediate constituent analysis, 91–93, 103
immediate constituent grammar, 93
incorporating languages, 70–72
Indo-European, 76n., 192
  reconstruction of, 195–196
Indo-European community, 167, 207–208
Indo-European languages, 68, 76n., 109, 190–192, 196–197, 207–215
Indo-Iranian languages, 209
Indonesian, 161, 217
infixes, 57, 59, 68
inflectional languages, 67–68, 71–72
initial string, 96–97
interjection, 4, 16
Interlingua, 109
intermediate string, 96
"internal" grammar, 95
internal open juncture, 50
internal vowel change, 58–59, 65, 75n.
International Phonetic Alphabet (IPA), 33–34, 40, 161
interpretive components, 102
intonation patterns, 46–50
intrusive "r," 174
Ionic dialect, 210
Irish, 32, 212
Iroquois, 222
isogloss, *see* dialect boundary
isolating languages, 67–68, 70–71
Italian, 13, 17, 129, 168, 184, 212
Italic languages, 212

Jabberwocky, 84
Jaberg, Karl, 171

James VI of Scotland, 8
Japanese, 67, 69, 132, 220
jargon, 177–178
Jespersen, Otto, 5–6
Jones, Daniel, 39
Jones, Sir William, 189
Jud, Jakob, 171
junctures, 49–50
  See also close; internal open; terminal junctures

Kabyl, 216
kanji, 159
Kawi, 197
kernel P-marker, 100
kernel sentence, 95, 99–100
  See also sentence, basic type
kernel string, 99–100
Kittredge, George L., 118
Kluckhohn, Clyde, 137
koiné, 210
Korean, 220
Korean Bamboo English, 180
Korzybski, Alfred, 143
kuo-yü, 182n.
Kurath, Hans, 171–172

Lamb, Sydney M., 140
Landsmaal, 214
Langer, Susanne K., 10
language, acquisition of, 3, 7, 11n.
  arbitrariness of, 14–16
  authority in, 186–188
  change in, 20, 201–203
  classification of, 66–67
  comparison of, 20, 66, 184–203
  creative aspect of, 104
  and culture, 12–13
  deductive versus inductive approach to, 82
  definition of, 14, 24, 94
  and dialect, 166–181
  and extralinguistic world, 134
  imitation of, 2–3
  and nationality, 12–13
  nature of, 12
  origin and prehistory of, 1–10
  as a patterned system, 14, 19, 78
  predictability of, 18
  scientific study of, 189–203
  as speech, 2, 12, 14
  style in, *see* speech, levels of
  and thought, 1–2, 11n., 19, 134, 136, 147, 197
  types of, *see* typological classification
  universals of, 104, 187
langue d'oc, 204n.
langue d'oïl, 204n.

Lapp, 221
larynx, 25, 28
laterals, 30–32, 37
Latin, 12, 20, 67–68, 80–81, 111–113, 116, 125, 128, 132, 184–196, 198, 201, 203, 212
Latvian, *see* Lettish
Lautverschiebung, *see* sound shifts
learned development, 149
Leibniz, Gottfried Wilhelm, 189
Lepsius, K. R., 198
Leskien, August, 199
Lettish, 68, 211
lexeme, *see* lexical word
lexical rule, 101
lexical unit, 116
lexical word, 140–142
lexicon, 97, 108
lingua franca, 209
linguist, 19–21, 34, 39, 42, 45, 56
linguistic atlas, 171
linguistic geographer, *see* dialectologist
linguistic geography, *see* dialect geography
linguistics, 19–20, 93, 104, 197
  American school of, 21
  See also comparative, descriptive; historical linguistics
lip position, 37, 39
Lithuanian, 68, 211
loan characters, 165n.
loan translations, 130
loanwords, 129–132, 199
logograph, *see* writing, logographic
Lowth, Bishop Robert, 80
Luce, Clare Boothe, 122
lungs, 25, 28

Magyar, *see* Hungarian
Mahrati, 209
Malay, 59, 218
Malayo-Polynesian languages, 217–218
Manchu, 221
Mandarin Chinese, 13, 44, 48, 168, 219
manner of articulation, 36–37
Manx, 212
Mao Tse-Tung, 13, 182n.
Maori, 218
matres lectionis, 160
Mayas, 155, 222
McDavid, Raven I., Jr., 171
meaning, 2, 18, 20, 34, 43, 46, 49–50, 53, 56, 82–83, 116, 135–150
  amelioration of, 146
  central versus marginal, 140
  components of, 135
  connotative versus denotative, 142–148

meaning *(continued)*
  extension of, 144
  external versus internal, 136
  grammatical versus lexical, 60–61, 85–86
  loss of, 144
  pejoration of, 146
  range of, 136, 144
  restriction of, 145
  and symbol, 10
  unit of, 142
Melanesian, 217
Melanesian (English) Pidgin, 180
Mencken, H. L., 167
metaphor, 140
Meyer-Lübke, Wilhelm, 198
Micronesian, 217
Middle English, 202
Miklosich, Franz von, 198
Min dialect, 219
minimum free form, 56
mnemonic devices, 154
Moabite, 215
Mongol, 221
Mon-Khmer languages, 219
monogenesis, 9
monophthong, 42
morpheme, 55–74, 75n., 78, 91, 97, 100
  bound versus free, 56
morphemics, 66
morphological word, 141
morphology, 21–22, 66, 105n.
morphophonemic changes, 65, 69, 75n., 76n.
morphophonemic rules, 75n., 101
morphophonemics, 66
morphosyntactic level, 21
Mouth-Gesture theory, *see* Ta-Ta theory
Muller, Max, 5
Murray, Lindley, 80

Nahuatl, 188, 222
nasal cavity, 29–30
nasal sounds, 29–32, 37
nasalization, 45
national language, *see* official language
native language, 8
native speaker, 43, 55, 93–95
Neo-Grammarians, 195, 199
Neo-Latin languages, *see* Romance languages
neologism, 114
nodes, 96–97
noncontinuants, 29
non-European languages, 32, 37, 188, 198, 215–223
Norman Conquest, 127

normative grammar, *see* prescriptive grammar
Norwegian, 184, 214
notched sticks, 155
noun phrase, 92, 96, 99–100
nouns, 18, 46, 49, 57–58, 60, 63, 70, 72, 75n., 77n., 97, 110–111, 121
Nynosk, *see* Landsmaal

official language, 13, 169–170
Ogden, Charles K., 134–135
Old Bulgarian, *see* Old Church Slavonic
Old Church Slavonic, 211
Old English, 20, 109, 116, 126, 194
Old French, 20, 111, 131
Old High German, 169, 194
Old Icelandic, *see* Old Norse
Old Iranian, 209
Old Norse, 190, 194, 214
Old Persian, 209
Oneida, 70
onomatopoeia, *see* sounds, imitation of
onomatopoeic word, *see* sound-imitative words
oral cavity, 28–29, 32
ordering of rules, 98
organs of articulation, *see* speech, organs of
orthography, 62, 162–164
Osthoff, Herman, 199

P-marker, *see* phrase structure marker
P-rule, *see* phrase structure rule
Paget, Sir Richard, 3
Pahlavi, 210
palate, 25, 29, 36–37, 41
Pāṇini, 185–186, 209
pantomime, 3
Papuan languages, 218
paradigms, 58–60
  derivational, 58
  inflectional, 60, 71
parent language, 76n., 184, 190, 201
passive transformation, 99
  See also T-passive rule
past participle, 62–63, 75n., 101, 106n.
past tense, 58, 62–64, 75n.
Pei, Mario, 26
perfect tense, 59
performance, 95, 104
Persian, 131
Petit-Nègre, 180
pharynx, 29
philosophical grammar, 187
Phoenician, 215
phonation, 25
phoneme, 28, 35, 39, 43–50, 53, 74
  segmental versus suprasegmental, 46

phonemic analysis, 44–46
phonemics, *see* phonemic analysis
phonetic spelling, *see* sounds, representation of
phonetician, 34, 39
phonetics, 27–50
phonography, 156
phonological component, 101
phonological law, 199–201
phonological phrase, 48
phonology, 21–22
  comparative, 191
phrasal stress, 49
phrase structure component, 99, 103
phrase structure marker, 98, 100
phrase structure rule, 97–99, 101–102
Phrygian, 7
pictograph, *see* writing, pictographic-ideographic
pidgin languages, 179–180
  Pidgin English, 180
Pike, Kenneth L., 48
pitch, 2, 46–49, 67
Plattdeutsch, 214
Plato, 5
plosives, 29–30, 192–193
plural, 58–60, 62–65, 71, 74–75n., 76n., 129
point of articulation, 35–37
Polish, 211
polygenesis, 9
Polynesian, 217
polysemy, 140–141
polysynthetic languages, *see* incorporating languages
Pooh-Pooh theory, 4
popular development, 149
popular etymology, *see* folk etymology
portmanteau word, *see* blending
Port-Royal grammar, 187, 204n.
Portuguese, 130, 213
positional variant, *see* allomorph; allophone
Prākrits, 209
prefixes, 57–60, 69, 111–115
  See also affixes
prepositions, 54, 57, 60–61, 113
prescriptive grammar, 80
present tense, 58, 61–62
prestige dialect, 169
Primitive Germanic, 204n., 213
primitive language, 6–7, 12
primitive societies, 8, 12, 152
Priscian, 186
Provençal, 188, 213
Prussian, 211
Psammatichos, 7

Punjabi, 209
Pyles, Thomas, 118

Quechua, 222
quipus, 155

Rask, Rasmus, 190–194
rebus, 157
Received Standard English, 170, 176
reduplication, 59–60
reference, 135, 138, 141–142
   See also meaning, range of
referent, 135, 140
relevant feature, see distinctive features
Renaissance, 113, 128
resonance chamber, 28–29
resonants, 32
retroflex glide, 32
Révész, G., 6
Rhaeto-Rumansch, 13, 212
Richards, I. A., 134–135
Riksmaal, 214
Roberts, Paul, 43, 136
Robins, R. H., 24, 197
Romance languages, 68, 135, 184, 198, 201, 205n., 212–213
Romance philology, 198
Romany, see Gypsy language
root, see base
   triliteral, 59, 68
Rosetta Stone, 216
Ruanda, 217
Rumanian, 213
runes, 148, 214
Russian, 11n., 13, 76n., 123n., 130, 179, 185

Samoan, 218
Samoyedic languages, 221
sandhi, 66
Sanskrit, 68, 131, 185, 186–194, 201, 209
Sapir, Edward, 1, 21, 137
Sardinian, 213
Sassetti, F., 189
satem languages, 205n.
Saussure, Ferdinand de, 21, 24
Scaliger, J. J., 188
Scandinavian languages, 192
Schlegel, Friedrich, 191
Schleicher, August, 195–197
Schott, W., 198
Scots-Gaelic, 212
Scottish, 17, 32
semantic categorization, 138

semantic change, 144–150
   See also meaning, amelioration of; extension of; loss of; pejoration of; restriction of
semantic component, 102, 136
semantic field, see reference
semantic unit, see meaning, unit of
semantic word, 141–142
semanticist, 142
semantics, 135, 150
   descriptive versus historical, 147
semasiography, 156
sememe, see semantic word
semiconsonant, see semivowels
Semitic languages, 68
Semito-Hamitic languages, 215
semivowels, 31–32, 37
sentence, 18, 55, 58, 60, 70, 83–85, 91, 92, 95, 98–99, 103
   basic type, 92–102, 106n.
   complex type, 94, 96, 99, 102
   derived, 93, 95, 99
   as structural pattern, 86
   underlying structure of, 99, 101
sentence frame, 61, 84
Serbo-Croatian, 211
Sheard, J. A., 118
Shluh, 216
shortening, 119
Siamese, see Thai
sibilants, 30, 62
singular, 18, 58, 62, 64–65
Sinitic languages, see Chinese
Sino-Tibetan languages, 219
Sioux, 222
Skeat, W. W., 177
slang, 178–179
Slavic languages, 68, 101, 211
Slovak, 211
Slovenian, 211
Smith, Henry Lee, Jr., 49
sound image, 15
sound-imitative words, 7, 16, 23n.
sound shifts, 192–194, 198–199
sounds, 2, 4, 6, 12, 15–17, 22, 24–50, 56, 61
   aspirated versus unaspirated, 43–44
   correspondences of, 190, 192
   description of, 27–32
   imitation of, 4, 7, 9, 15, 16, 23n.
   representation of, 32–35, 41
   system of, 17, 22, 24, 41
   transcription of, see sounds, representation of
   unit of, see phoneme
   voiced versus voiceless, 28, 37
Spanish, 15, 17–18, 45, 47, 130, 139, 141, 184, 213

speaking circuit, 24–25
speech, 25–26, 35–37, 176–181
  anatomy of, *see* speech, physiology of
  development of, *see* language, origin and prehistory of
  levels of, 176–179
  organs of, 16, 25–26, 35–37, 41, 51
  parts of, *see* form class
  physiology of, 25–26, 50
  "r"-colored versus "r"-less, 40, 174
  regional and social variations of, *see* dialects
  standard versus substandard, 176
  standardization of, 181
speech areas (Eastern U.S.), 173
speech community, 15, 19, 42
speech process, 24–27
spelling, *see* orthography
sphere of reference, *see* reference
spirants, *see* fricatives
Stammbaum theory, 196
stem, *see* base
Stoic philosophers, 136
stops, *see* plosives
stress, 46–47, 49, 117
structural ambiguity, 85–86, 103
structural grammar, *see* descriptive grammar
structural linguistics, *see* descriptive linguistics
structural signal, 85–86, 89–90, 94
structuralism, 83
structuralist, 22, 46, 82–83, 91, 94–95, 104, 136
structure word, *see* function word
Sturtevant, Edgar, 14, 162
subordination, *see* embedding
substitution test, *see* commutation test
substratum, 193, 205n.
Sudanese-Guinean languages, 216–217
suffixes, 57–59, 69, 99, 106n., 109, 110–112
  diminutive, 110, 123
  nonnative, 114–115
  pseudo, 115
  See also affixes
Sumerians, 3, 154
supraglottal cavities, 29
suprasegmental phonemes, *see* intonation patterns
surface structure, 102–104, 204n.
Swahili, 58, 69, 161, 217
Swedish, 9, 39, 184, 214
Sweet, Henry, 81
Swiss German, 169, 204n.
syllabaries, 157–161
  Cherokee, 158
  kana, 159

syllabaries *(continued)*
  West Semitic, 158–161
syllabic nucleus, 31, 41–42
syllable, 46, 49–50, 56, 158
syllable sign, 157–158
symbol, 96–97, 135, 155
  arbitrariness of, 14–15
  and object, 15
  phonetic versus phonemic, 35
  vocal, 14
symbolism, 6, 9, 14–15
synchronic linguistics, *see* descriptive linguistics
synonym, 41
syntactic component, 101–102
syntactic phonology, *see* sandhi
syntactic structure, 22, 91, 102
syntax, 21, 66, 95
synthesis, index of, 72
synthetic languages, *see* inflectional languages
Syriac, 215

taboo, 147
Tahitian, 218
Tamil, 219
tap, *see* flap
target language, 21
Ta-Ta theory, 4
taxonomic grammar, 93
telescoped word, *see* blending
Telugu, 219
tense, 19, 57–60, 98–99
terminal contour, 48–49
terminal juncture, 49–50
terminal string, 96–99, 103
terminal symbol, 96
test frame, 86–89
Thai, 48, 219
Thomas, Charles K., 40
Tibeto-Burmese languages, 219
Tokharian, 208
tone (tonal) languages, 48
tones, 48
tongue, 3, 12, 25, 31–32, 36
  position and height of, 37–38
Tower of Babel, 9, 19
T-passive rule, 100
traditional grammar, *see* grammar, tradition in
Trager, George, 49
transferred meaning, *see* meaning, central versus marginal
transform, 95, 99–100
transformation rule, 95, 99, 103
transformational analysis, 93–104
transformational-generative grammar, 75n., 93, 95, 102, 136

transformationalist, 103–104
translation, 139
triconsonantal root, *see* root, trilateral
trilled sound, 31–32
triphthong, 31–32, 41–42
T-rule, *see* transformation rule
Tuareg, 216
Tungus, *see* Manchu
Tupi-Guaraní, 223
Turkic languages, 221
Turkish, 39, 69, 131, 161, 221
typological classification, 66–67, 197

Ukrainian, 211
Ullman, Stephen, 150
unreleased sound, 34, 43–44
Uralic languages, 221
Urdu, 209
usage, 79, 82
utterance, 54–55, 86–89, 94
   "minimum free," 91
uvula, 36

variants, *see* allomorph; allophone
Varro, 186
Vedas, 185, 207
Vedic Sanskrit, 207
velum, *see* palate
verb phrase, 92, 95
verbs, 18, 46, 57–70, 97–99, 191
   strong versus weak, 75n., 106n.
Verner, Karl, 194
Verner's Law, 194
vibrant, *see* trilled sound
Vietnamese, 48, 70, 161, 219
vocabulary, 21, 63, 108–133
   Indo-European, 208
vocal cords, 25, 28, 49
vocal organs, *see* speech, organs of
vocoids, *see* vowels
voicing, 28, 43
vowellike sounds, 32–33, 37, 42
vowel harmony, 69
vowel marks, 160
vowels, 18, 28, 32, 37, 39–41, 58, 61–62
   classification and description of, 37–39

vowels *(continued)*
   nasalized, 30, 45
   rounded versus unrounded, 39
   simple versus complex nuclei, 41
   syllabic versus nonsyllabic, 31, 42
   tense versus lax, 41

wampum, 155
Welsh, 212
Wenker, Georg, 171
wh-words, 51n.
Whitney, William Dwight, 82
Whorf, Benjamin Lee, 137, 139, 205n.
William of Normandy, 127
word class, *see* form class
words, 50, 53–58, 60, 91, 99, 108–132
   compounding of, *see* composition
   creation of, 23n., 113–114, 121–122
   order of, 18, 67
      See also syntax
   origin of, 147–148
writing, 9, 12, 62, 153–164
   alphabetic, 159–161
   demotic, 157
   hieratic, 157
   hieroglyphic, 157
   logographic, 156–157
   origins of, 154
   pictographic-ideographic, 155
   syllabic, 157–158
   word-syllabic, *see* writing, logographic
written language, 32
written records, 3, 20, 154
Wu dialect, 219

Xhosa, 217

yes-no question, 52, 101
Yo-He-Yo theory, 5

Zend, 209
zero allomorph, 64, 75n.
Zeuss, Johann Kaspar, 198
Zulu, 217

71 72 73 74 75   10 9 8 7 6 5 4 3 2 1